The Supreme Awakening

Vasugupta's Śhiva Sūtra Vimārśinī

WITH KṢEMARĀJA'S COMMENTARY

Revealed by

Swami Lakshmanjoo

John Hughes, Editor

Lakshmanjoo Academy

Published by:

Lakshmanjoo Academy

First Edition:
Copyright © 2001 by Uiversal Shaiva Fellowship
Second Edition:
Copyright © 2007 by Universal Shaiva Fellowship
Third Edition:
Copyright © 2015 John Hughes

Third Edition first published by Lakshmanjoo Academy 2015

Printed in the United States of America

For information, address:
Lakshmanjoo Academy
http://www.lakshmanjooacademy.org

ISBN 978-0-9837833-8-1 (Hard Cover)
ISBN 978-0-9837833-7-4 (Soft Cover)

This book, *ŚhivaSūtras: The Supreme Awakening,* is revealed by the twentieth century's great philosopher saint Swami Lakshmanjoo. This spiritual treasure, gifted by God to the sage Vasugupta for the upliftment of humankind, is considered to be one of Kashmir Shaivism's most important scriptures. Here, Swami Lakshmanjoo gives the reader a penetrating vision of the glorious journey of the Supreme Awakening; the traveling from limited individuality to absolute oneness with God. This secret teaching, contained within these pages, is revealed by Swami Lakshmanjoo for the first time. Drawing on his own experience Swami Lakshmanjoo, basing his rendering on the esoteric commentary of Abinavagupta's chief disciple Kshemaraja, shows us the way home.

Contents

Expanded Contents

Introduction

The series of twenty lectures derived from the revelations that comprise this book began on 7 June 1975, at the ashram of the preeminent Kashmir Śaivaite philosopher/saint Swami Lakshmanjoo. Lakshmanjoo, known to his devotees as Swamijī, lived on the eastern side of the Kashmir Valley on a hill overlooking the famous Dal Lake just near the famous Mogul garden, Nishat. The area surrounding Swamijī's ashram has for centuries been sanctified by the sacred feet of great Śaivaite masters. Abhinavagupta and others frequented this peaceful tract of land and enjoyed the beautiful orchards that spread majestically over the hillside. To the north, within walking distance, is the valley of Harvan where, at the foot of Mahādeva Mountain, the *Śiva Sūtras* were revealed centuries ago to the great sage and Śiva devotee, Vasugupta.

Swamijī met with us in the morning once or twice a week in a small glassed-in lecture hall, its mud walls adorned with the illustrations of gods, goddesses, and the pictures of saints and holy men. Those attending these lectures—about eight in all—gathered at nine in the morning at the entrance of the ashram and waited for Swamijī to come and open the gate. I remember the excitement I would experience each morning in anticipation of his lecture. I knew that these talks were filled with precious knowledge. This doesn't mean that I fully understood everything Swamijī taught us but I did have a clear intimation of its importance. I was convinced that these lectures contained a secret knowledge that held the key to the human predicament.

Here, humankind was being given the understanding and means to obtain liberation from the bondage of *saṁsāra*—the endless cycle of birth and death.

Upon opening the gate, Swamijī would greet us warmly and invite us to follow him along a short path to the building that housed the lecture hall. After entering the hall, we would each find our own place on the soft Kashmiri rugs covering the mud floor across from Swamiji, who would face us sitting cross-legged on a rug behind a small table where he placed his Sanskrit copy of the *Śiva Sūtra Vimarśinī.* In preparing to give the lecture, Swamijī would wait patiently while he was fitted with a lapel microphone and while I checked to see that the tape-recorder was working. Swamiji was always concerned about the lectures being recorded and would never start until I gave him the assurance that everything was in working order.

The recording of Swamiji's lectures first began in 1971. I had arrived in Kashmir for the sole purpose of asking him if he would teach me Kashmir Śaivism. His reply was, "Yes . . . if you have enough time I will be willing to teach you." I then asked him if I could record his lectures. He agreed readily, saying, "It would be a good idea to make recordings of my lectures." As time passed and I continued my studies, I meticulously recorded everything that Swamiji said during our meetings. One day, before commencing our class, Swamiji turned to me and said, "I am very pleased with your continued efforts to tape-record and preserve my teachings. Before, I was concerned that the tradition and understanding of Kashmir Śaivism would be lost with my passing from this world. Now, however, because there are audio recordings of my teachings, I am hopeful that the true understanding of Kashmir Śaivism will be preserved and will not be lost."

Although he was obviously well-versed in all aspects of Indian and Śaiva philosophy, Swamiji never approached any teaching from a detached scholarly point of view. Sitting at his feet and hearing him translate and explain the *Śiva Sūtras,* I realized that these sūtras and their true understanding was not at all foreign to his own experience. In fact, I understood that in explaining the *Śiva Sūtras*, Swamijī was actually revealing his own experience. I have heard it said somewhere that the philosophy of Kashmir Śaivism is the mystical geography of awareness. How true this seemed to be. Sitting at Swamijī's feet, I understood that he had realized this geography. It was his own home. He was not like a scholar describing the ocean while standing on the shore. He was the ocean. This makes the translation presented here even more real and personal. It is for this reason that I emphasize that this book stands as a revelation and not as a strict translation.

The *Śiva Sutras*

Kashmir Śaivism is a system of philosophy known as the Trika system. The Sanskrit word *trika* means "threefold." In Kashmir Śaivism, *trika* is used to refer to the threefold signs of humankind and their world. These three signs are Śiva, Śakti and the bound individual *(nara)*, and the three energies of Śiva. These three energies are *parā śakti*, supreme energy; *parāparā śakti*, medium energy; and *aparā śakti*, inferior energy. Trika philosophy explains that the realm of *aparā śakti*, the lowest energy, is found in states of wakefulness *(jagrat)* and dreaming *(svapna)*. The domain of *parāparā śakti*, the medium energy, is established in the state of sound sleep *(suṣupti)*. And finally, the province of *parāśakti*, the supreme energy, is found in the fourth *(turya)* state. These three primary energies represent the threefold activities of the world. The philosophy of Trika Śaivism declares that the whole universe and every action in it, whether spiritual, physical, or worldly exists within these three energies.

In his book, *Kashmir Śaivism, the Secret Supreme*, Swami Lakshmanjoo tells us that Trika philosophy is intended for any human being without restriction of caste, creed, or color. Its purpose is to enable the aspirant to rise from individuality to universality. Trika Śaivism is composed of four schools of practice and philosophy. These are the *Pratyabhijñā* system, the *Kula* system, the *Krama* system and the *Spanda* system. All four of these schools of Kashmir Śaivism accept and are based on sacred scriptures called *āgamas*. The word *āgamas* refers to the sacred teachings that exist within Lord Śiva. And so these scriptures, as *āgamas*, are understood to be Śiva's revelation.

In Śaivism, there are 92 *āgamas*, delineated as follows: the monistic *Bhairava Śāstras*, which are supreme *(parā)*, number 64; the mono-dualistic *Rūdra Śāstras*, which are medium *(parāparā)*, number 18; and the dualistic and inferior *(aparā)* *Śiva Śāstras* number 10.

Because the *Śiva Sūtras* were revealed to the sage Vasugupta by Lord Śiva, they are also considered a divine revelation and as such are accepted as *āgama śāstra*. In fact, in revealing the absolute monism central to the philosophy of Kashmir Śaivism, the *Śiva Sūtras* are considered to be one of the most important *āgamas* of Trika Śaivism.

Sūtras are short sentence statements, many times without a formal verb, which, like a string, run through and bind together that which they are revealing. There are three complete commentaries and one smaller commentary available on the *Śiva Sūtras*. These commentaries are the *Śiva Sūtra Vimarśinī* by Kṣemarāja, the *Śiva Sūtra Vārttikam* by Bhaṭṭa Bhāskara, the *Śiva Sūtra Vārttikam* by Varadarāja and a brief commentary known as the *Śiva Sūtra Vṛtti* by an unknown author. Kṣemarāja, the author of the *Vimarśinī*, lived in the tenth century C.E. Bhaṭṭa Bhāskara, the author of the *Śiva Sūtra Vārttikam* lived in the eleventh century C.E. Varadarāja, the author of the other *Vārttikam* on the *Śiva Sūtra*, lived in the fifteenth century C.E. It is not known when the *Vṛitti* was written but because it corresponds so closely with the *Vimarśinī* of Kṣemarāja, it is thought that it must have been written during the time of Kṣemarāja.

Kṣemarāja, the commentator

Kṣemarāja is the author of the commentary known as *Vimarśinī*, upon which Swami Lakshmanjoo bases his rendering of the *Śiva Sutras*. Swamijī tells us that Kṣemarāja was the chief disciple of the great Kashmir Śaivaite philosopher-saint Abhinavagupta, who lived in the tenth century C.E. Kṣemarāja was a prolific writer who possessed a keen philosophical intellect. His writings possess a command and understanding of one who has actually lived the experience he is explaining. The authority expressed in his writings also suggests that he was spiritually quite advanced. But because he wrote about the deepest and most subtle of human spiritual experiences, his writings are said to be complex and hard to understand. For the most part, in writing about a most refined and universal experience, Kṣemarāja had to employ a language and cognitive framework suitable to express that reality. Those who have not actually experienced the ultimate universal reality central to the philosophy of Kashmir Śaivism will not have acquired a point of reference with which to understand it. Explaining the nuances of the universal experience to those who can only imagine it, is like trying to explain the third dimension to those who can only experience two dimensions.

Along with the *Śiva Sūtra Vimarśinī* of which the present work is a translation and elaboration, Kṣemarāja also wrote the following works:

Pratyabhijñāhṛdayaṁ (text on the philosophy of *Pratyabhijñā*)
Spandanirṇaya (commentary on the *Spanda Kārikā*)
Spandasandoha (commentary on the first verse of the *Spanda Kārikā*)
Parāprāveśikā (a short introduction to the thought of Kashmir Śaivism)
Commentary on *Svacchanda Tantra*
Commentary on *Netra Tantra*
Commentary on *Śivastotrāvali of Utpaladeva*
Commentary on *Stavacintāmaṇī of Bhaṭṭa Nārāyaṇa*
Commentary on *Vijñānabhairava* (only about 25 verses exist)

Organization

The *Śiva Sūtras* are divided into three parts. According to Kṣemarāja, the three parts correspond to the three means *(ūpāyas)* for the attainment of liberation *(mokṣa)*, as revealed by Kashmir Śaivism. The three *ūpāyas* for traveling from individual limited consciousness to universal God consciousness are *śāmbhavopāya, śāktopāya* and *āṇavopāya*. The first and highest means is called *śāmbavopāya*. The second means, for aspirants of medium qualifications, is called *śāktopāya*. The third means, called *āṇavopāya*, is regarded as inferior.

Abhinavagupta, drawing from the *Malinīvijaya Tantra*, defines *śāmbavopāya* as the *upāya* wherein the aspirant achieves entry *(samāveṣa)* into supreme consciousness just by the grace of his master, without adopting any process. He does not use thought *(dhyāna)*, *mantra*, or any other aid to meditation. *Śāktopāya* is defined as the *upāya* where the aspirant achieves mystical entry *(samāveṣa)* through contemplation of the mental object that cannot be spoken or recited. *Āṇavopāya* is defined as the *upāya* where mystical entry takes place through concentration on parts of the body *(sthāna-prakalpanā)*, contemplation *(dhyāna)*, recitation *(varṇa)*, taking the support of the breath *(uccāra)*, and *mantras*.[1]

The means of traveling from limited consciousness to universal consciousness depends on the ability of the aspirant. Abhinavagupta tells us in the *Tantrāloka* that the aspirant should always try for the highest and best thing first. Failing that, he should try for the next best, and so on. Thus, in his *Tantrāloka*, he has defined and elaborated the highest *upāya*, *Śambavopāya*, first. His descriptions of *śāktopāya* and *āṇavopāya* follow.

And so it is that the *Śiva Sūtras* also start with the highest and most refined means. The first awakening explains the highest *ūpāya, śāmbhavopāya*; the second awakening explains *śaktopāya*, and the third awakening explains *āṇavopāya*.

1. Swami Lakshmanjoo, translation and commentary on *Tantrāloka* 1.167, 1.169; October 1975 tape-recording in possession of the editor.

Mahādeva Mountain

Shiva Rock

First Awakening

The *Śiva Sūtras* are the sūtras of Lord Śiva himself. Kṣemarāja, a disciple of Abhinavagupta, has provided us with a commentary on them. He begins with an introductory verse.

> I surrender my body and mind to that supreme God consciousness of Śiva, who is the whole universe and who is one in many. It is from Him that the *Rudras* and the *Kṣetrajñās*[1] arise and it is in Him that they rest.

This universe, which is a world of consciousness, is filled with and is one with the supreme state of God consciousness. God consciousness is *spanda*, a unique reality of supreme movement filled with nectar and an outpouring of the supreme bliss of independence.

Kṣemarāja says, "Although I know there are many commentaries existing on *Śiva Sūtras*, I find they all differ from each other and are all incorrect. Therefore, taking the protection of my masters and scriptures, I will present a new and fresh approach in commentating on these *Śiva Sūtras*."

Some time before in the valley of Kashmir, at the foot of Śrī

---

1. *Kṣetrajñās* are those beings who have achieved the fullness of God consciousness through spiritual practice. *Rudras* are those beings who are eternally filled with God consciousness.

Mahādeva Mountain, there lived a great devotee of Lord Śiva named Vasugupta. He was absolutely unique and purified by the grace of Lord Śiva. Filled with devotion, Vasugupta did not accept the theory and teachings of Buddhist philosophers.[2] Having purified his heart by the teachings of siddhas and yoginīs,[3] he was determined in meditating on Lord Śiva.

After some time, Lord Śiva, having decided to elevate the great master Vasugupta by filling him with true knowledge, appeared in a dream. In this dream, he told Vasugupta that at the foot of Mahādeva Mountain, there is a great boulder and under this boulder are inscribed his sacred verses (sūtras). He then directed him to find these sūtras and to practice their teaching. "If you do this," he said, "you will discover the truth of the reality of God consciousness."

Vasugupta awoke from his dream and set off in search of the great rock. Eventually, he found the rock just where Lord Śiva said it would be, at the foot of Mahādeva Mountain. As soon as he touched it, it turned over and there, on the underside, he found the engraved sūtras described by Lord Śiva.

He was awestruck and filled with joy. He began intense study and reflection on these sutras. He read them thoroughly and exhaustively, concentrating and meditating upon each one, seeking to grasp its true and hidden meaning. Through this profound study and reflection, he gained the understanding and knowledge the sūtras contained. He then began to share the theory and secrets of these sūtras with his chief disciples, Bhaṭṭakallaṭa and others. Simultaneously, he revealed the sūtras in a book called *Spanda Kārikā*. Kṣemarāja further clarified these *spanda* verses in his work entitled *Spanda Nirṇaya*.

Now the Śiva Sūtras will be explained.

The first sūtra of the *Śiva Sūtras* explains that the reality of

---

2. *Nāgabodhi siddhas.*

3. *Siddhas* are those saints who are hidden, who do not reside in physical bodies. They reside in subtle bodies and are all pervading. *Yoginīs* are female *siddhas*.

the universe is the real self. This self is not false. This is contrary to the theories of those philosophers who argue that the individual being is always individual being and universal being is always universal being. For these philosophers, universal being will never be united with individual being and individual being will never be united with universal being. This first sūtra, on the other hand, states that individual being is one with universal being. The reality of this whole universe is God consciousness. It is filled with God consciousness.

1. caitanyamātmā

The independent state of supreme consciousness is the reality of everything.

In this verse, the word *ātmā* means "the reality of everything." Supreme consciousness, "*caitanyam*," is the reality of everything. Why? Because the one who has not come into consciousness does not exist at all. The act of consciousness is the same in the conscious and the unconscious. For the one who is conscious, the act of consciousness is there. For the one who is not conscious of the act of consciousness, it is also there in the background.

So, the conscious being is the being who makes others conscious. This being is independent in all knowledge and every action. Such a reality is called *caitanya,* which means "complete independence." All knowledge and all action are united in one consciousness—completely independent God consciousness. Only *Paramaśiva* possesses this completely independent God consciousness.

From earth to *Anāśrita Śiva*[4] all beings are dependent on the conscious being, Śiva. Although the complete, independent state of Śiva possesses many divine aspects—such as being eternal,

4. *Anāśrita Śiva* is that state of Śiva where universal existence is excluded from his own nature because of the apprehension that universality

all-pervading, completely full and all-knowing—these divine aspects are not unique to Śiva. They could also be found in other beings. The singularly unique aspect of Lord Śiva is complete independence, *svātantrya*. This complete independence is not found anywhere except in the state of Lord Śiva.

In this sūtra, the state of complete independence is indicated and accomplished through the use of the word *caitanya*. On the other hand, the author would use the word *cetanā*[5] if he were to declare that other aspects, in addition to the aspect of complete independence (*svātantrya*), also existed in the state of Lord Śiva. But only one aspect exists and that is *svātantrya*. The other aspects, such as being all-pervading, completely full, filled with bliss, etc., do not exist. It is only this one aspect, *svātantrya*, that is revealed by the word *caitanya*. This indicates that the word *caitanya* means "the independent state of consciousness."

The independent state of consciousness is the self. It is the self of everything, because whatever exists in the world is the state of Lord Śiva. So Lord Śiva is found everywhere.

We have already seen that different aspects of Lord Śiva do not exist at all. Now I will show you why these "different aspects" are to be excluded from those of Lord Śiva. If, for the moment, we accept that different aspects of Lord Śiva do exist, then we must ask the question: Are these aspects filled with *svātantrya*? If they are not filled with *svātantrya,* then they are insentient *(jaḍa)* and without consciousness (*anātmā*). If, however, the aspects are also filled with the independent consciousness of Lord Śiva, then why not just accept independent consciousness? Why postulate those independent aspects at all?

And, at the same time, if the state of God consciousness exists in the fullness of independence, and if time, space, and form are separate from the independent state of consciousness, then they would not exist at all. Time would not exist, space would not exist, and form would not exist. If, however, we accept these aspects, thinking that he is eternal, timeless, and the cause of the universe, then if they are accepted as indepen-

5. *Cetanā* means "consciousness," "awareness," while *caitanya* refers to that state that is entirely independent in all knowledge and all action.

dent, they are filled with consciousness. If, however, they are not independent, then they have been carried away from God consciousness and they cannot exist at all in the state of Lord Śiva.

Now, if all individual beings are filled with consciousness, then where is the difference in these beings? There can be no difference. So, all individual beings are one universal being.

Let us examine the theory of the *malas*, the veils of ignorance. Where does this ignorance exist? How can we say that ignorance exists? If ignorance is removed from God consciousness, it does not exist at all. So where does it exist? If ignorance is filled with the independent state of God consciousness, then it is not ignorance at all, but fullness of God consciousness. So ignorance cannot be found. Then what is it that remains? What is left? There is only independent supreme God consciousness—which is the reality of the self.

What if, for the time being, we were to say that the veil of ignorance exists before you are realized, and that afterwards, when you are realized, it does not exist? Then, if ignorance does not exist after realization, it is the truth that it did not exist at all. Why? Because at the time of realization, the aspirant realizes and knows that ignorance does not exist at all. So that ignorance never exists. Whatever he called ignorance existed, but it was not actually ignorance; it was really non-fullness of knowledge.

Kṣemarāja talks about those aspirants who are on the path, who meditate day and night, and do not achieve anything. He says these aspirants are the same as ignorant people. This is not the real state of Śiva. The real state of Śiva is full realization. When full realization takes place, that is the fullness—the reality—of independent God consciousness. Until then, nothing has happened. Aspirants who practice day and night and do not achieve anything are just like ignorant worldly persons bound up in *saṁsāra*. The reality of the self only exists when you are filled with the independent state of supreme God consciousness (*caitanya*). Until then, everything is useless and worthless.

So, there are not individual states of being, there is only the universal state of being, and that is one. This is why, in the very first verse, the author has explained that God consciousness is one in many.

Now we can explain this verse another way. When a master teaches his disciples by asking them, "Who is the self?" the disciples reply by saying, "The body is not the self, the breath is not the self, the intellect is not the self, voidness is not the self, this universe is not the self, the tradition of the atheists is not the self, the tradition of the Vedas is not the self, the tradition of the Buddhists is not the self and the Mādhyamika school of Buddhism is not the self." Then the master asks, "What is self?" And he answers his own question by saying, "Independent supreme God consciousness is the self and nothing else."

The independent state of God consciousness is also found in the individual states of body (*śarīra*), breath (*prāṇa)*, intellect (*buddhi*) and void (*śūnya*). In the body, he is above the body. In breath, he is above the breath. In intellect, he is the super intellect. In voidness, he is full. In nothingness, he is everything. This is the reality of universal I (*aham*).

Mṛityuñjidbhaṭṭāraka also gives the same exposition of the self:

> This independent supreme state of God consciousness is the nature of the self, which is found in every *śāstra*. It is the reality of the supreme self *(paramātman).* Beyond all coverings, it is fully exposed.

The *Vijñāna Bhairava* says the same thing.

> In each and every being exists the independent state of God consciousness. You must find this state of God consciousness. To accomplish this, concentrate on the totality of individuality, the state of universal consciousness. If this is done, you will conquer the differentiated state of world and will be carried above the individuality of consciousness. (*Vijñāna Bhairava* 100)

This is also expressed by Vasugupta in two verses of the *Spanda Kārikā*:

> If, through deep meditation, you examine the classes and activities of organs known as the organs of cognition and the organs of action, you will find in them the supreme independent state of God consciousness. (*Spanda Kārikā* 1.6, 1.7)

Kṣemarāja now gives another exposition of this first sūtra. He says that, in the verse, the word *ātmā* means "form." Thus the meaning is: "This supreme independent state of God consciousness (*caitanya*) is the form." But the author has not revealed whose form. He simply says that this supreme independent state of God consciousness is form. If it is not said whose form it is, you must conclude that this is the form of everything. So, the independent supreme state of God consciousness is the form of everything. It is the form of the nose, it is the form of the eye, it is the form of the face, it is the form of the arm, it is the form of the limbs. And even more than that: It is the form of an animal, such as a sheep; it is the form of a tree; it is the form of everything in this world.

The independent state of God consciousness is not only the form of the existing world, it is also the form of the nonexistent world. In the nonexistent world, you find the milk of a bird. Have you ever seen the milk of a bird? Of course not! But the milk of a bird also exists in the supreme independent state of God consciousness. Why? Because it can be thought. You can think of the milk of a bird. So, anything that can be thought exists. Although it may be nonexistent, it exists in the supreme independent state of God consciousness.

The formulation of the milk of a bird would never occur if it did not exist in consciousness. But it does exist in consciousness, and it can be conceived in thought. So formulations such as the son or daughter of a barren woman exist in the supreme independent state of God consciousness. Kṣemarāja, therefore, concludes that nonexistent things also exist in God consciousness.

This is so because of the process of thinking. Thinking takes place in our intellect. That intellect exists in our consciousness and that individual consciousness exists in the supreme state of God consciousness. So everything exists. Whatever you think exists and whatever you do not think also exists.

How can these objects exist without the knowers of these objects? It is because of the knowers of these objects that these objects exist. So, the knower and the known are one. And it follows that there is nothing right and there is nothing wrong. Everything is filled with God consciousness. Whatever you do is divine and whatever you do not do is divine as well. Whatever you commit is divine, and whatever you do not commit is also divine. The individual being is filled with the universal state of being.

The independent supreme state of God consciousness is the formation of the universe. Therefore, how can you choose some means out of all the universe for its realization? If you choose some means from the universe, that too is that which is meant. Therefore, whatever means you select, say, *prāṇāyāma*, *dhāraṇā*, *dhyāna*, or *samādhi*[6] such a way is filled with God consciousness. Therefore, that is not actually means, that is, in reality, meant. That is the end, not the means to that end. So, there is no choosing various means, there is no process, there is no *sādhanā*.

If, for the time being, you declare that things are not filled with God consciousness, even then they are dependent on the supreme state of God consciousness. They cannot be known, they cannot exist, unless they are found and realized in the supreme universal state of God consciousness. And the supreme state of God consciousness can never be covered by anything. Why? Because the covering cannot exist without supreme God consciousness.

It is also said in the revered scripture *Ucchaṣma Bhairava:*

> You must know that the state of independent supreme God consciousness is existing in the same way, beyond your individual state, as your shadow exists. Although you try to cross it and

6. These four means form part of the eight limbs of yoga as set forth in Patañjali's *Yoga Sūtra*. Traditionally, *prāṇāyāma* is understood to be the control of the breath, *dhāraṇā* is concentration, *dhyāna* is meditation and *samādhi* is absorption. See sūtra 6 of the Third Awakening for the expanded Kashmir Śaiva explanation of these "limbs of yoga."

> overtake it with your footsteps, you will never succeed. It cannot be overtaken just as the head cannot be in place of the foot.

This means that the supreme state of God consciousness can never be realized by any separate means; it can only be realized by the means that is filled with God consciousness. So then there is no need to realize anything; it is already realized. Just as one's shadow can never be overtaken, the supreme state of independent God consciousness can never become objective. It is never found, it is never realized. Why? Because it is the state of the finder, the state of the realizer.

In *Spanda,* it is revealed in these verses:

> In which state this whole universe is existing, that is in the real sense the reality of being. (*Spanda Kārikā* 1.2, 1.5)

It is concluded, therefore, that the supreme reality of *Śaṅkara's*[7] consciousness is that it is in a state of movement. It is not fixed or situated in any one place. It is located everywhere. Wherever there is space, it is there. Wherever there is not space, it is there. It is in space and beyond it.

---

7. *Paramaśiva* (Supreme Śiva).

The nature of limitation is located on the surface of *āṇavamala*. When *āṇavamala* exists, the other two *malas*, *kārmamala* and *māyīmala*, are also existing. When *āṇavamala* has ceased to exist, then these other two malas will also vanish.

This is said in *Svacchanda Tantra*:

> We have concluded that the word *caitanya* means the complete freedom of universal consciousness. Because of the impurity *āṇavamala*, which is attached with *kalā* (limited action) and *vidyā* (limited knowledge), *caitanya* (independent universal consciousness) is lost. It is absorbed in *rāga* (attachment) and limited by *kāla* (time). It is confined in the bondage of *niyati* (attachment to a particular object).[9] This limitation is strengthened by the limitation of the ego. It is absorbed in the body of *prakṛiti* and ever united with three *guṇas, sāttva, rājas* and *tāmas*. It is established in the reality of *buddhi* (intellect).[10] This Universal I is limited in individual I. It is limited by the mind, by the organs of knowledge, by the organs of action, by the five *tanmātrās*[11] and finally, by the five gross elements. *(Svacchanda Tantra)*

It is said in the *Mālinī Vijaya Tantra* that *kārmamala* also binds one's reality of *caitanya:*

> This action, good or bad, gives joy and sadness. (*Mālinī Vijaya Tantra* 1.24)

---

9. Because of *niyati*, you think, "This house here is my house. That other house is your home. It is not my house." In reality, though, this is not your home, but *niyati* has made you think that it is your house. This is limitation caused by *niyati*.

10. Beyond intellect, there is *caitanya*. When *caitanya* becomes limited, it is transformed into the nature of the intellect, the intellectual state, and it becomes intellect.

11. The five *tanmātrās—śabda* (sound), *sparśa* (touch), *rūpa* (form), *rasa* (taste) and *gandha* (smell)—are subtle elements attached and corresponding to the five great gross elements: *ākāśa* (ether), *vāyu* (air), *tejas* (fire), *jala* (water) and *pṛithvī* (earth).

When there is joy,[12] one is deprived of sadness, sadness is carried away. So, sadness is there and it is carried away. When sadness is there, joy is carried away. So when there is joy, there is also sadness. And when there is sadness, there is also joy. When there is one, there is the other. It is said in *Śrī Pratyābhijñā*:

> *Kārmamala* and *māyīyamala* always reside in *āṇavamala*. It is the foundation of these two, which are no other than contracted particular knowledge. *(Pratyābhijñā Kārikā)*

Contracted knowledge is particular (*viśiṣṭa*), not universal (*sāmānya*). If you know this particular object, that is particular (*viśiṣṭa*) knowledge.[13] If you know the universe, that is universal (*sāmānya*) knowledge. It is said in *Pratyabhijñā:*

> In this field of *āṇavamala*, differentiated knowledge is *māyīya mala*. When the doer is not properly recognized,[14] that is *kārmamala*. That gives you repeated births and deaths, enjoyment and sadness. When there is enjoyment, there is sadness and when there is death, there is life. *(Pratyābhijñā Kārikā)*

Karma is either good or bad. Whenever you do any action, it will be a good or a bad action. With good actions, you will fall, with bad actions, you will fall. There is no way of rising with any action. You may do good or you may do bad. Bad actions carry you downwards, good actions carry you downwards. Only independent action carries you to the Lord. And this is not actually action, but *svātantrya*. Action is always limited and always good or bad.

---

12. The bliss (*ānanda*) of one's own nature is different from the joy being referred to here, which is the joy of everyday life. *Ānanda* is not joy. *Ānanda* is universal joy. That universal joy is bliss, whereas the joy and sadness we are discussing is the pleasure of the organs.

13. When you perceive an object, you have to ignore something that is not that object; when you perceive that other object, then you have to ignore the previous object. This is a limitation. Through this process, knowledge is contracted and limited. This is particular (*viśiṣṭa*) knowledge. In ultimate reality, there is no other, there is only one.

14. "Not properly recognized" means being not universally realized.

But now the question can be asked, how does this threefold *mala* become the cause of bondage?

4. jñānādhiṣṭhānaṁ mātṛikā //

The Universal Mother commands this triple knowledge.

Mātṛikā, the Universal Mother, is the master director of the triple knowledge consisting of *āṇavamala*, *māyīyamala* and *kārmamala.* Here, the word *mātṛikā* means *ajñātā mātā. Ajñātā mātā* is the state where universal energy is known in the wrong way. When universal energy is known in a correct way, it is simple *svātantrya śakti.* When it is known in the wrong way, it is energy of illusion and it is called *māyā śakti.* So *mātṛikā* is both. *Mātṛikā* means *ajñātā mātā* when universal energy is not known correctly and *svātantrya* when it is known correctly. This means that *svātantrya* controls the three instruments of bondage. *Svātantrya* is your own will! If you bind yourself or if you free yourself, both are under your control.

The threefold *mala*, which was defined earlier, is first "the feeling of incompletion" *(apūrṇammanyatā)*; second, "differentiated knowledge" *(bhinnavedyaprathā)*; and third, "the impressions of pleasures and pain" *(śubhāśubhavāsanā).* The administrator of these threefold *malas* is the Universal Mother, who pervades all the letters of the alphabet from *a* to *kṣa.* This mother not only pervades the world of the alphabet *(vācaka),* but she also pervades the world of objects *(vācya)* designated by those letters. *Vācya* means the world or objects designated by words, which are created by a combination of letters. For example, in the sentence, "This is a chair", the word "chair" is spelled C-H-A-I-R. This is the world of letters. And the object called "chair" sitting in front of you is what is nominated by that word "chair." This is the world of objects. The objects of this world are known by the words that refer to them. Thus the Universal Mother pervades not only letters, but also objects designated by letters and words. Universal Mother is the creator of the universe.

When universal energy, residing in the field of *māyā*, possesses differentiated and constricted knowledge, she appears to be limited, and thinks such thoughts as, "I am not full," "I am weak," "I am stout," "I am the only fortunate person in the world," or "I am a great master," "I have so many disciples," "I am a world renowned teacher."By these words, these letters and these objects, she is sometimes filled with grief, sometimes with wonder, sometimes with joy, sometimes with anger, and sometimes with attachment. And so what finally happens to this victim? This mother (*mātṛikā*) does something terrible. She makes this victim her plaything.

This Universal Mother *(citi*[15] *mātṛikā)* resides in the center of *brahmarandhra.*[16] Around that mother, seated at her feet are the organs of knowledge, the organs of action, mind, intellect and ego *(pīṭheśvari).*[17] These *pīṭheśvaris* become very fearful *(mahāghora).* At every turn, they[18] invariably create illusion and continually strive to bind him even more. Here, the mother *(mātṛikā)* is the essential factor and *pīṭheśvarīs* are the agents.

This is a verse from the *Timirodghāṭṭa*:

---

15. *Citi* means consciousness.

16. The *brahmarandhra* is a subtle opening existing at the top of the skull which is pierced by the force of *cit kuṇḍalinī* when, traveling up the central vein, it rises from *mūlādhāra cakra* to the top of the skull. It then penetrates the subtle opening of *brahmarandhra* and moves from the body to the universe, the great ether of consciousness.

17. These are all *pīṭheśvaris* for the one who has become the play of the mother. The one who is the player is not played by mother. He is existing in the state of being player.

18. The deities of these organs of action, organs of knowledge, mind, intellect and ego are *gocarī, khecarī, dikcarī,* and *bhūcarī.*

> In *brahmarandhra* there is the Universal Mother. Around her are gathered all the deities who delude the one she is playing with. But the one who is a player with mother is not deluded at all.

And the way he becomes the victim of pleasure and pain is by the words that he hears. For example, he will hear the words "our business has decreased," even though it has not decreased. When he hears that his business is ruined, he will be the victim of grief. And when, on occasion, he hears that his business is doing well, he will be the victim of pleasure. In both cases, he is played by *mātṛikā*. He becomes the victim of grief, the victim of pleasure, the victim of sex or the victim of enjoyment. These are the good and bad things we face in our daily lives. But the one who is player, he will never be sad. All these things will be enjoyed by him. He is aware of his nature. He will never be bound.

The objective world *(vācya)* is the world that is named. The subjective world are the names *(vācaka)* of those objects. When you unite the objective and the subjective states, that is bondage. When they are kept separate, then there is no bondage.

If somebody tells you your father has died, and if you associate this word "father" with your real father, that is bondage. If you keep it separate then there is no connection between the word "father" and your real father. There will only be a collection of letters F-A-T-H-E-R I-S D-E-A-D. You won't be bound by this. If you are bound, then you will be the victim of grief or pleasure. So it is the written characters of letters that gives rise to the wheel of energies.

When the Universal Mother *Mātṛika* kisses each of the fourfold energies of the lord, *ambā, jyeṣṭhā, raudrī* and *vāmā*, each energy has its own distinct fruit. When she kisses the energy of *ambā*, then you are kept from either rising or falling. You are held at the same place. When she kisses the energy of *vāmā,* you are given the fruit *saṁsāra*. When she kisses the energy of *raudrī,* you are unable to make any decisions, either good or bad. When she kisses the energy of *jyeṣṭhā,* you rise to the knowledge of your own nature.

By kissing these four energies, you are deprived of your real nature of universal consciousness. Not even for a moment are you situated in one-pointedness. Your organs of action and organs of knowlege lead you to the external, not the internal, world. Thus, these threefold *malas* are correctly said to bind your own nature. This is explained in these two verses of *Spanda*:

> When by hearing some sound, good or bad, you are carried away from your own nature . . . (*Spanda Kārīkā* 3.13)

and

> The energies of Lord Śiva are always determined to cover and conceal your own nature. (*Spanda Kārīkā* 3.15)

Now, the author establishes the means that causes these three kinds of bondage—*āṇavamala*, *māyīyamala* and *kārma mala*—to vanish, resulting in your resting in the desired state of consciousness.

5. udyamo bhairavaḥ //

That effort— the flashing forth of active awareness—that instantaneously makes universal consciousness shine, is Bhairava.

There are two kinds of effort, passive and active. Here we are concerned with active effort, not passive effort. Active effort is elevating . It is effort that, when it flows out in active consciousness, makes one's universal consciousness shine instantaneously. Active effort is *bhairava* because it carries one to the state of *bhairava.*

And active effort that takes you abruptly, in one flight, to your consciousness and causes the supreme knowledge of being *(pratibhā)* to radiate is *bhairava,* because all energies are diluted and digested in one energy, *svātantrya śakti.* It is also *bhairava* because the whole universe is filled with *svātantrya*, and because here all differentiated perception ends.

Active effort is called *bhairava* because it becomes the means of carrying you toward the state of *bhairava.* This kind of effort is found in real devotees whose consciousness is always introverted in the awareness of God consciousness. This is the meaning of this sūtra. It is also said in *Mālinīvijaya Tantra*:

> The penetrative inescapable state of trance, which absorbs your individual being, is called *śāmbhava samāveśa.* Because of the

> elevating infusion of power from the master, this *śāmbhava samāveśa* is experienced by one who is capable of keeping away all thoughts and impressions. (*Mālinīvijaya Tantra* 2.23)

Our masters explain this verse in this way. When you are capable, then your master will uplift you. If you are not capable, he will not be successful in carrying you there. This means you must be capable of absorbing this kind of awareness.

In *Svacchanda Tantra* it is also said:

> Oh Pārvatī, all *mantras* are successful for the one who contemplates on his own self as one with *bhairava* because he is always one with that awareness of consciousness *(samāveśa)*. *(Svacchanda Tantra)*

In this verse from the *Svacchanda Tantra,* "contemplates" means "to meditate on the introverted active state of elevating consciousness." This is explained in *Spanda* in the following verse:

> Take one thought. Contemplate on that one thought with unwavering concentration. Then, when another movement rises in your mind from that first thought, that is *spanda* and that is *unmeṣa.*[19] You have to observe it yourself and that will be *spanda.* (*Spanda Kārikā* 3.9)

Here it is explained how, after instantaneously taking hold of supreme consciousness, one attains establishment in *bhairava,* by which establishment he destroys the threefold bondage of ignorance. And if supreme consciousness is not held in an instant, it won't be held at all.

---

19. *Unmeṣa* means "opening the eyes." Here, we must understand that when one "opens the eyes," he is revealing his nature and when he "closes the eyes," he is hiding his nature.

Now, in the next sūtra, the author explains how, by the intensity of meditation (*parāmarśa*), the external state of dualistic consciousness is absorbed in nondualistic consciousness.

6. śakticakrasaṁdhāne viśvasaṁhāraḥ //

By establishing and meditating on the wheel of energies, the differentiated universe comes to an end.

Bhairava, which has already been explained, carries you to the highest summit of active consciousness and is found together with *svātantrya śakti*. How is *svātantrya śakti* found as one with *Bhairava*? You will find Her as one with *Bhairava* by keeping your organs in action, and then by establishing yourself inside, observing the action within. This is *Bhairava mudrā*. The supreme energy of *Bhairava* holds both the successive movement and nonsuccessive movement[20] of the collective totality of energies. But in fact, here there is neither a successive way or a nonsuccessive way of meditation. Why? Because, both nonsuccessive and successive ways of meditation require something to meditate on. Here there is nothing to meditate on.

So, in the state of *svātantrya śakti,* there is no meditation. It is not the means *(upāya)* of *śāmbhava*, or *śākta*, or *āṇava*. It is

20. "Non-successive movement" is just a point; there is no space. There is no journey in "non-successive" movement. It occurs in one flash. "Successive movement" occurs in stages 1,2,3,4. The "non-successive" *akrama* movement is embodied in the means known as *śāṁbhavopāya* and the "successive" *krama* movement is embodied in the means known as *śāktopāya* and *āṇavopāya*.

anupāya and beyond *anupāya.*[21] Supreme energy excludes *śāmbhava, śākta* and *āṇava upāyas* and, at the same time, they are all included. The state of *svātantrya śakti* excludes everything and also includes everything. This is the state of *svātantrya śakti.* Why would they be excluded? They would be excluded because the way does not exist at all. There is no way to go, there is no traveling. From the point you start, that is what is to be held. You have to hold that starting point and that is all. Although this *svātantrya śakti* is both successive and nonsuccessive, it is above that. Why? Because it is the supreme energy of Lord Śiva, which is absolutely independent awareness.

The play of creation, protection, and destruction is the recreation of *svātantrya śakti.*[22] Where? In the ground of her own nature (*svarūpa*). Right from the element earth *(pṛithvī)* up to the state of the supreme perceiver *(para pramātṛi).* When the heroic yogī meditates with continuous contemplation on that collective class[23] of energies of Śiva *(śakti cakra),* which is found in only one energy, *svātantrya śakti,* he destroys this dualistic universe right from *kālāgni rūdra*[24] up to *śāntātītā kalā.*[25] You must understand though, destruction does not mean that it is destroyed. Although it is individually

---

21. In Kashmir Śaivism there are three *upāyas* (means), *śāmbhavopāya, śāktopāya,* and *āṇavopāya.* In addition to these three *upāyas* another called *anupāya* is also mentioned. The Sanskrit word *anupāya* literally means "no *upāya.*" As the name implies, *anupāya* is not actually an *upāya,* for in *anupāya* there are no means. The one who has attained *anupāya* has only to observe that nothing is to be done. Just to be is enough. In *anupāya* the aspirant experiences that everything is filled with his own God Consciousness. In fact, *anupāya* is the unexplainable reality of the liberated aspirant.

22. Here, in examining means, the creation of means is found in *āṇavopāya,* the protection of means is found in *śaktopāya,* and the destruction of means is found in *śāmbhavopāya.*

23. The wheel of energies.

24. *Kālāgni rudra* rests in the element *pṛithvī. Pṛithvī tattva* is the lowest element of the 36 *tattvas.*

25. *Śāntātītā kalā* is the abode of Lord Śiva. It is found in the subtlest element, *śiva tattva.*

found, externally found, or found in his own awareness, the heroic yogī feels that the entire universe has become one with the fire of supreme consciousness. The secret teaching is contained in special *tantras* that remain unwritten and have been orally transmitted from master to disciple.

It is also said in *Bhargaśikhā śāstra*:

> When, at the time of meditating on the wheel of energies, he digests and destroys everything–death, the sphere of time, the collection of all activities found in the world, the totality of all emotions, becoming the object of all perceptions,[26] becoming the object of one thought or various thoughts—in his own supreme being he causes that whole to enter in that supreme consciousness of God.

The *Vīravala Śāstra* also says the same thing:

> That consciousness, where everything is destroyed and the totality of thirty-six elements is burned to ashes, should be perceived in one's own body, shining like *kālāgni rūdra*.[27] *(Vīravala Śāstra)*

The Mālinī Vijaya Tantra also says the same thing.

> The one who meditates on that unspeakable and indescribable being gains entry into his own nature by that trance called *śākta samāveśa*. (*Mālinī Vijaya Tantra* 2.22)

Now, the author of the commentary, Kṣhemarāja, tells us that he will not give us any further clarification because the *Mālinī*

---

26. Whenever you perceive an object, you become one with that object.

27. *Kālāgni* resides in the left big toe. You have to imagine fire coming from *kālāgni* and this fire burns your body so that nothing, no substance of the body, remains unburned. You must imagine that your whole body has become ashes and the highest peace of God consciousness will shine in your consciousness, in your knowledge. This practice is set out in the *Vijñāna Bhairava,* where you are instructed to imagine that *kālāgni*, the fire of God consciousness, has risen from the point of your big left toe.

Vijaya Tantra teaches us that this state and power of contemplation will only appear in the one who serves the feet of a master. He says that a more vivid explanation must come from the mouth of the master.

This is narrated in *Spanda Kārikās* in this first verse and in the last verse:

> By whose twinkling of the eyes, in their opening and closing, this whole universe is created and destroyed . . . (*Spanda Kārikā* 1.1)

> When one is unflinchingly focused to one-pointedness, then he enters in his supreme consciousness . . . (*Spanda Kārikā* 3.19)

There is no difference between a mystical trance *(samādhi)* and the world of action *(vyutthāna)* when the world of dualistic perception is completely digested in one's own consciousness.

7. *jāgratsvapnasuṣuptabhede turyābhogasaṁbhava*[28] //

Such a heroic yogī experiences the expansive state of turya in the differentiated states of waking, dreaming and deep sleep.

When that aspirant, who is a hero in meditation, through the flashing forth of active awareness[29] instantaneously makes universal consciousness shine *(udyamo bhairavaḥ)*, then for him the expansive state of *turya*[30] occurs in all states, waking *(jāgrat)*, dreaming *(svapna)* and deep sleep *(suṣupti)*. For this yogī, all the states of experience, waking, dreaming and deep sleep, are one with *turya*. He does not experience any differ-

28. Some commentators of these *sūtras* argue that the word "*saṁbhava*" should be replaced by the word "*saṁvit*" because the word "*saṁvit*" gives a more vivid explanation to the reader. In that case, the *sūtra* would read "*jāgrat svapna suṣupti bhede turyābhoga saṁvit*" which means, "the differentiated states of waking, dreaming and deep sleep, the expansive state of *turya* is held in consciousness *(saṁvit)*." If the word "*saṁbhava*" is correct, then it means "takes place, occurs." If the word "*saṁvit*" is correct then it means "it is held."

29. This heroic yogī possesses active, not passive, power of meditation. What is active meditating power? Active meditating power exists when there is no yawning, no leaning, and no other thought interfering during meditation. It is actively one-pointed awareness. Passive meditation will carry you towards nothingness. It is only a waste of time. Whenever you meditate, you must meditate in an active way.

30. *Turya* means "the fourth." When the individual subjective body travels in absolute subjective consciousness and becomes that subjective consciousness, this is the fourth state, *turya*.

ence between this world and the state of *samādhi*. This happens to that yogī who is a great yogī, with advanced development of awareness.

It is said in the *Candrajñāna*:

> Just like the moon, shining in the sky, beautiful like a flower, captivating the mind, instantaneously fills this world with happiness. In the same way, when this heroic yogī wanders about in this world, with the rays of his knowledge, he purifies and fills it with supreme bliss right from hell *(avīchi)* to śiva. *(Śrī Candrajāna)*

In the *Spanda Kārikā,* it is explained in this verse:

> In the differentiated states of waking, dreaming and deep sleep, that supreme consciousness of *turya* is found as one. (*Spanda Kārikā* 1.3)

Now, in the next three sūtras, the author explains the three states of consciousness, waking *(jāgrat)*, dreaming *(svapna)*, and deep sleep *(suṣupti)*.

8. jñānaṁ jāgrat //

External organic knowledge constitutes the waking state.

External organic knowledge *(jñānam)* is not knowledge of the self; it is dualistic knowledge.

9. svapno vikalpāḥ //

Internal perceptions and thoughts compose the dreaming state.

The Sanskrit word *vikalpāḥ* means "internal perceptions." If internal perceptions are found in the waking state, it is also dreaming (*svapna*).

10. aviveko māyāsauṣuptam //

Forgetfulness and the negation of awareness is the dreamless state or māyā.

That which is the object of everyone because it is from the external organic world comprises the waking state (*jāgrat*).

Those objects which are created in one's own mind and become perceptions of only one individual constitute the dreaming state. In the dreaming state, thought is predominant.

And when you are absolutely unaware, unable to differentiate your being—not being present where you are—this ignorance, this negation, is the state of deep sleep. This state is one with *māyā*. It makes you absolutely deluded about your nature. So, although it is the dreamless state *(suṣupti)* that is explained here, you must understand that the state of *māyā*, which must be discarded, has the same explanation.

Up to this point, we have explained the three states of consciousness, waking, dreaming, and deep sleep. You must now understand that each of these states contains three additional states. Thus in the waking state there are three states, in the dreaming state there are three states, and in the state of deep sleep there are three states. And these three additional states are waking, dreaming and deep sleep. So there is waking in wakefulness, dreaming in wakefulness and deep sleep in wakefulness.

You must know that in the waking state, whenever you find that there is external organic knowledge, that is wakefulness in the waking state. When there are only thoughts in the waking state, that is dreaming in the waking state and when there is unawareness (*moha*), the negation of your self, in the waking state that is deep sleep in the waking state.

These three states also exist in the dreaming state. When, while dreaming, there is some subjective knowledge and you are conscious of dreaming, feeling that you are dreaming a dream, that dreaming state is called wakefulness in the dreaming state. When, while dreaming, you are given completely to perception without any awareness of that subjective consciousness, that is the dream state within a dream. And when these dreams are not remembered at all, that is the deep sleep state within a dream.

Now, take the state of deep sleep. Where can wakefulness be found in the deep sleep state? Where can wakefulness exist when there is the absolute negation of thoughts and awareness? Although thought does not exist in the state of deep sleep, there is a point before entering the state of deep sleep where one feels that he is going to get complete rest. This is wakefulness in the deep sleep state. When the impressions of the deep sleep state remain, causing one to think upon waking that he was sleeping and does not know anything, this is dreaming in the state of deep sleep. In the dreaming state of deep sleep, there are impressions and there are thoughts of these impressions, but these are not gross thoughts. Rather, these are thoughts held in a subtle way. They are thoughts in the state of impressions. The completely thoughtless state is deep sleep in the state of deep sleep.

Now we will analyze these three states: waking, dreaming and deep sleep from the yogic point of view. When a yogī is completely one-pointed in meditation *(dhāraṇā)*, that is the waking state. Here the yogī is aware at the beginning of meditation that he is meditating and he is one-pointed about meditating. This is active, not passive,[31] meditation. For yogīs, the state of meditation is called wakefulness because here the yogī is given to one-pointedness.

---

31. In passive meditation, when you sit for meditation you may sit and think of someone else. When you sit for meditation, you must sit with consciousness. That is active meditation.

When one-pointedness is breaklessly maintained as the continuity of one thought, that, for the yogī, is the dreaming state. For the yogī, this state of dreaming is higher than wakefulness. And, for yogīs, higher still is the state known as deep sleep. This state exists when both the state of objectivity and the state of subjectivity instantly vanish. This is *samādhi*, the thoughtless state of consciousness, and it is deep sleep for yogīs.

This is why in *Mālinī Vijaya Tantra* the three states—wakefulness, dreaming and deep sleep—are shown one in another. In the waking state, there is wakefulness; in the waking state there is dreaming; and in the waking state there is deep sleep. Also in the dreaming state as well as in deep sleep there is wakefulness, dreaming and deep sleep.

Also from the *yogic* point of view it is explained:

> *Abuddha* is the state of wakefulness in wakefulness. *Buddha* is the state of wakefulness in dreaming, *prabuddha* is the state of wakefulness in deep sleep. And *suprabuddha* is the state of wakefulness in the fourth state *(turya)*.

So these threefold states, waking, dreaming and deep sleep, are explained from the worldly point of view and the yogic point of view.

The heroic yogī, who has destroyed this entire universe by meditating on the collective wheel of energies and through that process has achieved the expansive state known as "the fourth" *(turya)*, and who embraces everywhere, in waking, dreaming, deep sleep, and also in *turya*, the all-pervading oneness of God consciousness, ascends to and is established in that supreme summit of *turya*, the state known as "beyond the fourth" *(turyātītaṁ)*.

It is said in this sūtra:

11. tritayabhoktā vīreśaḥ //

The one who enjoys in the oneness of awareness all of the three states—waking, dreaming, and deep sleep—becomes the master of all organic energies.

When this yogī, through meditating on the wheel of energies *(śakticakra)*, apprehends the threefold state of waking, dreaming and deep sleep as absolutely free from all dualistic thoughts, filled with the nectar of bliss *(ānanda rasa)* and completely mixed with *turya*, then this yogī has truly relished these three states in the oneness of awareness. He is one who, enjoying the oneness of these three states in *turya*, becomes *vīreśaḥ*, the master of all active organic energies.[32]

This heroic yogī is simultaneously aware of where objectivity and where subjectivity exist in the three states of waking, dreaming and deep sleep and is never stained by them.[33] This kind of yogī enjoys the unrivaled kingdom of the

---

32. He is a master of organic energies, not organic organs. Why is this distinction being made? Because there are two classes of organs, one is organic organs *(indriya vṛittis)* and the other is organic energies *(indriya śaktis)*. Organic organs are organs found everywhere in every individual being. Organic energy, on the other hand, is found only in yogīs because yogīs are always aware. They are aware when they see, when they touch, when they smell, when they hear, when they taste, when they produce sounds, and when they talk. Yogīs who are the masters of the active organic energies are called heroes *(vīras)*.

33. For example, you see an object such as a chair. When you see this object, the chair is the object but in this experience there is a subject, an experiencer who experiences, who sees, this chair. The one who experiences

universal self. He is filled with supreme bliss and becomes master of heroes (*vīras*) who are dedicated to digesting the sense of difference in the universe. He is said to be one with *Manthāna Bhairava*, which is *Bhairava* who churns everything, all objectivity, all cognition and all subjectivity, into one consciousness, producing a supreme undifferentiated mixture of universal consciousness. This is how it is explained in very rare *Tantras*.

On the other hand, the ordinary worldly man, who is not like this heroic yogī, is played by the three states, waking, dreaming and deep sleep. He is just like a beast. And so also that yogī who has not attained this supreme state of consciousness, he too is not the master of all active organic energies. He is also just like a beast. This is very well explained in sacred texts such as the *Svacchanda Tantra*:

> The yogī, who has adopted independent yoga and because of that independent yoga is moving in an independent way and is situated in an independent state, gets entry in an independent being. (*Svacchanda Tantra* 7.260)

In *Spanda Kārikā*, the explanation is given in the following verse:

> The knowledge of that spanda is held by him in the same way in waking, dreaming and deep sleep. (*Spanda Kārikā* 1.17)

In the waking state, the knowledge of that *spanda* is not less than it is in the dreaming state or in the state of deep sleep and vice versa. This yogī experiences that the state of *turya* is identical in all three states.

---

internally that this is a chair, that is the subject and this chair is the object. These two, subject and object, are found in all the three states, waking, dreaming and deep sleep. In ordinary life, when someone experiences an object, such as a chair, he is aware of the object and unaware of the experiencer, the subject. Here, in this same experience, the yogī experiences the objective world and the subjective world simultaneously. When he is experiencing the object, he is concurrently experiencing the subject, the experiencer. And, at the same time, he is above these and so he is never stained by them.

Now the author asks this question. Does such a yogī have any characteristics that would lead one to surmise that he is established in the state of *paramaśiva*? The answer to this question is yes, there are signs. The author now explains in this sūtra the signs by which we can determine that a yogī is established in that supreme state of Lord Śiva.

12. vismayo yogabhūmikāḥ //

The predominant sign of such a yogī is joy-filled amazement.

This yogī is filled with joy and amazement. The Sanskrit word *vismaya* means "amazement completely filled with joy." Just as a person seeing some wonderful object is amazed, in the same way, this yogī is filled with amazement who, in the objective world of senses, experiences entry in his own self filled with consciousness, which is unique, intense, always fresh and uncommonly charming, and by which entry all his varieties of organs are filled with blooming, ever smiling, one-pointed joy.

What kind of amazement is this? This yogī, upon entering into that limitless state of bliss *(ānanda)*, is never satiated with the experience. On the contrary, he feels bathed with the amazement of joy. This is the predominent state of yoga of a yogī who has become one with the supreme Lord, the supreme *tattva*, Śiva *tattva*. And by this, you can surmise that he has ascended to the state of Śiva.

On the other hand, to perceive at the place of rectum (*mūlādhāra*) a joyful state of consciousness or to perceive effulgent light between the two eyebrows are not the states of such a yogī. These are to be discarded. There is only one sign of such a yogī and that is that he is filled with amazement overflowing with joy. It is said in *Kulayukta Śāstra*:

> When yogīs perceive the state of the self by their own effort, then in their own self they perceive the fullness of wonder filled with joy. *(Kulayukta Śāstra)*

Here in this verse is the conclusion reached in *Spanda Kārikā*:

> When he perceives his own nature through subjective perception, then he perceives that he is one with this reality. For him, being wonderstruck and filled with wonderful joy, there is no possiblility of traveling the path of repeated births and deaths. (*Spanda Kārikā* 1.11)

Such a yogī, established in this kind of yoga, filled with the wonderful state of joy,

13. icchā śakttirūmā kumāri //

His will is the energy of Lord Śiva and it is called umā *and it is called* kumāri.

or,

For such a yogī, his will is one with the energy of Lord Śiva, unobstructable, completely independent, always given to play.

His will is the energy (*śakti*) of Lord Śiva. And, his will is not only energy it is also called *umā* and *kumārī*. The author has provided these three names for the will of such a yogī.

The will of the yogī, who has attained complete entry into the state of Bhairava and become one with supreme Bhairava, is the energy of Lord Śiva. It is one with *umā*. Here, in this sūtra, the word *umā* does not refer to the wife of Lord Śiva. Here the word *umā* refers to the independent energy of the supreme Lord (*svātantrya*).

The will of this yogī is also called *kumārī*. The Sanskrit word *kumārī* can be translated and understood in a number of ways. It could be that *kumārī* refers to that energy that plays in the universe, creating, protecting, and destroying it. But why use this definition? Because in Sanskrit grammar, the word *kumāra* is contained in the meaning of *krīḍā*, which means "to play." *Kumārī*, therefore, means that energy that is always given to play.

There is another meaning of *Kumārī*. *Kumārī* can be understood as *kuṁ mārayati*. Here *kuṁ* means the differentiated perception in this world and *mārayati* is the energy that destroys differentiated perception and directs it into one's own nature.

That is *kumārī*. Also, *kumārī* can be understood to mean "virgin." In this context, what do we mean by the word "virgin"? Here "virgin" is to be understood as referring to that girl that has never been enjoyed by any other agency. She is one who has established her own nature in the state of enjoyer. She is enjoying her own nature in her own way. She does not require any other vehicle for enjoyment. This is *kumārī* and this is the state of being virgin. This kind of girl is always one with her own nature. She is not looking to the opposite sex for satisfaction. There is still another way to understand the meaning of *umākumārī*. At the time when Umā was virgin, she was completely detached from the world of enjoyment. When she had given herself to perform penance in order to receive the blessing of Lord Śiva, her mind was one-pointedly focused only on Lord Śiva. She was always one with that being of Śiva. In the same way, the desire of such a yogī is completely one-pointed. He always wills entry in his own nature and nothing else. This is how our masters have explained the meaning of this *sūtra*.[34]

So this kind of yogī, established in yoga in all three states and filled with joyous amazement, does not, like ordinary people, possess gross desire in his mind. On the contrary, his energy of will is always one with the supreme energy of Lord Śiva and, therefore, there is no power that can obstruct it. This verse in the *Svacchanda Śāstra* is saying the same thing:

> Lord Śiva's energy of will (*svātantrya śakti*) is one with *devī* (goddess) who, as His energy, is known by many different names. This energy of will is concealed with the magic of yoga and, named *Kumārī*, is desired by every being. (*Svacchanda Tantra* 10.727)

Everyone wants to have this kind of will so that whatever he desires, he gets. In the *Netra Tantra*, the same thing is explained:

---

34. On the other hand, some other commentators of the *Śiva Sūtras* have argued that in place of *śaktirumā*, the word *śaktitamā* should be used. If you accept this substitution, then in explaining the word *śaktitamā*, you can conclude that the meaning of this sūtra is "the will of this yogī is filled with knowledge and action."

Oh Pārvatī! His will is one with my will, my supreme energy. It is one with myself and rises from my own nature.[35]

The energy of the will of this yogī has become the cause of the entire universe because the energy of this yogī is one with the energy of Lord Śiva, just as heat is one with fire and rays are one with the sun. In the same way, his energy is one with the self of Śiva. (*Netra Tantra* 1.25–26)

This is concluded in *Spanda Kārikā* in this *śloka.*

He does not infuse the power of will in his senses but when he wills, it is done. He does not crave for any desire but, because he possesses the strength of supreme I, when he desires, he wills, and it is accomplished. (*Spanda Kārikā* 1.8)

---

35. His will doesn't rise from the senses. His will rises from the nature of the being of Lord Śiva.

To such a great yogī who has such a great will, desire . . .

14. dṛiśyaṁ śarīram //

This entire perceived world is his own self.

or

His own body is just like an object to him.

In this sūtra, the Sanskrit word *driśyam* means "perceived objective world." So in this case, the sūtra would be translated "This entire perceived world is his own self." It can also be translated in a different and opposite way. The alternative translation would be "He perceives his own body just like an object." He does not perceive his body with the oneness of I consciousness. Why? Because he has no ego for that body.

These are two ways this sūtra is to be translated. One, this whole objectve world is his own self and two, his own body is an object. In the first way of translating this sūtra, emphasis is on the reality that because he is one with every being, he perceives the perceived world of objects, the objective world, as his own self.

In the second way of translating this sūtra, the yogī's perception of his body as an object is stressed. But here the perception of his body as an object is not perceiving his body in a subjective way, as we do. Our perception of our body is suggested in such statements as, "I am strong, I am very weak." But who is weak? The self is not weak. Because the body is weak, you say I am weak. You perceive your body as one with your own I consciousness. But this *yogī* does not. He perceives his own body, and not only this body, but the gross body of wake-

Now the author furnishes another means to attain such a state of yoga.

16. śuddha-tattva-saṁdhānādvā'paśuśaktiḥ //

Or by aiming at the pure element of Śiva, he possesses Śiva's unlimited energy.

In the sūtra, "the pure element" *(śuddha tattva)* refers only to supreme Śiva. Now, what do we have to do with that? We have to make this universal objectivity enter in that supreme consciousness of pure Śiva. You must see that this universe is residing in that pure element. There you will never find any impure object. Everything will appear to you as divine.

When you target, which means "aim at," and then perceive that this whole universe is existing in the pure state of Śiva, in this way you will discard and be separated from the entangling energy that binds you with the wheel of differentiated perception. Instantly, you will become one with this universal state that is just like the pure element of Śiva *(sadāśiva)* and you will become master of the universe.

This is also said in *Lakṣmīkaulārṇava Tantra*:

> The yogic powers which are attained with the perfection of an initiation from a great master, when compared with this supreme universal consciousness, are not equal to its sixteenth part. These yogic powers are nothing in comparison. They are all to be discarded. You have only to own and maintain this universal-I *(mantra vīrya)*.

That is called *saṁdhāna*. The Sanskrit word *saṁdhāna* means "aiming." Aiming and entry, aiming and enjoying, aiming and feeling, aiming and attaining. And it is not only aiming, for this is just what we do when we meditate. We may meditate for one hour, two hours or three hours and during this time, we are always aiming, aiming, aiming. We are only aiming. But we have to aim once and for all. Aim and attain it. That is what is called *saṁdhāna* (aiming).

The *Vijñāna Bhairava* also speaks in the same way:

> With one-pointed attention, you must feel and perceive that this universe and your body are simultaneously one with God consciousness. Then the rise of that supreme God consciousness takes place. (*Vijñāna bhairava* 36)

This is also explained in *Spanda Kārikā* in this verse:

> For such a yogī who has this kind of perception, this world is a playground. Always filled with joy, he is never sad. Doubtlessly, he is liberated while living *(jīvan mukta)*. (*Spanda Kārikā* 2.5)

For such a yogī who possesses such exalted knowledge,

17. vitarka ātmajñānam //

Any inference of such a yogī is knowledge of his own real self.

Whatever this yogī thinks, whatever he confirms, is one with the knowledge of his own self. It is his constant perception, "I am Lord Śiva, one with the universe." This kind of perception[37] is his personal knowledge.

This is also quoted in *Vijñāna Bhairava*:

> The supreme Lord (Parameśvara) is all knowing, all doing and all pervading. The yogī thinks, "My self is one with the Lord because the aspects of Śiva are my aspects." By attentive meditation on this, one becomes one with Śiva. (*Vijñāna Bhairava* 102)

In *Spanda* it is also said:

> . . . this is said to be the real one-pointedness of thought. (*Spanda Kārikā* 2.7)

In this verse of *Spanda Kārikā*, we are told that the individual-I becoming one with the universal-I is knowledge of one's self.

37. In this sūtra, the word *vitarka* not only means inference, it also means perception.

For such a yogī, it also happens that,

18. lokānandaḥ samādhisukham //

The joy of his samādhi *is bliss for the whole universe.*

Whatever joy he feels while he is in *samādhi* is said to be the insertion of bliss for the whole universe. This yogī doesn't have to do anything. He only has to remain in *samādhi* and he will carry the whole universe into that supreme bliss.

In the sūtra, the Sanskrit word *loka* is to be explained in two ways. Whatever is perceived is *loka* and the perceiver is also *loka*. The one who is the perceiver of everybody is *loka* and the object that is perceived is *loka*. When the objective world and the subjective world are simultaneously in movement together, what happens is

> All individual beings perceive the objective world as separate from the subjective world and the subjective world as separate from the objective world. In this regard, there is a special exception for yogīs. When yogīs perceive the objective world, they perceive the subjective world in the objective world and the objective world in the subjective world. For these yogīs, the objective world and the subjective world is not different in their consciousness because their subjective God consciousness is held everywhere. (*Vijñāna Bhairava* 106)

According to such teachings found in the *Vijñāna Bhairava,* when a yogī resides with full awareness in the state of subjectivity, with the full joy of experiencing his own nature *(camatkāra)*, this is said to be the joy of his *samādhi* (mystical rapture).

The same is quoted in *Vijñāna Bhairava*:

> When a yogī meditates that the entire universe or his body is simultaneously filled with the supreme bliss of the joy of the self, then through the flow of that joy, he becomes one with supreme joy. (*Vijñāna Bhairava* 65)

This is narrated in *Spanda Kārikā* in this verse:

> This is said to be the achievement of supreme amṛita. (*Spanda Kārikā* 2.7)

There is another explanation of this sūtra given by masters and that is, "Whenever this yogī, who is always residing in his own self *(svātmārāmā)*, is introverted and established in his own self, then he naturally enjoys the bliss of *samādhi*. Anyone who sees this and thinks that this yogī is enjoying the bliss of *samādhi* will, at that very moment, also enter into *samādhi*. This is just like seeing a cobra not from distance, but face to face."

When you see a cobra and it bites you, you will be filled with the poison of that cobra. In the same way, when you observe a yogī who is established in the joy of *samādhi* and you understand that he is experiencing the joy of this *samādhi*, you will at once also relish the joy of this *samādhi*. This reveals how this bliss is bestowed on the whole world. But how does this observer enter in that state?

> The bliss of that yogī penetrates the nature of that observer who sees and feels that he is in bliss. Then he also abruptly becomes one with that bliss.

From this quote taken from the *Candrajñānagrantha*, quoted earlier in the commentary of sūtra 7, you can see that he has given the same kind of explanation of this statement "the whole world is enjoying the bliss of *samādhi*" (*lokānanda samādhi sukham*).

What yogic glory has this yogī achieved?

19. śaktisandhāne śarīrotpattiḥ //

By infusing his energy of will, the embodiment of that which is willed occurs at once.

He does not have to pray to Lord Śiva to bestow a boon on his devotees or on those who have come to take his refuge. He just has to infuse his energy of will thinking, "let this man achieve this," and it becomes true. That is the meaning of *śakti sandhāna*. Here, with his supreme energy of will, he aims at the object that is desired by his devotee and the manifestation of that object takes place immediately without any encumbrance. This has already been explained in the sūtra 13 of the First Awakening,

> For such a yogī, his will is one with the energy of Lord Śiva, unobstructable, completely independent, always given to play.

Whenever he aims the energy of will completely, not as an afterthought or superfluously but willing from the core of his heart, then what he wills must happen. Because of that force of will, whatever is desired comes true.

This is also quoted in *Mṛtyuñjayabhaṭṭāraka* (the *Netra Tantra*),

> The very moment he has willed something to happen, the power of that will begins to move for its accomplishment. The will of this yogī is faultless and beyond the imagination of a human being. And it is not only will, it is also knowledge and action.

> The energy of will of such a yogī is said to be the energies of all gods and goddesses. Whenever he wills wholeheartedly, his will is unstoppable. This is the cause of everything with fire because it works abruptly and moon because it shines in supreme peace. Everything exists in the will of this yogī. (*Netra Tantra* 7.36–40)

In *Lakṣmīkaulārṇava Tantra*, the glory of targeting his will is explained in this verse:

> Initiation cannot be successful, powers will not really shine, the mantra received from his master will be useless, its proper recitation[38] will not be understood and yoga will not be achieved unless the will of such a yogī is focused. (*Lakṣmīkaulārṇava Tantra*)

This is expressed in *Spanda* in this verse.

> A yogī with attachment to the world attains the objects of his desire, which are necessarily manifest by the Universal Lord, just by inhaling and exhaling along with focusing his will. (*Spanda Kārikā* 3.1)

He has to focus his will along with inhaling once and exhaling once and the desired object is attained. There is no time, no space, no waiting. He only inhales and exhales along with focusing his will and it is realized and he has achieved it.

But this kind of achievement is only attained by those yogīs who have attachment for the body, attachment for disciples, attachment for the public. It is for these yogīs, who have slightly come down from God consciousness, that this kind of power takes place. For elevated yogīs, these powers do not arise. Elevated yogīs are always focused in their own supreme way of God consciousness. They do not care for these powers or for matters of the world.

---

38. When aspirants first recite their mantra, they cannot understand how to recite it. But eventually a time comes when, after reciting it blindly, they learn the reality of its recitation. That is *mantrayukti*. *Mantrayukti* comes by itself after a constant period of recitation. And this *mantrayukti* will not take place unless there is focusing of the will of such a yogī.

But for those yogīs, who have not erased the impression of body consciousness from their minds, and whose internal consciousness is diverted to external consciousness[39] whatever they want to create, whatever they want to occur, takes place because Lord Śiva manifests their desired objects simply by their breathing in and breathing out once. Whatever they want to create, whatever they want to occur, those things take place because *prakāśa* and *ānanda*[40]give rise to these two breaths as *soma* (moon) and *sūrya* (sun) and the energy of *prāṇa śakti,* which is residing in the center of these two.

This is the meaning of this verse of *Spanda*:

> In the same way, in dreaming state he can dream any dream he wishes. (*Spanda Kārikā* 3.2)

This is not exactly like the concept of *māyā* for *Śaivities* or *prakṛiti* for the *Vedāntins*. For *Vedāntins, prakṛiti* controls the dreaming state and for Śaivaites, *māyā* is the controller of this state. Such a yogī, however, can dream any dream he wishes. He is not concerned with the consciousness of *māyā* or *prakṛiti*. So also in the dreaming state, he can dream whatever he wishes to dream. This is called the independent world of the dreaming state *(svapnasvātantrya).* So, this yogī's waking state is not the only independent state. For this kind of yogī, both the waking state and the dreaming state are independent.

---

39. Unless external consciousness is maintained, no power can be achieved. Powers come only by maintaining external consciousness. Otherwise, what is the use of power when there is always internal consciousness? In internal consciousness, you are always powerful, always blissful. In internal consciousness, there is no need of anything. In internal consciousness, you are full and complete. Incompletion rises in the external world, not the internal world.

40. Here, inhaling is *prakāśa* and exhaling is *ānanda.*

This yogī is fully conscious everywhere. Even when he dies, he is fully conscious. He knows where and when to die in God consciousness. The one who is not aware of that God consciousness, he is unaware everywhere, in each and every aspect of his movements from waking to dreaming to deep sleep. Whenever he goes to the dreaming state, he doesn't know from which point he has entered the dreaming state. When he comes out from the dreaming state, he does not know when he came out from the dreaming state and entered the waking state. And, when he enters the dreamless state, he doesn't remember the point when he entered. Naturally, therefore, he doesn't remember the point of death. On the contrary, the one who remembers these three points will also remember the point of death. He will also be conscious and aware there. The point here is awareness, awareness must be developed. The more you develop awareness, the more you are near to God consciousness.Kṣemarāja tells us that he has explained this idea thoroughly in his commentary on *spanda*.

By the glory of the supreme energy of will of such a *yogī*, other powers also come into existence.

20. bhūtasaṁdhāna-bhūtapṛithaktva-viśvasaṁghaṭṭāḥ //

By the greatness of this achievement of the energy of will, the yogī can focus his awareness and heal the sick and suffering, separate elements from his body and be free from the limitations of space and time.

By the greatness of this achievement of the energy of will *(icchā śakti)*, this yogī can concentrate on some particular person who is sick, who is suffering from pain or from sadness, and cause this sadness and suffering to leave him. That is the meaning of *bhūta saṁdhāna*. This is one power that this yogī attains.

When it is destined that this *yogī* has to suffer constantly for three years in his bed, he can temporarily separate that affliction from his body and keep it separately locked away. Once he separates this trouble from his body, he can continue with his daily routine without any hindrance. He has separated his trouble and kept it locked away. Let his body be painful, his consciousness is never painful. And whenever he returns from his daily routine and sleeps, he opens this box of trouble and that trouble enters his body again, causing him suffering. This is the meaning of *bhūta pṛthaktva*. This is the second power this yogī attains.

There is also a third power this yogī achieves. This power gives him the ability to be free from the limitations of time and space. With this power, he can enter a past or future world and see what has happened or what is to come. This power is called *viśva saṁghaṭṭa*.

The Sanskrit word *bhūta* means "that which exists." So, the body is *bhūta*, breath is *bhūta*, objects are *bhūta*. Simply by focusing on some object with his energy of will, this yogī's desired results are obtained. Whenever this yogī focuses his will on a person to cause that person, who can be either living or dead, to recover either here or in heaven or hell, that person will recover. He can lift that person from sadness in all the three worlds. Or to get rid of the pain in his own body, he can separate that pain from his body, enabling him to continue to do his work. Or he can enter that world and that universe which is far away in time and space. He can focus his mind on a distant city and see its past, present or future. This is explained in each and every Tantra in the chapters on practices (*sādhanā*), not in the chapters on attainments (*siddhas*). It is said in *Spanda*:

> By taking hold of spanda, the energy of will, even a feeble person becomes capable and fit to do whatever work he intends doing. The one who is filled with extreme and intense hunger can subside his hunger by focusing the force of the energy of will *(icchā śakti)*. (*Spanda Kārikā* 3.6)

And,

> The absence of awareness robs your body of the wealth of spirituality. This absence of awareness is created by your own ignorance. If you wash off that ignorance existing in you with spanda, the energy of will, then where does the possibility of the absence of awareness exist? (*Spanda Kārikā* 3.8)

And,

> Just as when an object is initially not clearly seen by ordinary people and then, when they put their attention on that object, they see it clearly and know what it is now and in any subsequent perception.[41] So, in the same way wherever and whenever any object is existing, you have only to focus your energy of will there and you can perceive that object in an instant. (*Spanda Kārikā* 3.5)

41. For instance, there is a rope lying on the ground. At first, the experiencer perceives that it is a snake. Then after perceiving it clearly, with awareness, he sees and understands that it is not a snake, it is a rope. So, at that time, he has clearly understood the object.

In the previous sūtra, limited yogic powers were explained. Now in the twenty-first sūtra, the author will explain unlimited yogic powers. When this yogī does not desire limited powers and is eager to attain the knowledge of universal being, then for such a yogī,

21. śuddhavidyodyāccakreśatva-siddhiḥ //

... pure knowledge rises and by that knowledge he becomes the master of the universal wheel.

For this yogī, pure knowledge rises and by that pure knowledge, he becomes *(cakreśvara)* lord of the universal wheel. This was just like Lord Kṛiṣṇa. Lord Kṛiṣṇa utilized his powers in a universal way, not a limited way. For example, Lord Kṛiṣṇa appeared in his universal form. That was the greatest yogic power. And furthermore, because he was master of the universal wheel, he displayed many additional powers. His powers were not limited. On the other hand, some yogīs will tell you that when you take your school examination, you will achieve a good grade, or they will tell you that you will be successful tomorrow in your business dealings. These powers are called limited powers.

If, however, you want rainfall to come and rainfall comes, the power that caused that rainfall is an unlimited power, a universal power. If you want an earthquake to happen, that is universal power. If you want the destruction of the whole universe, that is universal power. If you want the rise of happiness for the universe, that is universal power. When in the background there is no individuality, that is universal power. That is becoming master of the wheel of energies, *śakticakra*. By the rise of pure knowledge *(śuddha vidyā)*, the yogī exhibits universal power and becomes the master of *śakticakra*, the universal wheel.

When he concentrates his energy of will for attaining the universal state of being, he finds this pure knowledge arises in him, whereby he realizes, "I am the whole universe. I am not only my body, I am one with the universe." This yogī then attains the glory of the Lord, by which glory he becomes master of the universal wheel.

It is also quoted in the *Svacchanda Tantra*:

> The knowledge that he attains is unequaled supreme knowledge because he simultaneously attains the supreme glories of all knowledge and all action. *(Svacchanda Tantra)*

This is said to be the supreme knowledge of this yogī. But what is this knowledge? In the next verse from the *Svacchanda Tantra*, more is revealed about supreme knowledge.

> When the eternal aspect of Lord Śiva, the energy of svātantrya, is known, and supreme I consciousness is also in his knowledge, then the absence of supreme consciousness is kept away. This is why it is called pure knowledge, *śuddhavidyā*. (*Svacchanda Tantra* 6.396)

> You should be established in that supreme knowledge and reveal in your own nature the supreme light of supreme being. When that supreme light is revealed, you become one with Lord Śiva. (*Svacchanda Tantra* 6.397)

This is narrated in Spanda in this verse:

> When he pervades the whole universe including his individual being, then what is to be explained or spoken to him? He understands his state by himself. (*Spanda Kārikā* 3.11)

On the other hand, there are some yogīs who have no desire to create these universal yogic powers. In this regard, they are just like Rāma, the son of Dashratha. He did not possess or utilize any universal powers. He was above that. Because his mind was focused in his own nature, he didn't desire to have universal powers. Instead, he utilized his weapons, his strength and his energy.

In the next sūtra, the author explains what happens to this yogī when he desires to reside in his own state of God consciousness, peacefully, without creating universal agitation outside or inside.[42]

22. mahāhṛidānusaṁdhānān
mantravīryānubhavaḥ //

By the attentive continuity of meditation on the great ocean of consciousness,
the power of supreme I is attained.

Then, when this yogī meditates on the great ocean of consciousness with attentive continuity, the power of supreme I *(mantra vīryā)* is attained. In fact, this universe is created by this supreme energy of consciousness right from his internal energy of will to his energy of action.

Because there are so many currents rising in that universal consciousness, currents of sound, currents of touch, currents of smell, and so on, that supreme consciousness is said to be like a great ocean. All these currents are rising from that universal consciousness, which is absolutely pure and transparent. No one can stop this flow of supreme God consciousness, the depth of which is unlimited.

When he meditates on that supreme God consciousness by diverting all the flows of his organs to the introverted, not the extroverted, state, he obtains the state of supreme I *(mantra vīryā)* because the state of *mantra vīrya* is the power of all the letters of the Sanskrit alphabet beginning from the letter *a* and

42. Universal agitation is that agitation in which everyone is upset such as when an earthquake or other such disaster occurs.

ending with the letter *kṣa*. Why? Because all sounds rise from those letters. That sound is called *śabdarāśi*, the collective appearance of all letters. And the power and the essence of all those sounds is one sound, the soundless sound, the sound of I-being, *ahaṁ*, the supreme I and that is *mantra vīrya*. The yogī attains *mantra vīrya* not in an objective way but in a subjective way. Thinking and saying "this is *mantra vīrya*" is realizing it in an objective way. "I am *mantra vīrya*" is realizing it in a subjective way. This is said in the *Mālinīvijaya Tantra:*

> That supreme (svātantrya) independent energy of Lord Śiva is said to be one with Lord Śiva. (*Mālinīvijaya Tantra* 3.5)

In the *Mālinīvijaya Tantra,* the author has begun from this point where "the supreme independent energy of Lord Śiva is said to be one with Lord Śiva." From *svātantrya śakti* arise the energy of will, the energy of knowledge, and the energy of action. And then all universal energies flow outward. The center, therefore, from which all these energies flow, is *svātantrya śakti.*

So the author has explained that this energy of independence (*svātantrya sakti*) of Lord Śiva creates universal energies. It not only creates will, knowledge and action, but all universal energies are created by that one energy of Lord Śiva.

This is why the rise of supreme I is explained as being held everywhere by yogīs. It is held in "this," in "I," and also in "that." It is the universal first person held in the first person, in the second person and in the third person. It is the universal first person, not individual first person. As long as persons are concerned, these are all individual persons. The first person is "I", the second person is "you" and the third person is "he." When there is a universal person, then that is "I," that is "I" in "I," "I" in "you" and "I" in "him."

So that supreme energy of Lord Śiva *(svātantrya śakti)* is said to be just like the supreme ocean of consciousness. When the yogī concentrates on that supreme energy of Lord Śiva, he attains and experiences the state of *mantra vīrya* in the world of *mātṛikācakra* and in the world of *mālinī cakra.*

Mātṛikācakra is the successive creative way of I consciousness. *Mālinī* is the successive destructive way of I consciousness. The successive creative way of consciousness is synonymous with *ahaṁ* and the successive destructive way of I consciousness is synonymous with *mahaa* (pronounced *ma ha a*). The yogī experiences the state of I consciousness in both ways as creative and as destructive. It is well said in *Spanda* that:

> All mantras live in and get life from that one mantra of I consciousness. (*Spanda Kārikā* 2.1)

Thus, in this first awakening of *Śiva Sūtras*, the first sūtra is *caitanyam ātmā*, "God consciousness is your self."

So first, he has accepted the fact that this self is, in its real sense, consciousness. Consciousness is the self, not the body, not the mind, not the organs. What is the self? Consciousness is the self and when the state of consciousness is absent, or lessened, or becomes weakened, then you must know that the rise of *(malas)* impurities has begun. These impurities are three and they are explained in the second and following sūtras of the first awakening—*jñānaṁ bandha, yonivargaḥ kalā śarīram*, and so on. And that bondage is subsided by *udyamo Bhairava*, "the Bhairava which is the supreme flow of super effort." And then this entire universe is filled with divinity and all yogic powers, limited yogic powers, unlimited yogic powers or the internal residence of your own nature, are bestowed by that being.

Thus, this first awakening of the *Śiva Sūtras*, which is one with *śāmbhavopāya*, is explained. Though there are, many places, hints of *śāktopāya*, that *śāktopāya* is described only to make a distinction between *śāktopāya* and *śāmbhavopāya* and, therefore, to direct you towards *śāmbhavopāya*.

This is the end of the First Awakening.

Swamijī

Second Awakening

In the second awakening of the *Śiva Sūtras*, the author explains the second means of awakening, called *śāktopāya*.[1] The energy with which *śāktopāya* is concerned is not ordinary energy. This energy is the expansion, the commentary, of *mantra vīrya*, the commentary of I-consciousness.

At the end of the first awakening, the author introduced *mantra vīrya* because he wanted the idea to be fully revealed and explained in the second awakening. To illuminate the actual state of *mantra vīrya,* the author first explains the reality of mantra, and then the power of *mantra vīrya.*

---

1. The word *śāktopāya* refers to the "means" (*upāya*) pertaining to energy (*śakti*). *Śāmbhavopāya,* the first and supreme *upāya,* is *upāya* pertaining to *Śiva.* And *āṇavopāya,* the third and inferior *upāya,* is *upāya* pertaining to individual being. *Śāmbhavopāya* is explained in the First Awakening of the *Śiva Sūtras, śāktopāya* is explained in the Second Awakening, and *āṇavopāya* is explained in the Third Awakening.

The first sutra is the explanation of mantra:

1. cittaṁ mantraḥ //

Mind is mantra.

In this sūtra, there are two understandings of the mind and both are divine. The first understanding is that the mind is the thought of a sacred word. The second understanding is that mind is the thought of a sacred aspirant who is treading on the sacred path.

The Sanskrit word *citta* means "the thought of a sacred word." This thought is said to be the exposition of mantra. "Mantra," therefore, means sacred word. Sacred word is also the rise of words and sentences in the internal mind of the aspirant. This is also mantra because this aspirant, like a sacred word, is absolutely purified inside and outside. So the aspirant's mind is mantra and a sacred word also is mantra.

The author now explains this sūtra in these two ways. The word "mind" does not mean what we ordinarily understand by the word "mind." Here, the word mind means "that by which you become aware of supreme consciousness." So this mind is said to be that by which your self is exposed in its fullness. It is *vimarśa*—I consciousness—thought in two ways: in *prāsāda mantra* and in *praṇava mantra*. *Prāsāda mantra* is "the mantra of external flow." *Praṇava mantra* is "the mantra of external and internal flow." It is the internal flow in the external world and the external flow in the internal world.

Praṇava is the mantra where both mantras—the *mantra ahaṁ* and *mantra ma-ha-a*—arise. When the *mantra ahaṁ* arises, it is external, and when *ma-ha-a* arises, it is internal. When *aham* occurs, it is coming out from your supreme God consciousness and moving to objective God consciousness. This is traveling to objective God consciousness, not the objective world. When you rise from objective God consciousness to your subjective God consciousness, that is the rise of the *mantra maha-a*. So in both ways, these are the states of *praṇava*.

Prāsāda, on the other hand, is the state of the sacred word *sauḥ*. It is only external. It is rising from inside to outside. This is also rising. It is not falling when you move from inside to the outside world, it is a kind of rise. But it is the supreme rise when you rise in coming out and when you rise in going in. And this is the rise of *praṇava mantra*. When you only rise in one way, that is the rise of *prāsāda mantra.*

So in both ways, this is the state of *citta* (thought). It is said to be mantra because it is secret *(guptaṁ)*. It is not written, it lives in a secret world. When you recite this mantra, you are not reciting it with lips, but with consciousness. When you recite and you are aware of the *prāsāda mantra "sauḥ,"* of its occurrence in your own self, you will understand that this whole universe is the expansion of yourself. This is the kind of rise that occurs when you travel from the internal world to the external world.

It is *praṇava mantra* when you come out from the internal world and travel to the external world and then travel again from the external world to the internal world. So, it is said that this *praṇava mantra* is truly a mantra, for the word "mantra" is made up from *man* and *tra*. *Man* from the word *manana* means "causes you to reside in your own God consciousness." *Tra* from the word *trāṇa* means "protects you from all the evils of the world."[2] So when you focus your mind towards God consciousness, you are protected from all the horrors of the world. Here, this is the meaning of the word "mantra."

Now this exposition of mantra is explained in another way. Because the mind of this yogī is always purified and never thinks absurd thoughts, thinking only divine thoughts and being fo-

---

2. Here the word "evil" does not refer to the commission of what we ordinarily mean by "sin." Here the "evil" we are protected from is that of committing the greatest of all sins—coming out from God consciousness.

cused towards God consciousness, it is mantra. Whatever comes into the mind of this yogī is divine. So, all of his thoughts are divine and hence, his thought is also mantra.

> oṁ padmni oṁ
> oṁ nama śivāya
> svacchanda bhairavāya namaḥ

These sentences are collections of sacred words. Collections of sacred words are not mantras, but just a waste of time for the aspirant. In a real sense, these two—the aspirant's mind and a sacred word experienced as *prāsāda* mantra and/or *praṇava* mantra—are mantras.

The *Sarvajñānottara* also explains this in the same way.

> Those mantras which are recited with the lips and with the mind are not really mantras. *Devatas* and *Gandharvas*, all these great souls, have deluded themselves in thinking that these are actually mantras. And additionally, they are filled with tremendous pride thinking that they are verbally reciting the name of God. (*Sarvajñānottara* 16–17)

Those so-called mantras are not actually mantras. Mantra is divinity in the mind of the yogī or the flow of subjective God consciousness towards objective God consciousness or the simultaneous flow of subjective God consciousness towards objective God consciousness, and the flow of objective God consciousness towards subjective God consciousness.

In the *Tantra Sadbhāva*, this same thing is also explained:

> The life of all mantras is solely the energy of God consciousness. When that energy is absent, all those collections of words are useless just like a mass of clouds in the rainless autumn sky. *(Tantra Sadbhāva)*

In the *Śrīkaṇṭhīsaṁhitā Śāstra*, it is also said:

> The one who recites mantra for the sake of realizing God will never attain the reality of God consciousness. There is only one

> thing that a yogī must maintain and that is awareness, awareness of the union of objective God consciousness with subjective God consciousness and, in one driving push, the flow of objective and subjective God consciousness.

This is not a flow, it is a push. If you force it in this way, with great velocity, it will be just like a ball thrown against a wall. It will come to you again, and bring you back to subjective God consciousness. On the other hand, if you drive it slowly from subjective God consciousness to objective God consciousness, it will end in objective God consciousness and that is the state of *prāsāda*.[3] When you push it with great velocity, it will travel to objective God consciousness and then again return to your subjective God consciousness.[4]

This is narrated in *Spanda* in this verse:

> Because these words are digested along with the mind of the aspirant, they are said to be, along with the divinity of the yogī, one with divine God consciousness. (*Spanda Kārika* 2.2)

---

3. *Prāsāda* is the highest elevated state. When you are situated in *Prāsāda*—the highest state of God consciousness—you become filled with joy.

4. This is *krama mudrā* in its real sense.

2. *prayatnaḥ sādhakaḥ* //

(For such a yogī)
pauseless effort brings about his attainment of God consciousness.

This yogī's attainment of God consciousness is realized by his continued effort. His effort must be pauseless effort *(prayatna)*. That is *sādhaka*, the means for attaining God consciousness.

The mantra and its application, which was explained in the First Awakening of this scripture[5] and which is carried out at the very start of any movement, gives rise to the union of the worshiped and the worshiper. Here, just begin with some movement, any movement, and stop. Hold the beginning point of that movement with awareness. In Sanskrit, this state is called *anusaṁdhitsā*. By holding the very beginning of that movement, the goal of uniting the seeker of God consciousness with the God consciousness he seeks, the spiritual aspirant with that to which he aspires, the one who recites mantra with *mantra devatā*, that Lord for whom the mantra is recited, is achieved.

It is said in *Śrī Tantrasadbhāva*:

> Just as when a vulture, flying in the sky observes a piece of meat in that sky and immediately, with spontaneous effort, catches that piece of meat, so in the same way the elevated yogī directs his mind to that point of light *(bindu prakāśa)* of God consciousness.
>
> Or just as when the archer, placing an arrow on the string of

5. See sūtra 1.22

> a bow and then pulling back on that arrow and letting it go, where it flies swiftly, striking the point at which it was aimed. It is in this same way, O Devi, the supreme light of God Consciousness (*prakāśa*) is attained by just one thrust of awareness.

If the yogī is not successful in one push, he will not be successful at all. It must be attained in one thrust of awareness.

In some other place, it is also said:

> In its true sense, the knowledge of awareness is the state of mantra.

The explanation of this sūtra is that your effort must not be artificial (*akṛita*). It must be absolutely natural, filled with intense desire and fervent longing, and originating from the center of your heart. By that force, this great yogī directs his mind to that point of supreme God consciousness.

This is narrated in *Spanda* in this verse:

> The yogī must first possess such a determined longing that it will lead to the resolution, "I will sit until I attain the state of God consciousness or I will leave my body." The effort must be filled with such determination. It must not be passive effort, it must be active effort. That active effort itself is God consciousness. *(Spanda Kārikā* 2.6)

For such a great yogī, the mantra, universal I, and the splendor of that universal I is explained in this next sūtra.

3. vidyāśarīrasattā mantrarahasyam //

The secret essence of mantra is establishment in the body of the knowledge of oneness.

Here, knowledge means the supreme knowledge of oneness. It is, in the real sense, the supreme God who is the formation of the collection of all sounds. It is from this point that all sounds are created and stored. So, in another sense, it is the state of God consciousness that is one with the universe and filled with supreme I consciousness.

This is the essence of all mantras. By the words "essence of all mantras" is not meant the mantras such as *oṁ namaḥ śivāya, oṁ namo bhagavate vāsudevāya*, etc. These mantras are not mantras in the real sense. Mantra, in the real sense, is that supreme I consciousness. This is the secret about mantras.

This is also quoted in *Śrī Tantrasadbhāva Tantra.*

> All letters are actually one with mantra and those mantras are one with mother, the energy of Lord Śiva, and that mother is one with Lord Śiva himself.

Even though this explanation is secret and can't be exposed or explained, it is revealed in the *Tantrasadbhāva Śāstra* in this way. This is said by Lord Śiva to *Pārvatī*:

Oh Pārvati, there are those who are not maintaining the discipline as taught in the scriptures who do not believe that our master is one with Lord Śiva. They are crooked, attached to worldy pleasures and are not doing any spiritual practice. Because of these misdeeds I have extracted the splendor from their mantras. When that splendor is removed, these mantras become useless. For him who would wield these mantras, they are as good as letters. They have no value. You must have faith that the master is one with Lord Śiva. You must maintain discipline and character. You must not be given to attachment or worldly pleasures. When you live in this way, then your mantra will be filled with splendor and will remain successful.

Now the *Tantrasadbhāva* explains further:

That Divine Mother, who is filled with supreme light, has pervaded the whole universe up to *brahmaloka*. Oh devi, just as all letters are found in the first letter, the letter "*a*," in the same way, the whole universe is found in that Divine Mother.

Now I will explain to you some very essential characteristics of this Divine Mother. She is supreme, subtle, not limited to any particular school of philosophy or religion.[6] This Divine Mother, called *Kuṇḍalinī*,[7] is placed in the center of the heart.[8] There you will find that Divine Mother, just like a serpent in the sleeping state. Oh Pārvati, there she rests in deep sleep, not perceiving anything other than her own self in a place called *mūlādhāra*[9] by our masters.

In addition, this goddess, places in her body the moon *(chandra)*, fire *(agni)*, the sun *(ravi)*, all the stars (*nakṣatra*) and

6. She is not limited to any particular philosophy or religion because anyone—even a cat—can rise if Lord Śiva puts some force in that being.

7. She is called *Kuṇḍalinī* because she is internal power existing like a serpent in the shape of a coil. Actually, *kuṇḍalinī śakti* is the revealing and concealing energy of Lord Śiva. This *kuṇḍalinī śakti* is not different from the existence of Lord Śiva, just as the energy of light and the energy of the heat of a fire are not separate from the fire itself. *Kuṇḍalinī*, therefore, is, in the true sense, the existence of Śiva. It is the life and glory of Śiva. It is Śiva itself.

8. This heart is not the physical heart. This heart is the center of awareness. It is found everywhere in the body.

9. *Mūlādhāra cakra* is found near the rectum.

all the fourteen worlds *(bhuvanāni caturdaśa)* and still she is absolutely unaware that this is happening in her own nature.

But how to awaken her? He now explains how this is done.

This goddess cannot be awakened with force. She can only be awakened by *(nāda)* supreme I consciousness filled with supreme awareness. To awaken her, the yogī has to churn his point of one-pointedness in the heart, without break, again and again.

He must churn it by inserting sparks of awareness, one after another, again and again, in unbroken continuation. The process is to insert one spark of awareness. Let that one spark fade. Again, insert fresh awareness. Let that spark fade. Again, insert fresh awareness. This process must be continued over and over again in continuity.

Then, the body of energy, which is established in the body of the Divine Mother, *kuṇḍalinī*, is churned by this awareness. Because of this churning, this yogī will initially experience very intense lights seeming to come from all sides. Because of these lights and that *(nāda)* supreme I consciousness filled with supreme awareness, this *kuṇḍalinī* rises. In the body of that *kuṇḍalinī*, the yogī finds *bindu*.[10] This *bindu*, which is residing in the body of the Divine Mother *kuṇḍalinī*, has four projections radiating from its center.

The first projection is that of subjective awareness. The second projection is cognitive awareness. The third projection is objective awareness. And the fourth projection is digestive awareness.

Subjective awareness is awareness of the state of knower *(pramātṛi)*. Awareness of the state of knowledge is cognitive awareness *(pramāna)*. Awareness of the state of the known is

---

10. Here, *bindu* refers to the supreme semen *(vīrya)* that becomes agitated there. The formation of *kuṇḍalinī* is of that supreme semen. It is not individual semen. It is something beyond that, experienced only by yogīs. Because *kuṇḍalinī* is formed with the body of supreme semen, which is *bindu*, just imagine how joyous her formation would be!

objective awareness *(prameya)*. These three kinds of awareness rise from that center of that Divine Mother *kuṇḍalinī*.

The fourth projection is known as digestive awareness. This is that projection where subjective, cognitive and objective projections are digested in such a way that they are not differentiated one from the other. In the projection of digestive awareness, all these projections are one without distinction. In Sanskrit, this digestive projection is called *pramiti bhāva*, the digestive state of thought.

> O devi now you have to simultaneously put the churner and that which is to be churned in that body of *kuṇḍalinī*. By doing that, *kuṇḍalinī*, the Divine Mother, rises in a straight line. Here she is called *jyeṣṭhāśakti* because she is absolutely established between these two points, the point of subjectivity *(pramātṛi)* and the point of objectivity *(prameya)*.
>
> Then, when these two points (*bindu*) of subjective awareness and cognitive awareness are also agitated by the process of continual churning, that *kuṇḍalinī* gives rise to real pure supreme semen and that semen rises from bottom to top in the form of *kuṇḍalinī*. That *kuṇḍalinī* is known as the Divine Mother *rekhinī*. Here you won't find either the subjective or the objective projection because these are both diluted in the oneness of that supreme bliss resulting from the rise of supreme semen.
>
> At this point, when this semen rises, this yogī immediately comes out from his internal state because he cannot tolerate the joy he is experiencing, which is the creation of that nectar.[11] There the Divine Mother is called *tripathā* because she takes the formation of the three centers. And then again the three centers, the subjective center, the objective center and the cognitive center, rise. And when all these three centers again rise from *kuṇḍalinī*, the energy of *kuṇḍalinī* is called *raudrī śakti* because it is that energy that puts obstacles in the way in the journey of final liberation.

---

11. This is a natural occurrence. He reaches this state of super intense joy and then he comes out from it. This is the way it happens to everyone who experiences this state.

The yogī must return inside again and again. He must not think that he has lost anything. He need not wait for the master's direction. Because the way of liberation *(mokṣa)* is stopped, he must continue to return inside again and again and maintain awareness of that oneness.

Then again she *(ambikā)* takes the form of the half moon, which is half inside and half outside.[12] And so, even if that supreme Divine Mother is only one, yet she takes these three formations, one for the inferior yogī, one for the yogī who wants to experience enjoyment and one for the superior yogī.

By virtue of these energies of the Divine Mother *kuṇḍalinī,* nine classes of letters have risen. The first is the class of letters from *a* to *visarga (avarga).* The next is the class of letters associated with *ka (kavarga).* The third is the class of letters associated with *ca (cavarga).* The fourth is the class of letters associated with *ṭa (ṭavarga).* The fifth is the class of letters associated with *ta (tavarga).* The sixth is the class of letters associated with *pa (pavarga).* The seventh is the class of letters associated with *ya (yavarga).* The eighth is the class of letters associated with *śa (śavarga).* And the ninth is the class associated with *kṣa (kṣavarga).* All these classes of letters have risen from that Divine Mother *Kuṇḍalinī.*

There are five sacred states of the self that rise from this *kuṇḍalinī* and they are the five mouths of Lord Śiva: *iśāna, tatpuruṣa, aghora, vāmadeva* and *sadyajāta.*[13] These mouths have appeared from this *kuṇḍalinī* so Lord Śiva can speak to the public, helping them and, by illuminating that which is to be known, teach them.[14]

---

12. This state is the real state of *krama mudrā,* which is ultimately experienced by blessed yogīs.

13. In the beginning of *satyuga,* Lord Śiva appeared in the form of *Svacchandanātha.* As *Svacchandanātha,* he had five heads and eighteen arms. His five heads came into manifestation through his five great energies: *cit śakti* (all consciousness), *ānanda śakti* (all bliss), *icchā śakti* (all will), *jñāna śakti* (all knowledge), and *kriyā śakti* (all action). These five energies appeared in his five mouths known as *īśāna, tatpuruṣa, aghora, vāmadeva,* and *sadyojāta.*

14. Because these five mouths rise from *kuṇḍalinī,* Lord Śiva is dependent on *kuṇḍalinī.*

> Twelve vowels also rise from this Divine Mother *kuṇḍalinī* and fifty letters also rise from the same Mother. And now consider the three kinds of speech: supreme, medium and inferior.
> The supreme speech is said to be centered in the heart. This supreme speech is the supreme sound, called *paśyantī*. The throat is the center of *madhyamā* speech and the tongue is the centre of *vaikharī* speech.

When something is to be said, it is first to be taken from one's heart. In the heart, there is no differentiation of letters or words; there is only consciousness. There is some force of what is to occur in the next moment. So in heart, it is just one point, one atom *(ekāṇava),* and that is called *paśyantī* speech *(vāk).* The next speech *(vāk)* is called *madhyamā vāk.* It is centered in the throat. And the third *vāk* is called *vaikharī,* and it is centered in the tongue. It exists when you speak words.

> All these sounds appear in the tongue. So, this whole universe resides on sound. This is the process of sound and that sound is carried from that soundless center of *kuṇḍalinī.*

So, the supreme energy of supreme speech is the source of all speech. This is why all these letters emerge from the supreme center of that energy of God consciousness, the Divine Mother. And all mantras that are recited by spiritual aspirants *(sādhakas)* get their strength *(vīrya)* and splendor from that supreme *devī* of God consciousness, *kuṇḍalinī.* This is why it is said that *mātṛikā* and *mālinī*[15] both rise from this *kuṇḍalinī.*

Because the *Śiva Sūtras* are actually the most secret and essential thoughts of Lord Śiva, in explaining them we have referred to so many *tantras.* You should not be worried about our giving so many references. And if you still do not under-

---

15. *Mātṛikā* is the system of letters of the Sanskrit alphabet that begins with the first letter *a* and ends with the last letter *kṣa*. In the English alphabet this would correspond to the letters *a* to *z*. In Kashmir Śaivism, there is another understanding of the system of letters. In this system, the letters are not in order; it is an orderless world of letters. Such a system is one thing in all things and all things in one thing. In Kashmir Śaivism this system is called Mālinī.

stand what *kuṇḍalinī* actually is, even though we have given so many references to aid your understanding, then you should take hold of the feet of your master.

This meaning of the sūtra is narrated in *Spanda* in this verse,

> All mantras get their life from the Divine Mother *kuṇḍalinī*. She is the center of all mantras. (*Spanda Kārikā* 2.1)

Although the strength *(vīrya)* of the mantra is brought into existence by meditating on the supreme heart of I-consciousness, now and then, by the opposite will of Lord Śiva, the will of concealing *(tirodhāna)* his nature, some unfortunate men do not realize this I-consciousness and, on the contrary, satisfy their minds with limited yogic powers.[16] This next sūtra explains what will happen to these unfortunate yogīs.

16. For instance, flying in the sky, giving boons to disciples, etc.

4. *garbhe cittavikaso'viśiṣṭa vidyāsvapnaḥ*

When a yogī's mind is satisfied with the expansive body of illusion, then he falls in the world of differentiated perceptions and his knowledge of being is just like that of ordinary living beings.

Here, the Sanskrit word *garbhe* means that expansive body of the energy of illusion. That is *mahāmāyā*, the great illusive energy of Lord Śiva. The body of illusion that is being referred to are the limited yogīc powers (e.g., creating divine incense or the materialization of sacred ash to give to disciples, walking on water, flying in air, etc.). All these powers are existing in the sphere of *māyā*. When the yogī exhibits the world of limited powers and his mind becomes satisfied and does not move ahead, then for him, his knowledge of being is like the world of dreams; it is not knowledge at all. His knowledge is just the same as the knowledge held by ordinary worldly people. And so, like ordinary living beings, he falls and is established in the world of differentiation with various perceptions and thoughts.

This is also said in Pātañjali's *Yoga Darśana*,

> Those lights in the center of the eyebrows and divine sounds in the center of heart are obstacles for *samādhi*. (*Yoga Sūtra* 3.37)

The experiences that come in front of this yogī are called *samādhau upasarga*, obstacles to attaining real *samādhi*. These are obstacles for that yogī. For worldly men, on the other hand, they appear as great powers and they appreciate these powers. They say the yogī who possesses these powers is a real person, a real yogī. They applaud him, saying that he bestows these powers on his devotees.

This is narrated in *Spanda Kārikā* in this verse:

> As soon as *spanda* is meditated upon, the yogī perceives some divine light emanating between the eyebrows, he hears divine sound resonating in the heart, divine form appears in his sight and divine taste is experienced on his tongue. These are all just a disturbance in the state of real being and are to be avoided by those yogīs who wish to become fortunate. (*Spanda Kārikā* 3.10)

Then what happens to this yogī who puts these limited powers aside, even though they have appeared to him, and who holds in his mind the supreme state of I consciousness?

*5. vidyāsamutthāne svābhāvike
khecarī śivāvasthā //*

*The pure knowledge of God consciousness
effortlessly rises and this state of Śiva
is realized as one with the
state of khecarī.*

When this pure knowledge *(śuddha vidyā)*, which has been explained in previous sūtras, effortlessly comes into existence and when, by the supreme independent will of Lord Śiva, these limited powers subside and that real state of Lord Śiva comes into being, then this yogī flies in the ether of supreme knowledge. This is the state of *khecarī mudrā* that comes into existence for him. The state of *khecarī* is the state of Lord Śiva, who is the supreme embodiment of consciousness. Here the aspirant *(sādhaka)* becomes one with Śiva. This is the rise of one's own blissful state. This *khecarī* is not the *khecarī* described in these two verses:

> When the yogī is seated in *padmāsana*, he must put his mind, the master of all organs, in the center of the navel. He must sit erect until the time when the three ethers/voids, *śakti, vyāpinī* and *samanā*, come into existence for him.
>
> Then immediately this yogī should infuse the supreme void by taking hold of these three voids. By practicing in this way, this yogī enters in the *mudrā* of *khecarī*.

This state, described above, is not real *khecarī mudrā*. It *should* be avoided. What is real *khecarī mudrā*?

> When you are treading the way of totality *(kulamārgeṇa)*, you must see the totality in a piece of the totality. Take one part of the universe and see the whole universe existing there. That is the way of totality. So, just as its said in the *Tantrasadbhāva*, this *khecarī mudrā* is becoming one with supreme consciousness.

You must understand that everything is filled with completion. If only one individual being is there, you must understand and you must feel that in that one individual being all individuals exist.

Take, for example, one grain of rice. See the power that exists in that grain of rice. This one grain of rice has the power of producing not only a hundred plants but thousands, millions, billions of plants. Innumerable plants exist in that one grain of rice. So, one part of the world is complete in itself.

You must, when treading the way of totality, feel the voidness of differentiated perceptions in each and every being. This, in the real sense, is *khecarī*. It is this *khecarī mudrā* that is to be practiced.

So, the reality of this *khecarī mudrā* is just as it is explained in the *Tantrasadbhāva*, "becoming one with supreme consciousness." And when the agitation of that differentiated illusion of Lord Śiva fades into nothingness, then the power of all *mantras* and all *mudrās* (states) appears and is experienced by such a yogī.

This is said in *Kulacuḍāmaṇi Śāstra*:

> When, by one germ of creative being and one germ of existence, this *khecarī mudrā* is created *(mantra vīrya)* and then established *(mudrā vīrya)*, and when these two states appear to this yogī, then he is established in that supreme and peaceful state of Lord Śiva.

When that *mudrā* is created, it is mantra *vīrya* and when that *mudrā* is established, it is *mudrā vīrya*.

In the *Spanda Kārikās, mudrā vīrya* is incorporated in the explanation of *mantra vīrya* so there is actually no difference between *mantra vīrya* and *mudrā vīrya. Mantra vīrya* exists only at the beginning of creative energy and establishment in that creative energy is *mudrā vīrya.*

> When all these agitations end, then the state of Lord Śiva comes into being. (*Spanda Kārikā* 1.9)

Even though there are other subjects that are explained in this verse from the *Spanda Kārikās,* yet the subjects of *mantra vīrya* and *mudrā vīrya* are also alluded to.

For attaining these two powers, the power of creative energy *(mantra vīrya)* and the power of establishment in that creative energy *(mudrā vīrya)* . . .

6. gururupāyaḥ //

*The master (*guru*) is the means.*

These two powers can be attained only through the master (*guru*), no one else. But who is the master?

The one who demands that his disciples donate money to him or who requires his disciples to provide service to him, all in the guise of attaining enlightenment, is not the *guru*. Then who is the *guru*? The *guru* is that person who puts before you the reality of God consciousness. It is said that the *guru* is the means here because only he can make you realize the fullness of these two awarenesses, *mudrā* and *mantra*.

It is declared in *Mālinīvijaya Tantra:*

> Lord Śiva tells Pārvatī, "That master who is the cause of your attaining the creative energy of Lord Śiva and who then establishes you in that state is as good as me." (*Mālinīvijaya Tantra* 2.10)

In other words, that master is one with Lord Śiva. In *Spanda Kārikā,* this point about the master is not discussed; however, in the last verse there is this reference.

> I bow to that supreme and wonderful world of the master that gives rise to manifold ways of supreme thought that carry the disciple across the ocean of all doubts. (*Spanda Kārikā* 4.1)

Some other masters think, because of the teachings of the *Mālinīvijaya Tantra,* that the master is not a worldly being. For them, the master is, in the real sense, the supreme energy of Lord Śiva. In this regard, it is said in *Mālinīvijaya Tantra:*

> That is the wheel of all energies and that is the mouth of the master where everything is obtained. (*Mālinīvijaya Tantra*)

In the *Triśirobhairava Tantra,* it is said:

> The great energy of that great Lord is said to be the mouth of the master; hence, that energy, being the cause of understanding, is the means (*upāya*). (*Triśirobhairava Tantra*)

Therefore, when the master is pleased,

7. *matṛikācakrasambodhaḥ //*

*(The disciple attains) the knowledge of the wheel of the hidden mother (*Mātṛikācakra*)*

The disciple attains the knowledge of *Mātṛikācakra* only by the grace of the master, and not in any other way. What is *mātṛikācakra*? *Mātṛikā* is the mother who is unknown to the universe.[17] She is the creative cause of all *mantras* and all knowledge. The word "*cakra*" means "wheel." So *mātṛikācakra* literally means the wheel of the hidden mother.

Mātṛikācakra[18] is concerned with the theory of the Sanskrit alphabet from the letter "*a*" to the letter "*kṣa*." There are fifty letters. The fifty letters represent the existence of the whole universe. The universe is composed of thirty-six elements and the thirty-six elements are represented by the fifty letters. The

---

17. She is unknown to her children. Why? When you descend to the objective field, the creative energy is mother and this creative energy is unknown in the objective field. When you ascend to subjective consciousness, then creative energy is known. In the subjective field, she is not *mātṛika;* there she is *cit śakti*, the energy of consciousness.

18. In Kashmir Śaivism, there are two theories of the alphabet. These theories are known as *mātṛikācakra* and *mālini*. The theory being referred to here is the theory of *Mātṛikācakra*, not *Mālini*. *Mātṛikā* is the systematic reading of the letters of the alphabet from *a* to *kṣa*. *Mālini* is the combined, joined reading of these letters. In *mālini,* consonants are found in vowels and vowels are found in consonants. *Śakti* is found in Śiva and Śiva is found in *śakti*. When *śakti* and Śiva are found separately, that is the system of *Mātṛikā*. When Śiva and *śakti* are found together, combined in each other, that is the system of *mālini*. The theory of *mālini* is not explained in the *Śiva Sūtras*.

universe begins from *śiva tattva*, the element of Śiva, and ends in *pṛithvī tattva*, the element of earth.

The representative letters of Śiva, the first supreme element *śiva tattva,* are the sixteen vowels beginning from "*a*" and ending in "*ḥ*" visarga. The sixteen vowels represent, respectively, the existence of Lord Śiva, the thirty-sixth *tattva*. It is explained that in the thirty-sixth *tattva* there are five energies: *cit śakti*, the energy of consciousness; *ānanda śakti*, the energy of bliss; *icchā śakti,* the energy of will; *jñāna śakti*, the energy of knowledge; and *kriyā śakti*, the energy of action. These five energies combined together form the embodiment of Lord Śiva and that is *śiva tattva*.

In *Vedānta*, on the other hand, it is held that there are only three energies that comprise the embodiment of Lord Śiva. These energies are *sat, cit* and *ānanda*. *Sat* means "all existent, always existing," *cit* means "always conscious" and *ānanda* is "always blissful." This is the way *Vedānta* has explained the state of Śiva.

But Śaivism understands it differently. Śaivism argues that *sat* is not needed. It is already present. *Sat* is not an aspect of Lord Śiva. *Sat* is the reality of Lord Śiva. Why, therefore, call it an aspect?

Śiva tattva is explained in *Parātriṁśikā Śāstra* and in the *Tantrāloka:*

> The first movement (*kalā*) of supreme I consciousness (*ahaṁ vimarśa)* is unparalleled *(anuttara)* undifferentiated totality *(akula)*. And when it moves forward with the intention of creating His glory in the external world, it takes the formation of *ānanda*.

Here, the word *kalā* does not mean "part"; here *kalā* means "first movement." It is the first movement of Śiva. You should undertand that Śiva is always moving. Śiva is not stable, unmovable, unmoving, as *Vedānta* has explained. *Vedānta* postulates that anything that moves ultimately comes to an end. So any movable object will, in the course of time, expire. This theory of *Vedānta* is absolutely incorrect. Śiva is always in movement. He is the embodiment of movement (*spanda*). This is why everything, even one small blade of grass, is in movement. And, it is not only a blade of grass that seems to us to be living; even a rock is in movement. Rocks seem to us to be absolutely dead, without life. But there is also life in a rock. In the course of time, a rock undergoes change.

The word *anuttara* means "unparalleled, where there is no similarity." The word *akula* means "where the totality is not differentiated, it is only undifferentiated totality."

The first movement of the state of Paramaśiva was *anuttara*, unparalleled, and incomparable. But when Paramaśiva keenly observes his nature, his self, his reality again and again, he feels the blissful state of his own self. Otherwise, in this first move, he does not feel that blissful state at all. In the first move, there is only all consciousness. The blissful state is digested in that all consciousness in the state of *anuttara*.

And when He takes the formation of *ānanda*, the blissful state, it occurs only when He wants to observe it. For example, when you want to observe what you really are, that bliss comes. When you are not keen to observe your nature, your nature is in a natural way. You are who you are. When you do not observe again and again, then you are only filled with all consciousness. When you observe it again and again, then you feel the glory of your self. That is the formation of *ānanda*, the blissful state.

Śiva's glory is already created in the internal world of his being. In the next movement of Śiva, when he has the intention of creating his glory in the external world, the blissful state appears and that is the form of *ānanda*.

Anuttara, the unparalleled state of consciousness, is represented by the first letter in the Sanskrit alphabet, the letter *a*. The blissful state, *ānanda*, is represented by the second letter in the Sanskrit alphabet, the letter *ā*.

Then after *ānanda,* two more movements come forth, *icchā* and *īśana*. These two states of Lord Śiva come into existence after the existence of that blissful state *ānanda*. The first state *icchā* is the subtle state of will. What does he desire in this state of will? He desires nothing. He only desires his own nature. So the energy of will exists here just to treasure his own nature. It is the energy of will when he admires his own nature, expressed by, "Yes, I am possessing this state." And in the world of vowels, that state is represented by the letter *i*.

Then he takes another movement and that is the gross state of will. In the subtle state of will, he only admires his own nature. In the gross state of will, he not only admires his own nature but he wants to own that nature, he wants to have it, he wants to possess it. And that desire of possessing it will carry him down. Why? Because when he desires to possess it, this means that he feels he is not already possessing the nature of his own self. This means he is moving away from his own nature. This is the state of *īśana*. So, when he wants to possess the nature of his self which is full of consciousness and bliss, he wants to possess it in the state of *īśana,* and that state is represented by the letter *ī*.

After that, he produces another movement and that is *jñāna*. This first movement of *jñāna* is the state of *unmeṣa,* represented by the letter *u*. Here, he discovers that the universe is existing in his own nature which is full of all consciousness and all bliss. When he discovers this, then he begins another movement into the external world. In this next movement, he observes, "I want to find out what is existing in this self of mine." As soon as he desires to observe the differentiated realities existing in his own nature, the splendor of all consciousness and all bliss begins to move away. He now has the apprehension that this consciousness and bliss may be diminishing. It is not actually decreasing, but only the apprehension that it will decrease. This is the state of *ūnatā,* represented by the letter *ū*. The word *ūnatā* means "lessening." This state is the apprehension of the lessening of that supreme consciousness and supreme bliss that is His own nature.

When he has the apprehension that his supreme consciousness and supreme bliss will be lessened, he then diverts his will again into the internal world. He takes his will back again into his own nature and does not let it go out into the external world. This takes place in four ways. The first two movements are in the state of intention. The final two movements are in the state of establishment. First, he has the intention that this flow, this movement, must be diverted towards internal being and not the external world. He must take his will back to his own nature. Then there is the confirmation of that intention that it must be taken back. So these are two states, one is intention and the second is the confirmation of this intention.

Initially, there is only simple intention. This is what you find in lightning. When bolts of lightning are flashing forth from clouds, that is the first state. And when that lightning is observed flashing forth, that is the second state. So in the same way, first there is the intention of taking this whole movement into the internal world of consciousness, and second, there is the confirmation of this intention. This is represented by the letter *ṛi* and by the letter *ṛī*. The letter *ṛi* represents the intention of diverting his will again into the internal world. And *ṛī* is the confirmation of this intention. All this happens in the state of Śiva.

There are now two additional movements in this process of taking will into internal consciousness. First, there is the intention to return. Then there is the confirmation of the intention to return. Next, there is the establishment of this intention of again going back. And finally, this establishment is confirmed. These final two processes of establishment and the confirmation of this establishment are represented by the letters *lṛi* and *lṛī*. The short letter *lṛi* represents the establishment of carrying this entire process inside and the long letter *lṛī* represents the actual carrying of this whole process into his own nature so it rests in his own supreme being. These are four states of Śiva and they are in movement in one's own nature. Your state of consciousness is also in movement. Everything is in movement. But here it moves in his own nature, he does not come out of his own nature.

So, these four states are represented by the four vowels *ṛi ṛī lṛi lṛī*. Here, in these four movements, you get a glimpse of *ra* and *la*.

The semivowel *ra* gives you a glimpse of the first two movements and the semivowel *la* gives you a glimpse of the final two movements of carrying this whole process back into your own nature.

Accordingly, the whole process of universality is carried to one's own nature. Here, the whole universe is made one with His being of all consciousness and all bliss. Therefore, the four states residing in Śiva are said to be "filled with nectar" (*amṛita rūpeṇa*). These four letters are nominated by the great grammarian Pāṇini as *amṛita bīja* because they reside in one's own nature, which is filled with bliss. Here, there is no indication of moving outside into the external world.

At this point, there is no hope of creating the universe. The creation of universe has completely ended. Being completely inverted, this whole universe is carried back to his own nature. Nothing can be created now.

The grammarian Pāṇiṇi also designated these four letters, which represent these four movements, as the eunuch states of Śiva. They are called the eunuch states of Śiva because here Śiva has the impression that the splendor of his supreme state of being may be lessened. Fearing this, he does not have the courage to create.

Now what happens? In reality, Lord Śiva is always full, always blissful; nothing can diminish his nature. And it seems to him a great shame not to create this universe. So he takes another step to create this universe afresh. Now another movement takes place. This time, however, he does not infuse the power of creation in his will or in the will of his knowledge. This time he infuses the power of creative consciousness in his own self, which is *anuttara* and *ānanda* and then he infuses that creative power in his will. When that creative power again mixes in his will, he creates another internal world of his being. That world is the world of his energy of action. This energy of action is represented by four letters: *e, ai, o* and *au*. Not vivid (*asphuṭa*) energy of action is represented by the letter *e*, vivid (*sphuṭa*) is represented by the letter *ai*, more vivid (*sphuṭatara*) is represented by the letter *o* and most vivid (*sphuṭatama*) is represented by the letter *au*.

The four states of the energy of action *(kriyā śaktiḥ)* take place sequentially. First, the energy of action that is not vivid is the state of the triangle (*trikoṇa*). Why is this state of nonvivid energy of action said to be the state of the triangle? You already know that with the exception of the energy of consciousness and the energy of bliss, which are not to be included because they are one with Lord Śiva, there are three energies. These three energies are also not separate but, because they existed after the creation of the state of his *ānanda śaktiḥ,* they are being explained as separate. These three energies are the energy of will, the energy of knowledge and the energy of action. In the energy of will, only the energy of will exists. In the energy of knowledge, two energies exist—the energy of will and the energy of knowledge. In the energy of action, three energies exist—the energy of will, the energy of knowledge, and the energy of action. Therefore, the nonvivid energy of action is said to be the state of the triangle because in this energy of action there are three points, one point of will, one point of knowledge and one point of action.

In this first movement, Lord Śiva infuses his creative power, *anuttara/ānanda,* in will. Here, consciousness (*anuttara*) and all bliss (*ānanda*), the letters *a* or letter *ā,* are combined with the energy of will, the letter *i.* This first state of energy of action, the nonvivid energy of action, the state of the triangle (*trikoṇa*), is represented by the letter *e.* Now he infuses that creative power in knowledge. So *anuttara* or *ānanda,* the letters *a* or *ā* are combined with the energy of knowledge (*jñāna śaktiḥ*), the letter *u,* infusing their creative power in the energy of knowledge, and another state of the energy of action comes into existence and that energy of action is represented by the letter *ai.* This state of the energy of action is vivid energy of action. The purpose of this state is just to confirm that it is the energy of action that Lord Śiva is going to create, that this universe will be created in spite of the fact that the four states of the energy of will (*icchā śaktiḥ*) *ṛi, ṛī, lṛi* and *lṛī,* have entered into the state of eunuch. This is the power and the greatness of Lord Śiva's energy of consciousness (*anuttara*) and all bliss (*ānanda*).

And now, when *anuttara/ānanda* are again to infuse the creative power, it is infused not in will, as it was in the first movement, it is infused in *trikoṇa*. This infusion gives rise to the more vivid state of the energy of action called *ṣaṭkoṇa*.[19] This state is represented by the letter *o*. *Ṣaṭkoṇa* is the state where the whole universe is found in Lord Śiva and Lord Śiva is found in the universe. In this state, you won't find any difference between Lord Śiva and this created universe. You may call it "created universe" or you may call it "Lord Śiva"; it doesn't make any difference. If you want to see Lord Śiva, see him in blades of grass, he is there, vividly existing. Therefore, in the letter *e* he was not vividly existing. In the letter *ai* he is vividly existing. In the letter *o* he is more vividly existing. In the letter *au* Lord Śiva is most vividly existing.

The final state of the energy of action, represented by the letter *au*, will be found only in the universal state. That state is called *śūlabīja*, where the triple state of the three energies—will, knowledge, and action—is consumed in one universal point. This is why in this fourth state of energy of action all three energies of Lord Śiva—the energy of will, the energy of knowledge and the energy of action—are most vividly found. They are not found as vivid in the first state of the energy of action, the letter *e*, or in the second, the letter *ai*, or in the third, the letter *o*. They are found most vividly existing in the fourth, the letter *au*. It is in *au* that you will find Lord Śiva most vividly existing in the universe. So if you want to perceive the state of Lord Śiva as it ought to be perceived, in its real sense, you must enjoy this universe. You won't find the real state of Lord Śiva in *samādhi*. In the state of *samādhi*, you will find His nonvivid formation. You will find the exact state of Lord Śiva in the universe.

Up to this point, all of Lord Śiva's energies—the energy of consciousness, the energy of bliss, the energy of will, the en-

---

19. This is another movement of Lord Śiva. When the two movements *anuttara* and *ānanda* are reunited with the force *trikoṇa*—the letter *e*, which was already created—and when these two energies, *anuttara* and *ānanda*, come in contact with *icchā śakti* and *iṣana śakti*, then two triangles are united, creating two shapes with six angles. This six-angled star is composed of three male angles and three female angles and is shaped like the Jewish star.

ergy of knowledge, the energy of his four eunuch states, along with his not vivid energy of action, his vivid energy of action, his more vivid energy of action, and his most vivid energy of action—are explained completely. But what is represented by the next two vowels *anusvāra* "*ṁ*" and *visarga* "*ḥ*"?

The whole universe, beginning from the energy of consciousness (*cit śaktiḥ*) and ending in the most vivid energy of action (*kriyā śaktiḥ*) is no universe at all. In other words, it is the expansion of your own nature, nothing else. In reality nothing is created at all. It is only the glory of His own nature that you will find in this so-called creation. This state of knowledge and confirmation is represented by the letter "ṁ" *anusvāra*. Here, there is only a point (*bindu*). A point cannot be created; it is only one-pointed. After accomplishing this expansive state of activity, this entire active world is dissolved in one point. So, if you are created, if you grow up, if you become old, if you die, if you come again in this world, what significance is there in this? It is only the glory of your own expansion of being. There is no creation, there is no death.

But if nothing is created, then what is it that happens to make it seem that it is just like creation? After all, you do feel like it is being created. This is explained by the next state of Lord Śiva, *visarga* "*ḥ*". In the previous state of knowledge and confirmation represented by the letter "ṁ" *anusvāra*, we saw that the universe is just the glory of his own nature. There is no creation. There is only one point. The whole universe is dissolved in one point. So now, after creating these five energies of his nature, he creates the state of *visarga*. This sixteenth letter of the vowels is represented by the letter "*ḥ*". This state represents simultaneously the internal creative force and external creative force. Here, in this state of being of Lord Śiva, if you observe in one way, you will find that nothing is created. This is the internal creative force. If, on the other hand, you observe in another way, you will find that everything is created. This is the external creative force. So by observing in one way, nothing is created, and if at the same time you observe in another way, you will find that everything is created.

Here is a story that will help clarify this teaching, which is the supreme truth. In earlier times in this universe, there was a yogī and his name was Macchandanātha. He was considered to be a great yogī and he had many disciples. One day his chief disciple Gorakhanātha was traveling in a far off country. There to his surprise, he saw his master making love with a beautiful woman from a nearby town. Gorakhanātha was furious with his master for this unacceptable action. But his master had fallen in love with this woman and he married her. Living together, this master and his wife had many, many children. Gorakhanātha observed that his master was absolutely given to his wife and these children.

Then after some time, Gorakhanātha returned to his own country. He went to his master's *āśram.* Upon arriving at the *āśram,* Gorakhanātha was dumbfounded to find his master there in perfect *samādhi.* He knew his master was attached to his wife and children and yet here he was without his wife and children. Here he was, alone, absolutely given to *samādhi.* In fact, his brother disciples told him, his master had never left the *āśram.* He has always been here in his *āśram.* He had not gone anywhere.

Gorakhanātha was puzzled by this. Earlier he had seen his master, along with his wife and children, residing happily in that faroff place. Now he sees his master residing in his *āśram* absolutely given to *samādhi.* "What is happening?" Gorakhanātha thought to himself. To answer this, he again, through his yogic powers, returned to the far-off country and again saw his master totally given in love and affection to his wife and his children. Then Gorakhanātha was filled with awe and totally surrendered to his master. His master then explained to him, "From one point, you will see that I have fallen in love and am attached to the world, and from another point you will see that I have not fallen in love at all, that I am Lord Śiva."

So, if from one point you look to see what has been created, you will see nothing is created. You will see it is only the glory of your own I consciousness and nothing else. And yet, if you see from another point of view, you will see that everything is created. Such a state is represented by the Sanskrit letter *ḥ,* and is written in *Devanāgarī* as ":," two points in a vertical line, one above and one below.

Visarga is classified in three ways in Śaivism. The first *visarga* is concerned with Śiva. The second visarga is concerned with his energy (*śaktiḥ*). And the third *visarga* is concerned with individual being. The first *visarga* concerned with Śiva is called *para visarga*, the supreme creative energy of Śiva. The second *visarga* concerned with *saktiḥ* is called *parāpara visarga*, his medium creative energy. The third *visarga* concerned with the individual is called *apara visarga,* his inferior creative energy. These three energies are represented respectively by three letters. The supreme energy is represented by the second vowel of the alphabet *ā,* which is *ānanda śaktiḥ*. *Ānanda śaktiḥ* is the supreme energy of creation pertaining to Śiva. And the medium creative energy pertaining to *śaktiḥ* is *visarga*, *ḥ*, the sixteenth vowel of the Sanskrit alphabet. And finally, the inferior creative energy, which pertains to individual being *(jīva),* is represented by the letter *ha*, the last letter of the Sanskrit alphabet.

In addition to this, it is explained that the supreme energy of Lord Śiva, which is the first *visarga,* is called *cittapralayaḥ,*[20] because Lord Śiva does not have a mind. In place of mind Lord Śiva has only supreme independent consciousness of self. Because of this, the supreme creative energy is called *citta pralaya*.

The creative energy pertaining to his energy *(śaktiḥ)* is called *citta saṁbodhaḥ,* where the mind is fully aware, because here the possessor of that creative energy is *śaktiḥ*. This is the second *visarga*. Here, *śaktiḥ* means "all power." But power of what? It is the power of maintaining complete awareness of self. Here, the mind is fully aware without any differentiated thoughts. Differentiated thoughts do not arise. Here, there is only the awareness of one thought. This is why it is called *citta saṁbodha*.

20. The kind of *visarga* existing in the state of *ānanda śakti* and represented by the letter *ā*, is called *śāmbhava visarga*. This *śāmbhava visarga* is *cittapralayaḥ*. *Cittapralayaḥ* means "where your mind does not function." It is the thoughtless state. And so *śāmbhava visarga* is the thoughtless flow.

The third state of inferior creative energy is called *citta-viśrānti.* The state of *cittaviśrānti* is where one-pointedness is established. One-pointedness does not mean one-pointedness found in the *ekāgratā* state.[21] Rather, it is the one-pointedness of thought called *niruddhaḥ.* In this state, you do not have to maintain one pointedness; one-pointedness is automatically maintained. So, in *niruddhaḥ,* one-pointedness is not maintained with effort. *Niruddha* is effortless one-pointedness. One-pointedness maintained with effort is called the state of *ekāgratā.* And one-pointedness attained without effort—one-pointedness already existing—is called *niruddha.* This third *visarga* is called *citta viśrānti.*

There is, therefore, the perception in the state of Śiva of being introverted and the perception in the state of Śiva of being extroverted—internal and external. When you perceive all these states of Śiva internally, there you find the state of "*ṁ*" *anusvāra.* And when you also perceive that state externally, then you find the state of *visarga, "ḥ"* or : .

So when perception from the external point of view takes place, perception from the internal point of view already exists in Śiva. The perception from the external point of view will spread in the body of the whole universe. This body of the universe begins from the most inferior element, earth *(pṛithvī),* and ends with the most supreme element, which is the element *śaktiḥ,* not Śiva. Why is the supreme element *śaktiḥ* and not Śiva? Because Śiva is the source of all elements and pervades them all.

And now, when you move to external observation, in the world of the created embodiment of Lord Śiva, to observe what is created, what has happened in this creation, you will feel that five classes of consonants are created. That creation is composed of

---

21. The *ekāgratā* state of mind exists when you are determined to maintain your mind on one point with concentration. When you keep your mind in the state of being one-pointed, it will occasionally try to move to another object. You must be attentive in such a way that you prevent it from going to that object. When it goes to that object, you drive it back to its original point. This is the state of mind known as *ekāgratā.*

one class of five elements, one class of five *tanmātras*, one class of five energies of action and one class of five energies of knowledge.

As you know, Śiva has five energies: the energy of consciousness *(cit śaktiḥ)*, the energy of bliss *(ānanda śaktiḥ)*, the energy of will *(icchā śaktiḥ)*, the energy of knowledge *(jñāna śakti)* and the energy of action *(kriyā śaktiḥ)*. From the energy of his consciousness, the five great elements *(mahābhūtas)*—earth, water, fire, air and ether—have been created. Why are these elements created by his energy of consciousness? Actually, these five gross elements ought to be created by his energy of action, not his energy of consciousness. These five elements are the grossest created things in this universe. It has already been pointed out that Lord Śiva does not fear coming down into the gross world. This is the glory of Lord Śiva, that by his sweet will he comes down and he goes up again. So he rushes towards this extreme end of creation and by his subtlest energy of consciousness, creates the grossest element.

As we have seen earlier, in the energy of consciousness *(cit śakti)*, the other four *śaktis* exist. Also in the energy of bliss *(ānanda śakti)*, the energy of will *(icchā śakti)*, the energy of knowledge *(jñāna śakti)* and the energy of action *(kriyā śakti)*, all the other four *śaktis* exist. So in each and every energy of Lord Śiva, all five energies exist.

Both external perception and internal perception begin from *anuttara (cit śakti)*. But how does external perception unfold? External perception begins from *cit śakti (anuttara)* and *ānanda śakti*, the Sanskrit letters *a* and *ā*, which are one and filled with the five energies. From these two energies arise the five consonants *ka, kha, ga, gha* and *ṅa*. These five consonants represent the state of the five gross to grossest elements: earth *(pṛithvī)*, water *(jala)*, fire *(agni)*, air *(vāyu)* and ether *(ākāśa)*. Then from *icchā śakti*, the letters *i* and *ī*, five consonants arise and these are the consonants *ca, cha, ja, jha* and *ña*. These five consonants represent the states of the five *tanmātras:* smell *(gandha)*, taste *(rasa)*, form *(rūpa)*, touch *(sparśa)* and sound *(śabda)*. Then the two letters *ṛi* and *ṛī*, which are *anaśṛitaśiva*, along with five energies give rise to the five consonants *ṭa, ṭha, ḍa, ḍha* and *ṇa*. These consonants represent the five organs of action *(karmendriya)*. The five consonants *ta, tha, da, dha* and *na,* which represent the five organs of knowledge *(jñānendriya),* are produced by the same five energies through the letters *lṛi* and *lrī. Jñāna śakti,* the energy of knowledge, the letters *u* and *ū,* along with the five energies, gives rise to the five consonants *pa, pha, ba, bha* and *ma* and these produce the five elements *manas, buddhi, ahaṁkāra, prakṛiti* and *puruṣa.* So, from earth *(pṛithvī)* to *puruṣa* there are twenty-five elements, because five energies exist in each energy of Lord Śiva. Therefore, the energy of consciousness *(cit śaktiḥ),* the energy of bliss *(ānanda śaktiḥ),* the energy of will *(icchā śaktiḥ),* the energy of knowledge *(jñāna śakti)* and the energy of action *(kriyā śaktiḥ)* are all filled with *cit śakti, ānanda śakti, icchā śakti, jñāna śakti* and *kriyā śakti.* And therefore, these five energies are each filled with five energies and this calculates as five times five, which equals twenty-five.

The next four semivowels *ya, ra, la,* and *va* correspond to the six elements of *kalā, vidyā, rāga kāla,* and *niyati* along with *māyā.*[22] These elements of Lord Śiva are known as the six coverings *(ṣaṭ kañcukas),* which are reduced to four by combining *niyati* with *rāga* and *kalā* with *kāla.*

From the master grammarian Pāṇini's point of view, the six elements of Lord Śiva, *kalā, vidyā, rāga, kāla, niyati,* and *māyā,* pertain to the individual being. They do not relate to the elements because all these energies are found inside, not outside, the individual being. They are inside the thought and inside the perception of the individual being. For this reason Pāṇini has designated the letters *ya, ra, la,* and *va,* which represent these coverings, as *antaḥstha* because they remain inside the individual being.

On the other hand, in the *tantras* of our Śaivism, these five elements *niyati, kāla, ragā, vidyā, kalā* along with *māyā,* are called *dhāraṇā* because they give life to the individual being.

---

22. *Māyā* is the energy of illusion. *Kalā* is the energy of limited action. *Vidyā* is the energy of limited knowledge. *Rāga* is the energy of attachment to limited things. *Kāla* is the limitation of time. *Niyati* is the energy of being situated in only one particular place.

The individual being lives in these five elements. Without these five elements, the individual being has no life; there would only be the sphere of Lord Śiva. Therefore, in Śaivism we argue that these elements are not *antaḥstha*, being inside the individual being, rather they are *dhāraṇā* because they are what gives life to the individual being. The individual being is created and glorified by these coverings, for limitation is the glory of limited being.

When you subside these six coverings and move ahead, crossing the bondage of these coverings, differentiated perception vanishes and undifferentiated perception comes before you. Then your self is about to bloom into existence *(unmeṣa).* This blooming of the self is represented by the four letters *śa, ṣa, sa* and *ha.* The grammarian Pāṇini has designated these four letters *śa, ṣa, sa,* and *ha* as *ūṣma* letters because the Sanskrit word *ūṣmā* means that the internal light, internal fire, internal warmth, has again come forth. When this internal light, this internal warmth, comes forth, it is the state of *śuddhavidyā*, the state of *iśvara*, the state of *sadāśivaḥ* and the state of *śakti.* These states are represented by these four letters *śa, ṣa, sa,* and *ha.* The letter *śa* represents the state of *śuddhavidyā.* The letter *ṣa* represents the state of *iśvara.* The letter *sa* represents the state of *sadāśivaḥ.* And the letter *ha* represents the state of *śakti.* Here ends the world of the alphabet. This world is called *mātṛikācakram*, the wheel of the mother.

In this world of the alphabet, when creation ends, it ends in its fullness of being, in absolute supremacy, not in its fullness of inferiority. The creative world is found in its supreme state in the state of *sadāśivaḥ* which as we've seen above, is represented by the letter *sa.* This is the reason the author Kṣemarāja tells us that in the end of all this creation what is is exactly what ought to be, and this is filled with the nectar of supreme consciousness. This is the state of *sadāśivaḥ.* It is the state whose essence is captured in the experience "*aham idam,*" "I am this whole universe." In our philosophy, this letter *sa* is called *amṛita bīja,* the seed of nectar.

And in the end of that *amṛita bīja, prāṇa bīja* is created. This *prāṇa* is the life of Śiva. What is life for Śiva? Śiva's life is

Śiva's *śakti*. So *prāṇabīja* is the life of Śiva and that is *śakti*. This state of *śakti* is called *anāhata*, the automatic energy of Lord Śiva. It is represented by the letter *ha*. This letter *ha* is not to be recited; it is to be experienced. We, however, do recite the mantra *"so'ham."* In reciting *so'haṁ*, we recite *amṛita bīja*, *prāṇa bīja* and *anusvāra*. The letter *sa* is *amṛita bīja*, the letter *ha* is *prāṇa bīja* and *ṁ* is *anusvāra*. We recite it but this kind of recitation is incorrect recitation. Actually, these three letters cannot be recited at all; they are automatic. They are to be perceived, not recited. As long as you are reciting, it is an imitation of these letters. It is not real. And yet, in the beginning, you have to recite these letters. And then, when the reality comes in front of you, recitation ends. Then there is only the experiencing of these three letters: what *ṁ* is, what *amṛita* is and what *prāṇa bīja* is. This is why it is called *anāhata*. The Sanskrit word *anāhata* means that which cannot be recited. Why? Because it is impossible to recite.

So, this is the complete history of the universe that has been created from earth (*pṛithvī*) to *śakti*. This knowledge is the theory of *mātṛikācakram* which is referred to by Pāṇini in his sūtra:

> Put the first letter and put the last letter and combine them.

In perceiving, you should not perceive things one by one. See what is in the beginning and see what is in the end. Take these two and combine them and you have perceived the whole universe. This is *pratyāhāra*. To employ *pratyāhāra*, you take *anuttara*, the first letter *a* and *anāhata*, the last letter *ha* and combine them. But how can you combine them? They can't be combined. You can, however, unite them by means of taking them in one point. That one point is *anusvāra*, the letter *ṁ*. So the letters *a*, *ha* and *ṁ* when combined in one point become *ahaṁ*. This is *ahaṁ paramarśa*, the perception of universal I and it is the essence of *ahaṁ vimarśa*, the supreme mantra in our philosophy.

The Kashmir Śaivaite philosopher Utpaladeva has also explained this state of Śiva in this verse:

> Whatever is perceived is *prakāśa.*[23] It is the state of universal I. Carrying all that is perceived to your own nature, to that point of the self, and establishing it there is called *svātantrya.* It is called all action and it is called the universal glory of Śiva. (*Ajadapramātṛisiddhi,* 22–23)

Now, the author of this commentary, Kṣemarāja, reveals the secret of *mātṛikācakra.* In *mātṛikā,* there are three worlds, the subjective world, the cognitive world and the objective world. We are situated in the objective world. Being in the objective world, we are not aware of the cognitive world or the subjective world. The question is, how can we unite the objective world with the subjective world? The subjective world is found in *anuttara a* and the objective world is found in *anāhata, ha.* How, therefore, can these two very different worlds be united?

This question is answered by this precious secret of *mātṛikācakra,* which explains how to become successful in uniting the objective and the subjective world. First, you have to extract subjectivity from subjectivity and insert that subjectivity into objectivity. Then you have to extract objectivity from the real objectivity and insert that objectivity into inferior objectivity. Supreme objectivity is found in *ha* and supreme subjectivity is found in *anuttara, a.* Because *anuttara* has given rise to the five elements represented by the letters *ka, kha, ga, gha* and *ṅa,* inferior subjectivity is found in the letter *ka.* So you have to extract subjectivity from that real subjectivity of the state of *anuttara* and insert that subjectivity into objectivity in the letter *ka.* That is *pṛithvī* (earth); where we are actually situated. And then you have to extract objectivity from that real objectivity of *śakti* and insert that objectivity into another

23. Whatever you see, whatever you hear, whatever you smell, whatever you taste, whatever you touch is *prakāśa.* The sensation of touch, the sensation of smell, the sensation of taste, the sensation of seeing anything, whatever you perceive, not only think but perceive, with any or all of your five organs of perception, is called *prakāśa.*

inferior objectivity, which is *sa*. You must then unite that subjectivity *cum* objectivity and objectivity *cum* objectivity. This will create the letter *kṣa* which is the combination of *ka* and *sa*. The letter *ka* is the objectivity *cum* subjectivity, because subjectivity has entered into that objectivity, and the letter *sa* is objectivity *cum* objectivity because here supreme objectivity has come into inferior objectivity. Uniting them creates another *pratyāhāra* of *kṣa* (i.e., the combination of *ka* and *sa*).

This is the *śakti pratyāhāra*. It is the combination of one object with another object, not one subject and another object as was found in the combination of Śiva and *śakti* found in *mātṛikā*. This combination of *śakti* and *śakti* is found in this state of individual being. It is the unification of *śakti* with *śakti*, the unification of *ka* with the letter *sa,* that creates the letter *kṣa*. This is called *kūṭabīja*, or *bīja* that has arisen from female energy. Here, there is no utilization of male energy at all.

This philosophy of *mātṛikā* is supreme. The knowledge of *mātṛikā cakra* is perceived by that disciple who receives the grace of his master. What is that *cakra* (wheel)? It is the wheel of *mātṛikā* made of the five great energies of Śiva, the energy of consciousness (*cit-śakti),* the energy of bliss *(ānanda śakti),* the energy of will *(īcchā śakti),* the energy of knowledge *(jñāna śakti)* and the energy of action *(kriyā śakti).* All these energies together are called *cakras* because they move like wheels. This yogī does not feel that these energies in that wheel are separate from Śiva. On the contrary, he finds all these five energies filled with the nature of Śiva. This is the knowledge of *mātṛikā cakra.*

Here, in the *Śiva Sūtras*, we have briefly introduced the reader to the philosophy of *mātṛikācakra.* This philosophy is explained vividly and in great detail by our distinguished master Abhinavagupta in his *Tantrāloka* and in his commentary on the *Parātriṁśikā.*

In *Siddhāmṛita Tantra,* it is said:

> In fact, in this world of *mātṛikā,* the supreme hero is *kuṇḍalinī. Kuṇḍalinī* takes the roles of all these states. *Kuṇḍalinī* is the real heroine. She is not only the life of the world of *mātṛikā,* but filled with consciousness she is the germ of its root. And from

> that *kuṇḍalinī* arise the three letters *a, i* and *u. (Siddhāmṛita Tantra)*

In the beginning, in his system of the Sanskrit alphabet, the great grammarian Pāṇini also established three letters. These three letters are the letters, "*aiuṇ*"; "*a-i-uṇ*" is the first sūtra of Pāṇini. The letters *a, i* and *u* are first because *anuttara* is first as the letter *a*, *icchā* is second as the letter *i* and *unmeṣa* is third as the letter *u*. From these three letters all other letters are produced.

Now he explains how this takes place:

> The letter *ā* rises from the letter *a* and so on, until the flow of *visarga* arises. And from that *visarga* arise the letters from *ka* to *sa* and that is fivefold. *(Siddhāmṛita Tantra)*

> This awareness of I consciousness pervades in all the five supreme states. It pervades in the external world, in the internal world, in the world of sound, in the world of the supreme state and in the world of the supreme void. If this secret of *mātṛikā* is not realized, all the recitations of mantras are useless just like empty rainless clouds in the autumn sky. *(Siddhāmṛita Tantra)*

There are five supreme states of Lord Śiva. There is the external state of Śiva and the internal state of Śiva. The external state of Śiva is the heart of universe. The internal state of Śiva is the heart of the body. The heart of the body is not the physical heart. The heart of the body is in the state of perceiving and that is all-pervading. It pervades the whole body. For example, when an ant crawls on your foot, you are aware of it; that is the heart. That abode of awareness is that heart.

The external heart is the universe. This entire universe is the external heart. The internal heart is the heart abiding in one's own body and that is consciousness. Then there is the heart of sound. All sounds are produced from that soundless sound, that sound is called *nāda*. *Nāda* is sound that is not produced but which simply occurs. The fourth state is the supreme state of consciousness and the fifth state is the supreme state of supreme void.

> The qualification of a master is only this, he causes you to realize what is first and what is last and how to combine it. That master is to be adored in the same way people adore me (Lord Śiva).
> Once you realize the reality of *mātṛikā cakra,* whatever you do and whatever you say in your daily life will become divine and will be filled with that supreme universal consciousness of I. *(Siddhāmṛita Tantra)*

These are the sayings of Lord Śiva. You must not consider this master as an ordinary human being. This master is beyond humanity.

This teaching is also given in *Spanda* in this verse:

> This energy of action of Lord Śiva entangles Lord Śiva in the individual state of life. And when Lord Śiva realizes the nature of this energy of his own self, then it will cease to entangle him. It entangles only when it is not realized. Once it is realized, you are freed from all the bondages of life. (*Spanda Kārikā* 3.16)

Here ends the theory of *mātṛikā*.

For the yogī who is fully aware of *mātṛikācakra* . . .

8. śarīraṁ haviḥ

The establishment of I consciousness on the body becomes an offering in the fire of God consciousness.

When I consciousness *(pramātṛi bhāva)* is established on the body, the experiencer perceives, "I am this gross body in the waking state, I am this subtle body in the dreaming state and I am this subtlest body in the state of deep sleep." All worldly people have inaugurated *(abhiṣikta)* their I consciousness by inserting their I-ness in these three bodies. When I consciousness is established in these three bodies, they are called the three veils, the three coverings. You must remove I consciousness from these three bodily states, gross, subtle and subtlest, because when I consciousness is established in these bodies, then you perceive that you are these bodies.

I consciousness on these three bodies is called *śarīra*. For such a yogī, all these three bodies, including I consciousness, become offerings *(haviḥ)* in the fire of God consciousness. By these offerings, all these three states of I consciousness become one with God consciousness.

Because this great yogī offers these three flows of consciousness, causing them to be digested in the fire of God consciousness, only God consciousness and no other consciousness remains. This yogī finds the kingdom of God consciousness everywhere, in the gross body, in the subtle body and in the subtlest body. So in this way, he subsides I consciousness on these threefold bodies and he gains entry in God consciousness.

This is said in *Śrī Vijñānabhairava Tantra*:

> When all the five elements, all the organs and all the perceptions of the organs, including one's mind, are offered in the fire of the great voidness with the sacrificial ladle (*srukca*) of awareness, that is, in the real sense, the great fire sacrifice (*havana*). (*Vijñānabhairava* 149)

In *Timirodghāṭa Tantra* it is also said:

> When, in the fire of God consciousness, you subside the attachment to one whom you love, to the one who is your friend, to the one who is your close relative, to the one who fills you with happiness and to the one who is your beloved, then you are situated in the courtyard of the supreme ether of voidness. (*Timirodghāṭa Tantra*)

In essence, this is just to subside the oneness of I consciousness on these threefold bodies.

It is also said in *Bhagavadgītā*:

> The way of action of great yogīs is to offer all the actions of the organs of the senses and all the actions of breathing completely in the fire of the one-pointedness of God consciousness. (*Bhagavadgītā* 4.27)

The author Kallaṭa has explained the meaning of agitation this way in his commentary of *Spanda Kārikā*:

> When all agitations end, then the supreme state of God consciousness is revealed. (*Spanda Kārikā* 1.9)

In this verse, the word "agitation" refers to that state which exists when you put your I consciousness on these threefold bodies. When I consciousness on these threefold bodies is removed and inserted in God consciousness, then agitation ends. There is no further agitation.

9. jñānamannam //

(For such a yogī)
differentiated perception is his food

or
knowledge of his own nature is his food.

This yogī eats and digests differentiated perception in his own supreme nature of consciousness.

Previously in the second sūtra of the First Awakening of the *Śiva Sūtra*, we are told *jñānaṁbandhaḥ*, "bondage is differentiated perception." And when that differentiated perception is carried in God consciousness by great Śaiva yogīs, it does not live, it expires. Then, there is no residue of that differentiated perception. This is why he has said in the present sūtra, "differentiated perception is his food," because he takes it in and digests it in his own nature of God consciousness.

Previously, this point was communicated in this verse:

> In that state, where he carries all differentiated perception into one God consciousness and digests it, not only are differentiated perceptions digested but along with differentiated perceptions, death, time, all actions good or bad, all changes of life, all perceptions good or bad, and all discussions of the question of monism or dualism are also digested in that supreme oneness of God consciousness. (*Bhargaśikhā Śastra*)

This is one explanation of this sūtra. There is also another way to explain it. In this explanation, take the word *jñāna* to mean *knowledge of your own real self*, and not *differentiated perception*. Thus, the reading would be:

For such a *yogī*, knowledge of his own nature is his food.

So, in one way, because this yogī carries differentiated perceptions from the differentiated to the undifferentiated state, he has explained that all kinds of differentiated perceptions are this yogī's food. This yogī carries these differentiated perceptions from darkness to light, from sadness to joy. Everything for him is joyous, filled with light and glory. This is one way of explaining the word *jñāna*.

The other way to explain the word *jñāna* is that *jñāna* is the real knowledge of your own nature. This is his food and he is satisfied with this food. Being always satisfied with this food means he doesn't crave for physical food. Of course he eats, he does not starve himself, but he is not attached to food. He is always intoxicated in his own self because the knowlege of his real nature gives him complete satisfaction.

It is also said in *Vijñānabhairava*:

> Take any one means, in this world of one hundred and twelve means *(upāyas)*, for entering in God Consciousness, and meditate according to that means. The fullness you experience by practicing consistently day by day on that means will give you perfect satisfaction and perfect fullness of self. (*Vijñānabhairava* 148)

Here, the author says that it doesn't matter which means you take out of these one hundred and twelve ways. The fullness you experience through constant practice gives you perfect satisfaction and fullness of self.

This is stated in *Spanda* in this verse:

> Always maintain awareness in all your activities. (*Spanda Kārikā* 3.12)

If you lose awareness, then you are gone. You have destroyed the reality of life. You must, therefore, be aware. If you are fully aware of your thoughts, then you will not see any thoughts there. You can't be partially aware while thinking; this won't accomplish anything. Be fully aware of what you are thinking and you won't think anything. If you are aware of what is happening next, nothing will happen. If you are aware that you are dying, you won't die. If you are aware that you are going from wakefulness to the dreaming state, you won't go. On the contrary, by establishing this awareness, you will get entry into God consciousness. This is the greatness of awareness, that if you are always aware in continuation, always one-pointed and residing in the one-pointed state of God consciousness, you won't think anything. If, on the other hand, you are unaware, you will miss the reality of your life.

When this yogī does not maintain awareness in continuity, then, although he possesses the knowledge of God consciousness, there are many occasions when he lacks awareness. For example, if this yogī is aware of God consciousness now and after a short time he becomes unaware, missing that awareness, then again after a few minutes he is again maintaining that awareness, this is not the way to maintain awareness. Awareness must be maintained in continuity. And when this yogī doesn't maintain unbroken awareness, what happens to him?

10. vidyāsaṁhāre
tadutthasvapnadarśanam //

Although he is established in
God consciousness in samādhi,
yet not being able to maintain awareness,
after a short time he enters into the
dreaming state.

This is the meaning of this sūtra. When you have completely entered in *samādhi* and while in *samādhi,* you do not maintain your awareness wholeheartedly with great effort, then after a while you enter into the dreaming state. This happens to all yogīs. This losing awareness is the great crisis in the yogic world. All yogīs generally experience this state of losing awareness. And when they do, they go to the dreaming state because that state is subtler than the waking state.

In the world of experience and awareness, the grossest state is the waking state. A more subtle state is the dreaming state. More subtle still is soundless sleep. And the most subtle state is *samādhi.* So it is very difficult to maintain awareness in *samādhi.* There is only one way you can maintain awareness in *samādhi* and that is when your master is exceedingly pleased with you. When he is pleased with you, you will be able to maintain awareness; otherwise, it is impossible.

But the question is why, when you are in *samādhi* and are unable to maintain awareness, do you enter the dreaming state rather than the waking state? It is because in wakefulness you are more aware than you are in the dreaming state. For instance, say your father has been dead for two years. While you are in the waking state, someone says your father has come to visit. Will you believe it? No, you won't believe it. If, on the other hand, you had this same experience in the dreaming state, you would believe it. So you are not as aware in the dreaming state.

But here the question can be raised, if awareness is not as full in the dreaming state as it is in the waking state, then why is the dreaming state said to be more subtle than the waking state? Surely, the waking state should be the subtlest because there is more awareness in that state.

The dreaming state is more subtle than the waking state because the awareness existing in the waking state, which is more full, is awareness of the differentiated state. In fact, the awareness existing in the waking state, or in the dreaming state or in the dreamless state, is awareness of differentiated perceptions. In these three states, undifferentiated perception does not exist. This is the nature of these three states.

If you meditate more and more, and expand your awareness in meditation, then initially you will enter *samādhi* through the dreaming state because the dreaming state is subtler than the waking state and you can maintain awareness more easily in that state. Initially, you never enter *samādhi* while in the waking state. You will always enter by way of the dreaming state. When your awareness is fully established, then you can also gain entry into *samādhi* while in the waking state.

And those yogīs who do not have much capacity or ability to meditate enter *samādhi*, not in the dreaming state, but in sound sleep. If they continue meditating, then after some time they will get entry into *samādhi* in the dreaming state. And when their awareness is further strengthened and developed, they will gain entry to *samādhi* through the waking state. Once you enter *samādhi* through the waking state, that *samādhi* becomes the most firm. So this is the reason why, when that supreme knowledge of God consciousness is weakened by the lack of awareness, you enter the dreaming state.

When it is said that the supreme pure knowledge of God consciousness, which is the expansion of knowledge of one's own self, is destroyed by the lack of awareness, the destruction being referred to here is not real destruction. Saying the supreme pure knowledge of God consciousness is destroyed means this supreme pure knowledge of God consciousness subsides, it diminishes. And because of that lessening, the yogī enters the dreaming state and is thrown into the world of differentiated perception.

When, through meditating in continuity, your thought becomes ever more subtle, you will feel that you are about to go to sleep. Sleep comes for those who can not maintain awareness. Those who can maintain awareness do not fall asleep. They enter the gap, the junction of these two states of waking and dreaming. That junction is *turya*, the real state of being.

This is also said in *Mālinīvijaya Tantra*:

> This state of God consciousness was not explained to Pārvatī by Lord Śiva until he was absolutely and wholeheartedly happy with her. It was at that time he explained to her the way of entering God consciousness. This is the reason why, even though your master has initiated you wholeheartedly, you still can not maintain awareness in that state. There must be ample satisfaction in the heart of your master first, before the entry into God consciousness occurs. (*Mālinīvijaya Tantra*)

The supreme path of reality was not explained to Pārvatī by Lord Śiva when he was not pleased with her. It was only when Lord Śiva was absolutely pleased with Pārvatī, his life partner, that he explained to her the reality of God consciousness. So the entry into God consciousness takes place only when your master is absolutely pleased with you.

Hence, the fruit of this entry into God consciousness comes

after an utmost struggle. And even if that state of reality has come nearer to your awareness, even then you cannot maintain awareness there. It is very difficult to touch it. As soon as you want to touch it, you become unaware. You lose awareness. Your connection of awareness is severed at once. Kśemarāja tells us that if this happens, you must understand that your master was not really happy with you when he initiated you. Therefore, you must ask your master to initiate you only when he is completely happy with you. You must not pressure your master to initiate you. By using pressure, nothing can be accomplished. This is the teaching of Kṣemarāja. I don't necessarily agree with this point of view.

It is further stated in the *Mālinīvijaya Tantra:*

> The yogī who does not maintain awareness at the time he achieves supreme yogīc powers becomes detached from the awareness of God consciousness. This yogī has diminished his power of moving forward and the obstacles of life toy with him. (*Mālinīvijaya Tantra*)

At the point when a yogī attains supreme yogīc powers, his awareness may be prevented from further achievement because of his being so filled with the enjoyment of these powers. For example, a yogī gains the power of flying in the air. If at that time, because he is overjoyed—so happy to have gained so much—he becomes detached from the awareness of God consciousness, then his awareness decreases and his power of going forward on the path is reduced. Having weakened his power of going forward, through the attainment of these yogic powers, all the obstacles of life play with him.

In *Spanda,* in this verse it is said:

> The creative energy of Lord Śiva, becoming independent of that yogī who is lacking awareness, plays with him who now acts and experiences wakefulness and the dreaming state just like ordinary people. (*Spanda Kārikā* 3.3)

This yogī lacks awareness. He does not maintain the full awareness of God consciousness. Because of this, the creative energy of Lord Śiva, previously contingent on his maintaining awareness, becomes independent of him. This creative energy plays with him just like she does with ordinary people. In wakefulness he does what worldly people do and in the dreaming state he experiences what they experience. Now there is no difference between this yogī and the common person.

So no matter what happens, a yogi must maintain awareness in continuity. This is what we are being taught here.

This is said in *Mālinī Vijaya Tantra:*

> Do not become attached to *yogic* powers, be detached from them. *(Mālinī Vijaya Tantra)*

In *Spanda,* it is also said:

> The one who is always completely aware to apprehend the essence of *spanda* in each and every movement of life quickly gains entry in God consciousness in the very state of wakefulness. (*Spanda Kārikā* 1.21)

So, beginning from the first sūtra of this chapter, *cittaṁ mantraḥ*, "the yogī's mind is mantra," *śāktopāya* is explained, which is filled with *mantra vīrya* and with *mudrā vīrya.*[24]

> That means *(upāya)*, wherein one, by meditating only with thought, gains entry in God consciousness, through maintaining awareness on an object of perception which can not be uttered, is called *śāktopāya*. (*Mālinī Vijaya Tantra* 2.22)

In *śāktopāya,* the object of meditation is not differentiated perception; it is an object of your own nature which you meditate on with thought. This meditation is not accomplished through the recitation of mantra. It is only accomplished with thought. You must maintain awareness of that object. This is the way of *śāktopāya.*

---

24. See sūtras 1.22 and 2.5, for an explanation of *mantra vīrya* and *mudrā vīrya*

There are some yogīs who are treading on the path of *śāktopāya* who are unable to maintain awareness. For them, this last sūtra has been explained.

When this yogī's state of pure knowledge *(śuddha vidyā)* is destroyed by lack of awareness, he enters the dreaming state. At this point, his future is uncertain. God only knows what will happen to him. He has lost everything and from a yogīc point of view, he is a pauper.

So now, to aid this yogī, the author will explain the means called *āṇavopāya* whereby he can learn how, in time, he will be able to maintain awareness and thereby reach and secure entry into *śāktopāya* and, in the end, gain entry into *śāṁbhavopāya.*

This is the end of the Second Awakening.

Swami Laksmanjoo

Third Awakening

In the First Awakening, the explanation of *śāmbhavopāya* is given. In the Second Awakening, *śāktopāya* is explained. Now, in the Third Awakening, the explanation of *āṇavopāya* will be given.

In the first sūtra of the First Awakening, the definition of your own self is given. In the first sūtra of the Second Awakening, Kṣemarāja has again defined the reality of the self. And in the first sūtra of the Third Awakening, he also explains the reality of the self. But there is a difference in these three explanations.

The explanation given in the first sūtra of the First Awakening is for the self situated in his real way of being in *śāmbhavopāya*. So in that verse *(caitanyamātmā)*, he says, "Independent God consciousness is the reality of the self."

In the first sūtra of the Second Awakening, he says *(cittaṁ mantraḥ)* "the mind is mantra." In this sūtra, the author has descended slightly from "the real way of being" of the first sūtra of the First Awakening to the "experience of the impressions of thoughts." In this sūtra, he is residing in the world of the mind, not in the world of his real nature. But here his mind is so purified that it has become the embodiment of all mantras. And that embodiment of all mantras is *ahaṁ*, supreme I-consciousness.

Now, in the first sūtra of the Third Awakening, he again explains the formation of the self. Here though, the self is defined as being absolutely one with the limited state of thought which is the mind.

And while explaining the Third Awakening of the *Śiva Sūtras,* which is concerned with *āṇavopāyaḥ,* the means of the individual limited being, he will elucidate the formation of individual being.

1. ātmā cittam

Individual being is the mind entangled in the wheel of repeated birth and death.

Here, individual being has been transformed into the nature *(svarūpa)* of mind. But what kind of mind is this? It is not the mind filled with *(mantraḥ)*, the God consciousness of supreme I. It is that mind which is eternally saturated with the impressions of sensual pleasures.

This individual is attached to the three intellectual organs—mind, intellect and ego. The function of these three organs is as follows. First, understanding what is to be done is accomplished by the organ of intellect. Second, the thought of how to do it is accomplished by the organ of mind. Third, the ego is attached when we say, "this is to be done by me."

These three movements are the functions of the mind of that individual being. It is this mind of the individual being which is *ātmā*. Here the Sanskrit word *ātmā* does not mean "individual being." The word *ātmā* comes from the verbal root *ata*. In grammar, the meaning of *ata* is *sātatya gamane*, "who comes and goes, who is always in movement, moving in repeated births and deaths, being born and dying again and again." So he who is always entangled in the wheel of repeated births and deaths is *ātmā*. And that mind is *ātmā*.

Why does he move in repeated births and deaths? This happens when he neglects the knowledge of his own real nature. This individual being moves in various wombs, by possessing at different times either a *(sattvika)* pure state of thought, a *(rājasika)* active state of thought, or a *(tāmasika)* dull state of thought. And when at the time of death he is situated in the *sattvika* state, he moves to a higher life. When at the time of death he is situated in a *rājasika* disposition, he enters into those lives filled with luxuries. And when he is situated in a *tāmasika* mood, he enters into beasts, trees, or into other states of deadened consciousness. This is the nature of this *ātmā,* which is the substance of individual being.

On the other hand, the mind that has become one with God consciousness does not remain in this way. He moves in his own real nature. This is why the first sūtra of the First Awakening is *caitanyam ātmā*, "independent God consciousness is the reality of the self." So in this sūtra, the word *ātmā* in *caitanyam ātmā* was explained in such a way that you will understand that *ātmā* is no other than God consciousness. But here, in the present sūtra, *ātmā* is defined as a truly inferior being. This is the state of individuality. It exists when the supreme being possesses the state of individuality. Possessing this state and being shrunk from all sides, he becomes an individual being.

You should not think, therefore, that the author has explained *ātmā* in different ways. The explanation given for *ātmā* in the first sūtra of the First Awakening is correct in that state of being and the explanation given for *ātmā* in the present sūtra is correct in the present state of being, described above as "who comes and goes."

What happens to this individual being who has become one with the limited mind which is soaked in the impressions of worldly pleasures?

2. jñānaṁ bandhaḥ //

(For this limited individual), all knowledge is bondage.

Whatever knowledge this individual possesses is bondage for him. The meaning of the present sūtra is different from the meaning given for the second *sūtrā* of the First Awakening which is also *jñānaṁ bandhaḥ*. We've seen that this second *sūtrā* of the First Awakening is to be understood as *jñānaṁ bandhaḥ* and *ajñānaṁ bandhaḥ*, "Knowing differentiatedly is bondage and not knowing undifferentiatedly is bondage." But here, in the present sūtra, whatever knowlege he possesses in the state of limited individuality is differentiated knowledge. In this state, there is no possibility of possessing undifferentiated knowledge.

Depending on the three intellectual organs, intellect, mind and ego, the knowledge found here functions in three ways. The three intellectual organs first understand what is to be enjoyed, then establish that understanding, and finally attach ego to that understanding. And these three intellectual acts are one with *(sukha)* pleasure, *(duḥkha)* pain and *(moha)* illusion. *Sukha* is connected with the *sattvika* state of life, *duḥkha* is connected with the *rājasik* state of life and *moha* is connected with the *tāmasik* state of life. These three states of life are controlled by this limited knowledge of the individual being. Therefore, this kind of knowledge causes you to possess only differentiated knowledge, not undifferentiated knowledge. When he is entangled by these three kinds of differentiated knowledge, he travels in the world of repeated births and deaths in various ways and that, in reality, is bondage.

It is said in *Tantrasadbhāva Śastra,*

> Sometimes he is situated in the state of *sattva guṇa*. At other times, he is situated in the state of *rājas guṇa*. And, at other times he is situated in the *tāmas guṇa* state of being. In brief words, he is only residing in the perceptions of the *guṇas,* not beyond them. This is why, being disconnected with the previous state of life and united with the next state of life, he moves in various births and deaths. (*Tantrasadbhāva)*

This is told in *Spanda* in these one-and-a-half verses,

> When the five *tanmātras*[1] give rise to the three intellectual organs, intellect, mind and ego, then collectively there are eight organs. These eight organs are said to be *puryaṣṭaka* and they function in our dreaming state. This *puryaṣṭaka* prevents you from getting through to the reality of your self. When the reality of your nature is ignored, then you are dependent on enjoyment which cannot be refused. Because of this, you are played and entangled by the wheel of repeated births and deaths.
>
> Now you will be told how to end this wheel of repeated births and deaths. (*Spanda Kārikā* 3.17–18)

---

1. The five *tanmātras* are *gandha, rasa, rūpa*, *śabda*, and *sparśa*. These five *tanmātras* correspond to the five great elements *(mahābhūtas). Gandha tanmātra* arises from the element of earth *(pṛithvī mahābhūta). Gandha tanmātra* is the home of smell. *Rasa tanmātra* has come out from the element of water *(jala mahābhūta). Rasa tanmātra* is the residence of the impression of taste (*rasa*). From the element of fire *(tejas mahābhūta)* issues forth *rūpa tanmātra. Rūpa tanmātra* is the residence of form, where the impression of form resides. From the element of air *(vāyu mahābhūta)* rises *sparśa tanmātra,* which is the sensation of touch. And finally, rising from the element of ether *(ākāśa mahābhūta)* is *śabda tanmātra*, the *tanmātra* of sounnd

3. kalādīnāṁ tattvānāmaviveko māyā //

Being unable to possess the undifferentiated knowledge of the 31 elements, you live in those elements, from kalā to pṛithvī (earth), which are the expansion of the energy of illusion (māyā śakti).

In the scriptures, it is established that knowledge is enlightening and *ātmā* is also enlightening. It is said the *ātmā* and knowledge are in reality one. This is explained in this way in the *Śri Vijñānabhairava Tantra*:

> Knowledge is filled with enlightenment and the knower is also filled with enlightenment. Therefore, you can be enlightened completely by either knowledge or the knower. This is because in knowledge you will find the residence of the knower and in the knower you will find the residence of knowledge. These are not two different aspects of being, they are one aspect of being. Knowledge and the knower *(ātmā)* are, in the real sense, one. (*Vijñānabhairava* 137)

So, it is said, there you will find that knowledge is also filled with enlightenment. Knowledge, therefore, can only enlighten you, not deprive you of enlightenment. So, the question must be answered, how is it that in this sūtra you have explained that all knowledge is bondage?

The author answers by stating that he accepts as correct the theory that knowledge and the knower are one with one condition. It is only correct when, by the grace of the Lord, you know this whole universe is filled with knowledge and knower, that knowledge and knower are one, that "this" and "I" are one being. If you know it, then it is not bondage; if you don't know it, then it is bondage.

The thirty-one elements *(tattvas)* beginning from *māyā tattva* and ending in *pṛithvī tattva*, (earth) are the thirty-one elements existing in the world of illusion. *Saṁsāra* begins with the element *kalā* and ends with earth.

In the world of enlightenment, there are five elements *(tattvas)*: *śuddhavidyā, īśvara, sadāśiva, śakti* and *Śiva*. These five elements are pure. The thirty-one elements that comprise *saṁsāra,* being filled with ignorance, are impure. When you are not aware that everything is filled with divinity, with knower and knowledge, then you live in these thirty-one elements. You are unable to possess that undifferentiated knowledge that is the actual state of these thirty-one elements. When you do not possess undifferentiated knowledge of these thirty-one elements, then these elements are impure and are existing in the kingdom of *māyā*. By possessing undifferentiated knowledge, when you are aware that the knower is inside knowledge and that knowledge is inside the knower, then these thirty-one elements are recognized as one with the five pure elements and they are known to be divine and to be the expansion of your *svātantrya śākti.*

Kalā is the first element found when descending from your own real nature. Being limited by *Kalā tattva* is to be separated from possessing the energy of unlimited action. Because of *kalā tattva,* you possess the energy of limited action, limited creativity. And so also, possessing only some limited knowledge, you are disconnected from being all-knowing. In this way, you descend into the world of limitation where you finally enter into the state of *(pṛithvī)* earth, the grossest state of *saṁsāra*.

So, in descending from your own real nature, first there is *māyā* and the five *kañcukas,*which are six coverings which cover your real nature. Then there is *puryaṣṭaka*, which is composed of the five *tanmātras* (subtle elements), *manas, buddhi,* and *ahaṁkāra*. Then there are the five organs of knowledge, the five organs of action, and the five gross elements.

When you know these elements as differentiated and not as undifferentiated, thinking they are different from your own nature and not one with it, then you have descended. Even though in reality these thirty-one elements are one with that supreme being, still you think you are one with that differentiated reality. On the one hand, you think that actually the reality of being is not one with differentiated reality and on the other hand, you think that you are one with that differentiated reality. You think that you are one with your own body and God is not. When you understand in this way, then you have descended. And when you know that all bodies are my bodies and all bodies are universal bodies and you know you possess a universal body, knowing, "I am God," then you are truly elevated. For you, there is no possibility of again becoming immersed in this world of ignorance.

So, when you know you are one with that differentiated reality, you have come down. Descending in such a way, you are absolutely deprived of your real nature. That is *māyā.*

It is said in *Tantrasadbhāva*:

> The results of your God consciousness (*caitanya*) being fenced in by the five coverings is that you act in a limited way, know in a limited way, love in a limited way, live in a limited way and possess in a limited way. Being attached to this path with your organs of knowledge and organs of action, you are guided to walk the spiritual path in a limited way. Your attachment to this path is such that even if you meet an elevated soul who desires to show you the correct path, you will not accept his guidance.
>
> Consequently, in your world of illusion, where you remain filled with insecurity and fear, these limitations are bondage. Here, being completely dependent on that illusive energy of knowledge and being without real knowledge, you are continuously doing right or wrong. So, being completely entangled in that fence you become just like a beast. (*Tantrasadbhāva)*

In this verse in the *Spanda Śāstra,* it is also said:

> For those who are fully aware of God consciousness, all the organs of cognition, organs of action and organs of the intellect lead them to that supreme state of God consciousness. For those who are not aware, these same organs deprive them completely of that God consciousness. (*Spanda Kārikā* 1.20)

These organs, therefore, perform in two ways, depending on whether you are fully aware or not. Those who are deprived of awareness are pushed down into the field of ignorance. Those who possess the fullness of awareness, however, become completely elevated.

Therefore, to curtail this limitation of being:

4. śarīre saṁhāraḥ kalānām //

You must make all the circles (kalās) in your body enter one into the other from gross to subtle.

Beginning from *pṛithvī* and ending in Śiva, there are five circles. In this process of going from gross to subtle, you have to make one circle enter another circle. You do this by putting the effect in its cause, and then you put that cause in its cause, and then you also put that cause in its cause. And, in the end, you will find only Śiva existing everywhere. When Śiva is there, then you are one with Śiva. You can't be an observer of Śiva. There the observed and the observer become one.

To explain more clearly, from the element earth to *śiva tattva,* there are five circles or enclosures that form the boundaries for all the thirty-six *tattvas.* These five circles (*kalās)* are *nivṛitti kalā, pratiṣṭhā kalā, vidya kalā, śāntā kalā,* and *śāntātītā kalā.* You have to make these five circles (*kalās*) enter into each other in your own body, which is comprised of three states—waking, dreaming, and deep sleep. Here, you have to think that the grossest circle has entered in its nearest, more subtle circle, and that circle has entered in its nearest, still more subtle circle and so forth.

Nivṛitti kalā is situated in the grossest element, which is the element "earth" *(pṛithvī tattva).* The next circle is *pratiṣṭhā kalā. Pratiṣṭhā kalā* possesses the twenty-four elements from "water" *(jala tattva)* to *prakṛiti tattva.* The third circle is called *vidyā kalā. Vidyā kalā* possesses six elements. These are the sixfold coverings (*ṣat kañcukas*) *kalā, vidyā, rāga, kāla, niyati,* and *māyā*, the illusive energy of God. You find the fourth circle *śāntā kalā* in that supreme pure being, from *śuddha vidyā tattva* to *śakti tattva*. The fifth circle *śāntatītā kalā* is found in the first and subtlest element, Śiva.

So, to alleviate this state of being completely entangled in limitation, you have to practice going from gross to subtle, as outlined above. To do this, you must meditate and imagine that the gross state of *nivṛiti kalā* has entered into *pratiṣṭhā kalā*. Then you have to imagine that *pratiṣṭhā kalā* has entered into *vidyā kalā*, and *vidyā kalā* has entered into *śāntā kalā* and finally, that *śāntā kalā* has entered into *śāntātītā kalā*. When *śāntātītā kalā* exists, you are situated in the state of Śiva. Practicing in this way will subdue the differentiated state along with the grip of *māyā*.

Let it be the gross body, let it be the subtle body, let it be the subtlest body. This body is either gross as the five gross elements *(mahābhūta)*, subtle as *puryaṣṭaka*,[2] or subtlest as *sūkṣma śarīra*. In short, this gross, subtle, or subtlest body exists up to the circle of the thought of consciousness *(samanāntaṁ)*.[3] You have to make the gross body enter into the subtle body, and you have to make the subtle body enter into the subtlest body.

For example, be situated in your mind and think this gross world is only the invention of your mind. When you are situated in your mind, you are situated in the dreaming state. Although you are actually awake, you are in dreaming state. Now let that dreaming state enter into the dreamless state. In the dreamless state, you become thoughtless, one-pointed. At that time, you are very near to experiencing the state of *samādhi*. You must practice in this way to abolish the power of ignorance, the power of illusion.

---

2. *Puryaṣṭaka* is collectively composed of eight elements, the five *tanmātras*, *śabda, sparśa, rūpa, rasa, gandha,* the mind *(manas)*, intellect *(buddhi)*, and ego *(ahamkāra)*. As *puryaṣṭaka*, these eight elements function in our dreaming state. This is the substance of the subtle body.

3. *Samanāntaṁ* means "up to the state of *samanā*." *Samanā* is that state where the mind is totally destroyed with the exception of its impressions. The impressions remain. When one is burnt to ashes, the impressions of those ashes remain.

There is another type of meditation in which you imagine your gross body is consumed by flames and burned to ashes. Here, you must first meditate, imagining that this body pervades this whole universe, beginning from *Kālāgni Rudra*, the grossest point of world, and ending with *śāntātītā kalā*, the subtlest point of the world. Then put your attention on the big toe of your left foot and imagine that *Kālāgni Rudra,* vigorously producing its fire and burning brilliantly, is rising, consuming your body in flames so there is nothing left of your body but ashes. This kind of meditation uses the power of imagination. Ultimately, it will also be successful.

These two types of meditation are explained in these two verses of the *Vijñānabhairava*.

> You have to meditate that the grossest orbit of the world, *bhuvanādhava,* has entered into the more subtle orbit of the world *tattvādhva*. And then this subtle representation of orbit has entered into its subtlest representation of *kalādhva*. Gross has entered into subtle and subtle has entered into subtlest. And when, in the end, your mind becomes unminded, then you are one with God. There is no difference between your being and God. (*Vijñānabhairava* 56)

First comes the grossest representation of an orbit (circle) *(adhva), bhuvanādhva*. A more subtle orbit is *tattvādhva*. The most subtle orbit is *kalādhva*. The grossest circle is *bhuvanādhava* because it is defined in 118 worlds. The more subtle circle is *tattvādhva* because it is explained in 36 elements. The most subtle circle is *kalādhva* because it is explained in five circles.

This kind of meditation is called *laya cintanā* or *laya bhāvanā*[4] because you take your attention from the gross *(sthūla)* orbit to the subtle *(sūkṣma)* orbit and then to the subtlest *(parā)* orbit, absorbing one in the other. So here you take your attention to the grossest orbit and then you absorb that orbit in the more subtle orbit. And finally, you merge that subtle orbit with the most subtle orbit. This is the threefold movement of entries.

---

4. Absorption of thought.

This next meditation also uses imagination.

> The state of *kālāgni rudra* resides in the big toe of your left foot. Using your imagination, generate fire from that *kālāgni* and then, using that fire, completely incinerate your body. You must imagine your whole body has become ashes. Then the highest peace of God consciousness will shine in your consciousness. (*Vijñānabhairava* 52)

These kinds of meditation are found not only in this tantra, but in each and every tantra of Śaivism. This is why in the *Mālinī Vijaya Tantra*, the means associated with meditation and the means associated with imagination are explained as being in the inferior world of *āṇavopāya,* not *śāktopāya* or *śāmbhavopāya.* And so, these inferior means are not explained in the *Spanda Śāstra* because the *Spanda Śāstra* only explains *śāktopāya* and *śāmbhavopāya*, and not *āṇavopāya.*

5. nāḍīsaṁhāra-bhūtajaya-bhūtakaivalya-bhūtapṛithaktvāni //

The merging of the movements of breathing, controlling the gross elements, diverting attention from all objective senses and directing it towards the center of the movement of the breath, and removing your consciousness from the grip of the elementary field .

As you know, the Third Awakening of the *Śiva Sūtras* is concerned with the inferior *upāya, āṇavopāya*. When, in explaining *āṇavopāya* you reach the terminus, there you will find a touch of *śāktopaya*. And when you explain *śāktopāya* in a beautiful way, in the end you will find its terminus in *śāmbhavopāya*. These are the beginning and ending terminations of *śāktopāya*. So when the terminus of that point in *āṇavopāya* is found, there you will also find *śāktopāya* in *āṇavopāya* because the terminus is not only the ending point, but also the beginning point. As the *Spanda Śāstra* only explains *śāktopāya* and *śāmbhavopāya,* or that point or terminus where *āṇavopāya* ends and *śaktopāya* begins or commingles, it is in this context that you will find the *Spanda Śāstra* quoted in the Third Awakening of the *Śiva Sūtras*.

So, this process of meditation, which is not outside of *āṇavopāya*, is explained. In this sūtra, the other means of meditation which are interconnected with this process of meditation (*dhyāna*)—*prāṇāyāma, dhāraṇā, pratyāhāra* and *samādhi*—are explained.

In this sūtra the word *nāḍīsaṁhāra* means "merging the movements of breath." The word *bhūtajaya* means "attaining control of the gross elements." When you have control of the gross elements, then, when you suffer, you do not suffer internally. If you become feverish, internally you do not suffer any pain. In the sūtra, the word *bhūtakaivalya* means "taking the mind away from gross objects of senses and directing it toward the center of the movement of the breath." The word *bhūtapṛithaktvāni* means "freeing your consciousness from the grip of the elementary field." For example, if you have a painful leg, you separate your consciousness from the pain of that leg and you are without pain. These powers are what yogīs experience.

Now the commentator thoroughly explains this sūtra. The word *nāḍīsaṁhāra* means "merging the movements of breath in the central vein (*suṣumnā nāḍī*)." This is accomplished by maintaining awareness of the breath while inhaling and exhaling. By this "maintaining awareness of the breath," you direct and carry these movements of breath, both inhalation and exhalation, to the central vein.

About this process, the *Svacchanda Tantra* says:

> Take your breath out through the right nostril and in through the left nostril. This is the purification of all veins and the purification of the path toward final liberation (*mokṣa*).
>
> This retention of breath, (*prāṇāyāma*) is done in three ways—exhaling, inhaling and retaining. These three ways of the retention of the breath are gross and commonplace. There are, however, three other ways of retention which are internal and uncommon.
>
> You have to take your breath out in the center of the navel. Don't let your breath actually go out, just push it a bit in the center of the navel. This is internal exhaling. Then you should again take it to the center of navel. This is internal inhaling. So, first give it a push and then take it back in the navel. In this uncommon practice of breathing exercise (*prāṇāyāma*), you have to just push and then back, push and back, without breathing out or in. So here *kumbhakā*[5] functions in three ways. While

5. *Kumbhakā* is the restraining and controlling of breathing. The *Kumbhakā* referred to here is not a gross retention of breath but a subtle one, only done by advanced yogīs.

> breathing out it is not going away, it is already *kumbhakā*. When you breath in it is not going away. And when you retain it, it is there. So, these three processes of *prāṇāyama* are to be done in the center of the naval. (*Svacchanda Tantra* 7.294–96)

The word *bhūtajaya* means to achieve control of the five elements from earth to ether through contemplation.

This is explained in the *Svacchanda Tantra* in this way:

> Whenever you want to control the wind in your body,[6] you must, through contemplation, put your awareness on the big toe of your left foot. When there is insufficient fire in your body (less warmth in your body), you should meditate by putting your awareness in the center of the navel. When there is a lessening of the flesh in your body, you have to contemplate on earth while putting your awareness in the pit of your throat to increase that flesh. When there is a lack of water or you are flooded, then you must contemplate on water while putting your attention on the inner tongue (*ghaṇṭikā*)[7] just near the *tālu*. To attain all the powers that you desire, you must contemplate on the element ether (*ākāśa*) while putting your attention on your head. (*Svacchanda Tantra* 7.299–300)

The meaning of the word *bhūtebhyaḥ kaivalyam* is to be free of the elements. How is this accomplished? You must draw back (*pratyāharaṇam*) your mind from the objective field of sensory pleasures and concentrate it on the center of the breath.

So it is said in the *Svacchanda Tantra*:

> Direct your consciousness to the center of the navel and also direct your mind to that center, carrying it away from the organs of the senses. This fourth breathing practice *(prāṇāyāma)* is a calmed means of retention. (*Svacchanda Tantra* 7.297)

In this *prāṇāyāma,* there is no breathing out and in. This has already been explained. From the heart, you should direct your

---

6. Controlling wind relieves rheumatic pain.

7. *Ghaṇṭikā* refers to the uvula, a small, conical, fleshy mass of tissue suspended from the center of the soft palate.

consciousness to the center of the naval and at the same time, direct your mind, which is lost in objective pleasures, towards this center.

In the present sūtra, the words *bhūta pṛithaktvāni* mean "just to carry your awareness away from the gross elements." How does this happen? It happens when one's consciousness is not influenced by the elementary field.

About this subject, it is said in the *Svacchanda Tantra*:

> When you subside the force of all of the five gross elements, up to the stage of *unmanā* (beyond *samanā*), you become one with Śiva. (*Svacchanda Tantra* 7.327)

The words *nāḍīsaṁhāra-bhūtajaya-bhūtakaivalya-bhūta-pṛithaktvāni* found in the present sūtra give you the same sense as the words *bhūtasaṁdhāna bhūtapṛithaktva viśvasaṁghaṭṭāh* found in the twentieth verse of the First Awakening of *Śiva Sūtras,* which is concerned with *śāmbhavopāya.* So why has he repeated this sūtra again here in the awakening concerned with *āṇavopāya*?

There is a difference. The difference is when one is established in the trance of *śāmbhavopāya,* these powers come automatically, without effort, but for the practitioner (*sādhaka*) of *āṇavopāya,* these powers are attained only after applying effort to achieve them.

By yogic exercises, such as purification of the body *(dehaśuddhi),* purification of the elementary field *(bhūtaśuddhi),* purification of the breath *(prāṇāyāma),* the diversion from objective pleasures to your own consciousness *(pratyāhāra),* one-pointed concentration *(dhāraṇā),* meditation *(dhyāna)* and *samādhi*, powers are attained and one attains mastery of the elementary field. This kind of temporary power is achieved by yogīs because they are covered by illusion and are not, in the real sense, directed towards the universal consciousness of self. If you actually know your real nature, you will not care about these powers.

This is explained in the next sūtra:

6. mohāvaraṇātsiddhih //

These powers are brought into existence when a yogi's consciousness is covered by the energy of illusion (māyā).

Māyā is that which carries your consciousness away from the reality of the self. It is the energy of illusion. Due to this action of *māyā,* a covering comes into existence where you will achieve those powers explained in the previous sūtra. But in fact, due to these powers, the supreme consciousness of Lord Śiva does not appear.

This is said in *Śrī Lakṣmī Kaulārṇava Tantra*:

> That being who arose spontaneously *(svayaṁbhūḥ)* and appeared in this universe by his own free will *(svātantrya),* who is not entangled in the wheel of repeated births and deaths, who is the supreme state which is beyond various thoughts *(vikalpa)* and who is the eternal treasure is only Śiva and none else. All ac-

> tions of limited beings are witnessed by him. The one who is directed toward these limited yogic powers is carried away from the consciousness of Lord Śiva and is not capable of experiencing His nature. (*Lakṣmī Kaulārṇava Tantra* 11)

On the other hand, that yogī whose covering of illusion has subsided and who also practices these same yogic exercises such as *āsana, dhyāna, dhāraṇā* and *samādhi,* is not caught in the grip of these limited yogic powers. For him, these yogic exercises are unique. They are uncommon and are not experienced by ordinary people.

First, he explains the uncommon meaning of *aśana.* Ordinarily, *āsana* means to sit in some particular posture. First, your master directs you to sit in a posture such as that known as *padmāsana* or *svāstika āśana.*[8] He tells you not to lean, just sit up straight. You try to do whatever he tells you to do. This is done first. But for such an advanced yogī, *āsana* is also unique. What is that *āsana* for this advanced yogī?

> He is to direct his consciousness between his two breaths of exhaling and inhaling. After putting his consciousness in the center between these two breaths, he must hold his awareness in that center and there he must establish this power of awareness in continuity, not being diverted for even one moment. When he is established there, this is real posture *(āsana)* for this yogī. (*Lakṣmī Kaulārṇava Tantra* 8.12)

Now after *āsana,* this yogī must practice *prāṇāyāma.* For this yogī, however, this *prāṇāyāma* is unique.

> Initially, this yogī experiences the gross movements of breathing in and breathing out. Then after some time,[9] through the continuity of fixing awareness on these two breaths, his breath

8. *Padmāsana* is the seated pose sometimes referred to as the "lotus pose." This is the classic seated pose where the yogī sits cross-legged with the right foot on top of the left leg and the left foot on top of the right leg. When Lord Śiva is visually depicted, he is usually shown sitting in this pose. *Svāstikāśana* is another sitting pose known as the "auspicious posture."

9. "After some time" means, after half-an-hour, or after two days, or after one week, or after three weeks, or after months, or after years. . . .

> *(prāṇa)* becomes so very subtle *(sūkṣma vṛitti)* that even he can't observe when he is breathing in and breathing out. Following this subtle state of breath *(sūkṣma vṛitti)*, the state which is said to be beyond this subtle state *(sūkṣmātītā)* comes into existence. When this yogī experiences this state of *sūkṣmātītā*, he has the apprehension that he will lose consciousness of awareness but in fact, his maintaining continuity of awareness does not allow this to happen. Now this yogī experiences an internal throbbing (*spandana*) and this throbbing again vibrates his awareness in fullness. (*Lakṣmī Kaulārṇava Tantra* 8.13)

> When he is actually effecting this supreme *prāṇāyāma*, he experiences tremendous divine sounds rushing in his mind. Once this supreme *prāṇāyāma* is accomplished, this yogī will never fall from his reality of consciousness. This *prāṇāyāma* is explained in this way. (*Lakṣmī Kaulārṇava Tantra* 8.14)

Next is the yogic practice of *pratyāhāra*. In the practice of *pratyāhāra*, you are to divert your consciousness of mind from the senses toward your own self. For such a yogī, however, this is not really *prātyāhara*. For him, *prātrāhara* is something else.

> At this point, this yogī has the apprehension of falling again into wordly consciousness. Here, he must wholeheartedly maintain his awareness and avoid its becoming weaker. He must not mind the sounds that he is experiencing, whether they be good, bad, furious, frightening or threatening.[10] Then by remaining fully aware, he will gain entry into the supreme state of consciousness. This is called *pratyāhāra*. It cuts down and chops to pieces the bondage of ignorance *(ajñāna)*. (*Lakṣmī Kaulārṇava Tantra* 8.15)

---

10. When you leave these sounds aside, you should not remain inattentive to them. You should hear these sounds and not be afraid of them. When you allow them to frighten you and you become afraid, thinking, "It may do some harm to my body" or "No, no, no, I won't hear these sounds," etc., then you will come out and again you will be in the worldly field of consciousness. So, you should remain inattentive to these sounds, not shunning them and not giving them any importance.

The next yogic practice is *dhyāna.* What is the real *dhyāna* for such a yogī?

> When these sounds subside and he goes beyond the experience of them he attains that supreme state of ecstasy which is ineffable and which only he knows. This is actually *dhyāna.* (*Lakṣmī Kaulārṇava Tantra* 8.16)

Now for this yogī, what is the yogic practice known as *dhāraṇā*?

> When he holds the consciousness of Lord Śiva in continuity, eternally, without any break, that is *dhāraṇā.* (*Lakṣmī Kaulārṇava Tantra* 8.17)

What is *samādhi* for this yogī?

> When such a yogī experiences the state of universal consciousness of Lord Śiva, not only in his internal state of consciousness of self but also in the very active life of the universe, this is called real *samādhi.* (*Lakṣmī Kaulārṇava Tantra* 8.18)

So it is explained in the *Netra Tantra* that *dhyāna, dhāraṇā* and *samādhi* will also direct you toward the state of consciousness of Lord Śiva. So, the kind of *dhāraṇā* explained in the *Netra Tantra* will carry you toward the state of consciousness of Lord Śiva and that kind of *dhāraṇā*, which leads to the attainment of yogīc powers, will mislead you.

7. *mohajayād anantābhogāt sahajavidyājayaḥ* //

After conquering the field of illusion (māyā) by destroying its many impressions, one attains the victory of the pure knowledge of consciousness.

Māyā can not be eliminated until its last faint impressions are also destroyed. Until then, this illusion (*moha*) will not end. And when these remaining faint impressions are also overcome and destroyed, then one achieves the victory of the pure knowledge of consciousness.

What is illusion (*moha*)? Illusion is this completely differentiated universe filled with impressions and experiences. When this illusion is conquered *(jayāt)*, which means overcome *(abhibhavāt)*, then victory is achieved. But this only occurs when the last faint impressions *(saṁskārāḥ)* of this illusion are also destroyed. Through this pure knowledge *(vidyā)* is realized, where eternal aspects are revealed and supreme God consciousness is obtained. Then being victorious, you attain and hold this supreme pure knowledge of consciousness.

Therefore, the conclusion here is that in *āṇavopāya* one also is capable of entering into *śāmbhavopāya* after entering and completing *śāktopāya*. So first this yogī completes *āṇavopāya*.

Then he gets entry into *śāktopāya*. And when *śāktopāya* is completed, he gets entry into *śāmbhavopāya*.

It is also said in the *Svacchanda Tantra*:

> O Devi, up to *samanā*,[11] the collection of bondage is unlimited.

When you experience pure knowledge, you experience it in two ways: one, pervading and residing in God consciousness *(ātmavyāptiḥ)* and two, pervading universal God consciousness *(śivavyāptiḥ)*. If the experience of God consciousness takes place in the first way, that God consciousness is also bondage. You have to surpass that God consciousness *(ātmavyāptiḥ)*. Only experiencing that state of God consciousness will not transport you to that supreme limit of reality *(śivavyāptiḥ)*. Now Lord Śiva explains how God consciousness occurs.

It is said in the *Svacchanda Tantra*:

> Bondage is just differentiated knowledge. It is experiencing the objects of the world as separate from God consciousness. Here, you think that God consciousness is pure and consciousness in worldly life is impure. You must quit experiencing these kinds of bondage *(pāśas)* and focus your mind towards pure God consciousness. When you abandon this experience of bondage and direct your mind toward God consciousness, experiencing only yourself, that is known as the pervasion of God consciousness, the pervasion of the self *(ātmavyāpti)*.
>
> The pervasion of Śiva *(śivavyāpti)* is separate from and superior to the pervasion of God consciousness *(ātmavyāpti)*. When you experience, just as Lord Śiva experiences, that each and every object of the universe is completely filled with all knowledge, all action and all will, this is known as the pervasion of Śiva *(śivavyāpti)*. This is the only way to be directed towards the kingdom of consciousness (*caitanya*), the state of ultimate freedom *(svātantrya)*. (*Svacchanda Tantra* 5.434–35)

---

11. *Samanā* is that state where the mind is totally destroyed, with the exception of its impressions. When one is burnt to ashes, the impressions of the ashes still remain.

So, this scripture tells us that the pervasion of God consciousness *(ātmavyāpti)* is also an illusion that must be overcome. When it is overcome, then you will be capable of achieving the pure knowledge which is beyond the mind *(unmanā)*. That is the pervasion of universal God consciousness, *śivavyāpti*.

As it has been said in *Svacchanda Tantra*:

> When you experience casting aside the bondage of the bound individual *(pāśaḥ)* and put your consciousness in your own self, that is God consciousness. Then, after that, God consciousness is also to be abandoned and you must unite your consciousness in the pure knowledge of consciousness. There, because the mind *(manaḥ)* is only the collection of differentiated knowledge *(saṁkalpa)*, you will find that state where the mind *(manas)* is not existing at all *(unmanā)*.[12] (*Svacchanda Tantra* 5.393)

So,

> When you progress beyond the idea *(saṁkalpa)* of good and bad, of pure and impure, then actually, when you think deeply about it, there is no difference between individual consciousness and God consciousness. This is that supreme knowledge where you find universal God consciousness, the pervasion of Śiva *(śivavyāpti)*. There is no greater knowledge *(vidyā)* than this. (*Svacchanda Tantra* 5.394)

God consciousness is the same as the individual consciousness in which we are living. Our life is filled with individual consciousness. A yogī's life is filled with God consciousness. And a supreme yogī's life is filled with universal God consciousness. Individual God consciousness is the state of the mind (*manaḥ*). God consciousness is the state of self (*ātma*), and that self too is to be abandoned. Universal God consciousness is the state beyond mind (*unmanā*).

---

12. The mind *(manaḥ)* is only the collection of differentiated knowledge *(saṁkalpa)*. It does not matter whether it is pure knowledge or impure knowledge. Both of these exist in limitation, in the cycle of the mind in bondage.

Now *vidyā* (knowledge) is defined. There are three aspects found in *vidyā*: knowing (*vedana*), infusing your consciousness (*bodhanā*) and the disposal of materials that are alien to yourself (*varjana*).

> When knowledge *(vedana)* of the eternal aspects of Śiva—universal knowledge, universal will and universal action—is held and the knowledge of supreme God consciousness is also achieved *(bodhanā)*, and when the negation of universal God consciousness is abandoned and universal God consciousness is possessed *(varjana)* that, in reality, is called knowledge *(vidyā)*. You must establish yourself there and then the supreme light of universal God consciousness, which is the only cause of entering into your real nature, will appear. (*Svacchanda Tantra* 5.395–96)

Now, for that yogī who has achieved this kind of pure knowledge of universal God consciousness,

8. jāgratdvitīyakaraḥ //

The waking state is another form of his real nature of consciousness.

Wakefulness is not other than his own nature, his real nature of consciousness. It is another formation of his universal consciousness. In speaking of the waking state, the dreaming state and the state of sound sleep are also included. So for such a yogī, these three states, which are experienced in daily life, are not other than universal God consciousness.

The waking state (*jāgrat*) is another formation, another ray of his being, his expansion of self. For him, the waking state is not separate nor is it foreign. It is, on the contrary, another form of his expansion of universal Self. The divinity that he gains in the state of universal God consciousness is found by him to exist equally in the waking state, in the dreaming state, and in the dreamless state, deep sleep.

And then, after achieving the state of pure knowledge, this yogī pervades this supreme knowledge with oneness. He is always aware of his universal consciousness. So, for such a yogī, the waking state is the second form of his establishment of being. Where does this yogī find this state? This state of wakefulness is not found in "I"-consciousness. It is found in "thisness," because "thisness" is absorbed and digested in Universal God Consciousness. So, for such a yogī, this whole objective world is another way of his being, another way of universal consciousness. The state of God consciousness, on the other hand, does not digest "thisness"; it only digests "I"-consciousness.

So, this yogī realizes that the state of wakefullness is just another ray of his universal consciousness. For him, this whole universe is not separate from him. It is his own expansion. It is only the sparks of his own being.

It is said also in *Vijñānabhairava Tantra*:

> The universal consciousness of God is experienced in each and every way in this field of organic action *(akṣamārga),* whether it be hearing, touching, seeing, tasting, or smelling. So, when the aspects of universal God consciousness are always present and when that universal God consciousness is the main aspect of that yogī, his universal God consciousness is filled everywhere. It is never absent for in absence it is also not absent. (*Vijñānabhairava Tantra* 117)

This is the meaning of this verse. Whatever is found in this universe is existing in universal consciousness. So there is nothing to eliminate, nothing to separate from your consciousness. When universal God consciousness is the foremost aspect of this yogī, then everything is filled with his universal consciousness. It is never absent. For in absence, it is also not absent. If it is absent that means it is also existing because the absence of universal consciousness is also existing in universal consciousness. So, in the absence of universal God consciousness, he also finds the presence of universal God consciousness. For, in the absence, his being is present because he is aware that universal God consciousness is not existing. Similarly, it is existing in negation because negation also exists in universal God consciousness.

This is not the same in God consciousness because in God consciousness the negation of God consciousness is discarded. It is only in universal God consciousness that both the affirmation and the negation of universal consciousness are digested. So, if you know universal God consciousness, it is there and if you do not know universal God consciousness, it is there. Both knowing and not knowing are existing there because not knowing is also existing in that supreme being. Not knowing cannot exist without universal God consciousness, because not knowing is also existing in supreme being. So absence is also present.

It is also said in *Sarvamaṅgala Śāstra*:

> In this universe, there are only two aspects found—energy and the energy holder. Of these two, it is energy that is held in each and every part of the universe because this universe is, in fact, the existence of energy. And the energy holder is *Maheśvaraḥ*[13] himself alone. *(Sarvamaṅgala Śāstra)*

This universe includes everything, whatever you feel, whatever you hear, whatever you experience in the daily routine of life. That is the existence of energy. *Śaktimāna*, the energy holder, is the great lord (*maheśvaraḥ*), Lord Śiva himself.

So nothing is lost because when you lose something, you experience that there is something less. But that lessening of consciousness is also existing in universal God consciousness. If that lessening of consciousness is found as part of awareness, it will improve the functioning of that universal God consciousness. When, day by day, your consciousness becomes less and you are aware of it, nothing is lost. When a madman is completely mad and he knows he is mad, then he is not mad. If he is aware that he is mad, then he is not mad at all. But when he is unaware of his madness, then he is actually mad. So, when he is aware that he is actually mad, then he is not mad. When a yogī is aware that his nature of self has become less, then, because he is aware, it has not become less. The nature of the self is awareness. When awareness is held, everything is held.

13. *Maheśvara* means "Great Lord." It is another name for Lord Śiva.

Such a yogī always resides in the consciousness of his nature. For him,

9. nartaka ātmā //

The dancer in this field of universal dance is his self of universal consciousness.

What is this universal dance? It is everything that you experience in your life. It may be coming. It may be going. It may be birth, death, joy, sadness, depression, happiness, enjoyment. All of this forms part of the universal dance, and this dance is a drama. In this field of drama, the actor[14] is your own nature, your own self of universal consciousness. This self of universal consciousness is the one who is aware, he is the actor in this universal drama. Those who are not aware are not actors; they are played in this drama. They experience sadness, they experience enjoyment, they become joyful, they become depressed. But those who are aware, they are always elevated; they are the real players in this drama.

So it is your own self of universal consciousness which is, in fact, the actor. Why? Because he acts. The actor is he who conceals his real nature. When you conceal the real nature of your being and, to the public, reveal another form of your being, that is the behavior of acting. Because when any person, say, a person named Denise, is the real actor and, as an actor, she ap-

14. In the text, to illustrate the creation of this universe and the concealed nature of the creator, the metaphor of dancing is used not acting. But the Sanskrit word *nartaka* also means "actor." In English, the metaphor of dancing does not carry the same weight and connotation as the metaphor of acting. Therefore, to add clarity to the present discussion, I have changed the references of dancing to acting.

pears as Lord Kṛiṣṇa, as Lord Śiva, as a woman, as a child, as a silly fellow, then the real and actual state of her being is concealed. So for others, the actual state of her being is concealed and a superficial formation is revealed. But for her, the actual state of her being is not concealed. She knows she is Denise. At the time of becoming Lord Kṛiṣṇa or Śiva or Jesus Christ, she is aware of her being Denise. In herself, she knows she is really Denise.

So, Lord Śiva is the real actor. And although his nature of universal consciousness is concealed to the public, in fact, he knows that he is that reality. Actually, being filled with that awareness of universal God consciousness, he sometimes appears in the waking state, sometimes in the dreaming state, sometimes in the dreamless state, etc. This, however, is actually his play. It is not his real action. His real action is his being in his own universal God consciousness in each and every moment of revealing his differentiated forms. At the time of revealing his differentiated formation in the waking state, he diverts his universal consciousness in the state of wakefulness. And also in that state, he finds he is playing. Actually, this is play, he is not becoming that state. For although he has become the waking state, he has not actually become the waking state and he has not become the dreaming state or the state of deep sleep. In fact, he is already there in that universal God consciousness.

In the hymns composed by *Devī* contained in the seventh chapter of the *Tantras* known as the *Naiśvāsa Devī Maheśvaranartakākhye* it is said:

> In one way, O Lord Śiva, you are actually residing in your own nature, and yet you have put on different coverings. Covering that universal God consciousness in one way, it appears as wakefullness and covering it another way, it appears as the dreaming state or the state of deep sleep.

It is because of these coverings that this universal God consciousness is not found.

Bhaṭṭanārāyaṇa has also said in his *Śāstra*, the *Stavacintāmaṇi*:

> O Lord Śiva you have present in your own self the germ of universal existence from which this universe has expanded. It is from this seed that you create the drama of the three worlds, the drama of waking state, the drama of the dreaming state and the drama of the state of deep sleep. O Lord, you create these three types of drama from the sprouting of that seed which is already residing in your real nature. This is only the course of your action of awareness. Who else can act in this way to create this drama and then withdraw it again? (*Stavacintāmaṇi* 59)

The *Pratyabhijñā Śāstra,* which expounds *pratyabhijñā*, the way of recognition, the secret of all tantras, also says the same thing,

> O Lord, in this world which is absolutely unaware of what is existing, only you are aware. You are the creator of the drama of this universe. You are unique and the one who is actually awake in this dreaming state. (*Pratyabhijñā Kārikā*)

He has established the covering of the waking state, the covering of the dreaming state, and the covering of the dreamless state because he has to maintain the drama of the universe. It is for this reason that he takes good care of this covering. Otherwise, this covering has no meaning. Meaning only exists in universal God consciousness.

So, this entire universe is actually the result of a colossal universal drama which is taking place. And who is the hero in this drama? Here the part of the hero is played by the internal soul[15] who is also the universal soul in disguise.

---

15. There are three kinds of souls: (1) the internal soul composed of *puryaṣṭaka* (mind, intellect and ego along with the five *tanmatras*), (2) the external soul, the soul that resides in the body, and (3) the universal soul. The universal soul is not the player in this universal drama. The external soul is also not the player. It is the internal soul that is the player. It is the internal soul that resides in dreaming state, the state of deep sleep, and in the void state. It is this soul that remains after death.

In his theatrical costume, he steps into the play, which is this drama of the universe. Now, in the next sūtra his method of acting is explained,

10. raṅgo'ntarātmā //

The player is the internal soul.

In this universal drama this actor plays many different roles in various ways. For example he may play the part of Rāma or of Sītā, or he may play the part of Pārvatī, or so many other characters. This acting, called *abhinaya* in Sanskrit, is thought to be of three kinds: *sattvika*, *rājas*, and *tāmas*.[16] When the actor is portraying or acting the part of Rāma, the audience must feel that this actor is actually Rāma, not just a person pretending to be Rāma. They must totally disregard the fact that he is an actor. If the audience is convinced that this actor is actually Rāma, this is known as *sattvika abhinaya*. This is how great actors in this universal drama act, playing various parts in this world. *Rājas abhinaya* is that quality of acting where the audience feels that there is something of Rāma in the actor and yet they still feel that this actor is not actually Rāma. In *tāmas abhinaya,* the audience feels that the actor playing the part of Rāma is only an actor and nothing more.

Here in this universal drama, the actor is the internal soul. He is acting in this universe just to reveal that this universe is actually a universal drama. In the drama, this internal soul is

16. *Sāttvika abhinaya* is the dramatic portrayal attached to *sāttva guṇa*; *rājas abhinaya* is the dramatic portrayal attached to *rājas guṇa;* and *tāmas abhinaya* is the portrayal attached to *tāmas guṇa.*

the stage where he plays the parts of many various characters. And although this internal soul plays the parts of these many different characters, yet from the universal point of view the internal soul is only one.

And so, because this internal self has shrunk from the expansion of universality, it is this self in which the soul is residing in the dreaming state, in the state of deep sleep and in the void state. You should realize, however, that this internal self is not the external soul. It is the external soul which resides in the body in the waking state.

There, in that field of drama, the internal self steps in and begins his dance, revealing this drama of the world by infusing the movement (*spanda*) of his organs. Sometimes he is sad, sometimes he is weeping, sometimes he is laughing and all of this is his play. In actual fact, he is neither laughing nor dreaming nor sad nor joyous—he is one, just as he has always been.

This is already explained in *Svacchanda Tantra:*

> By entering into the subtle body found in the dreaming state *(puryaṣṭaka),* he journeys in each and every womb in this universe. He is known as the interior self *(antarātmā).* (*Svacchanda Tantra* 11.85)

Who are the spectators of this drama of that one who acts on the stage of the interior self?

11. prekṣakāṇīndriyāṇi //

His own organs are spectators.

Thus, for a yogī, the observers of this drama are his own organs. It is a yogī who discovers that this world, as universal movement, is actually a universal drama taking place. Here the actor in this drama is only one, the interior self (*antarātmā*), taking the part of so many beings, including even rocks.

This is experienced only by yogīs, not by worldly people. Worldly people are overwhelmed by sadness, by pleasure, by pain, etc. Yogīs are not overwhelmed in this way because they are absolutely aware of what they are doing in this world. The yogī knows that he is playing, and that this universe is just a drama, a play, filled with life, with death, with sorrow, with sadness, with joy, with happiness; filled with rising and with falling. He knows whatever happens in this world, it is just play.

Thus the cognitive organs of a yogī perceive the real nature of universal being in an internal, not external, way. And when that reality of the self is revealed by these organs, then inherent difference *(vibhāgam)* is totally destroyed and vanishes. His organs become filled with universal joy and absolute independence *(svātantrya)*.

This has already been said in *Vedānta:*

> There are very few heroes who experience the reality of their own nature in an internal rather than external way. These heroes are always established in their internal being. There the external way has vanished. (*Kaṭha Upaniṣad.* 2.4, 2.1)

And for such a yogī:

12. dhīvaśātsattvasiddhiḥ //

By means of a supreme intellect filled with the awareness of the self, this yogī experiences that he is actually acting.

In this verse, the word *sattva* means *sattvika abhinaya* (true acting). It is the real essence of acting. Through the attainment of the reality of his supreme intellect, this yogī achieves the state of *sattvika abhinaya,* where he feels and experiences that he is actually acting in this world. This differs from those yogīs who are acting in this world in the state of *rājas abhinaya.* In *rājas abhinaya,* yogīs feel they are acting in this universal drama on the sidelines. And there are some other yogīs in this world possessing *tāmas abhinayaḥ.* In this state, they feel they are only acting in this universal drama through imagination. Yogīs possessing *tāmas abhinaya* don't feel they are actually acting. But this yogī possessing *sattvika abhinaya* is certain that he is truly acting as each and every person in this world. This state of *sattvika abhinaya* occurs for only that yogī who possesses that supreme intellect filled with the awareness of self. This is the intellect that is absolutely pure and skillful in perceiving its real nature. By directing that kind of supreme pure intellect, the reality of self takes place in an internal manner.

In the external world of drama, true acting *(sattvika abhinaya)* also exists but it is not performed by ordinary actors. This kind of acting is only performed by great heroes who possess the reality of intellect. This true acting is the imitation of the fourfold conditions, which are *āṅgika, vācika, āharya,* and *sattvika.*

The first condition is *āṅgika*. *Āṅgika* is appearance conveyed by bodily actions. The hero who is playing this part must affect the bodily actions of the person being portrayed in such a way that the spectator will feel this is actually the body of the person being portrayed and not the body of the actor. The audience must be thrilled in perceiving that. These bodily actions are called *āṅgika abhinaya.*

The second condition is *vācika*. In *vācika,* the appearance is conveyed by words. Here the audience must feel that the words they are hearing are spoken by the person being portrayed and not by an actor.

Āhārya is the third condition. In *āhārya,* the appearance is conveyed by dress and ornaments. These dramatic costumes must be worn in such a way that the audience thinks these costumes are the actual dress of the person being portrayed and not the costumes of an actor. The kind of acting which causes the audience to feel the costumes being worn are not really costumes is called *āhārya abhinayaḥ.*

The fourth condition is *sattvika*. In *sattvika,* internal feelings expressed as the external manifestations smiling and weeping are convincingly conveyed. For instance, if his acting is *sattvika,* then if he is sad, he will make all of the spectators sad; if he is weeping, you will weep with him. If he is portraying sadness, then you will feel he is actually sad and filled with misery and you will also become miserable and sad. This is the way *sattvika abhinaya* is rendered by players in the external drama.

So, when this real nature is held by such a yogī, then,

13. siddhaḥ svatantrabhāvaḥ //

The state of absolute independence is already achieved.

In the verse, the word *siddhaḥ* means *saṁpannaḥ* (achieved). The word *svatantrabhāvaḥ* means the state of absolute independence. That absolute independence lies in all knowledge, all action and all will. By this absolute independence this yogī makes the whole universe dependent on him. This world is lying under the control of such a yogī. Whatever he wills in this universe will take place.

This was said by the great yogī *Śrī Nāthapāda*:

> You must own that energy of absolute independence which is really the energy of Bhairava.

In *Svacchanda Tantra,* it is also said:

> All elementary worlds, all individuals, all words and all sentences are absolutely dependent on and under the control of such a yogī, who is always intent on determining the reality of Śiva. Whatever he does and whatever he wills will do and undo. (*Svacchanda Tantra* 7.245)

For such a yogī:

14. yathā tatra tathānyatra //

This [absolute independence] is the same in the external world as it was in samādhi.

For this yogī, there is no difference between the independence experienced in *samādhi* and the independence experienced in the external state *(vyutthāna)*. He may reside in *samādhi* or he may be given to the activity of the world; his reality of independence is the same.

Wherever this yogī has experienced the reality of self in *samādhi*, that awareness is experienced by him in each and every aspect of external life. There is no difference for him in these two. Whether he remains in *samādhi* or outside *samādhi* in the external world, he is the same and his experience, his realization of the truth, also remains the same.

This is said in the *Svachandra Tantra*:

> He is always independent. He is independent here, he is independent there, he is independent everywhere. (*Svacchanda Tantra* 7.260)

And in *Spanda*, it is also said:

> That reality of the self, where unartificial[17] universal indepen-

---

17. Unartificial *(akṛitrim)* means that it is not imaginary. Some yogīs possess imaginary independence, which is artificial. These yogīs permeate their thinking with thoughts such as "I am independent" or "I am Śiva." To possess unartificial independence, they must actually be independent, they must be Śiva, not just imagine they are.

dence will shine, should be sought with great reverence. (*Spanda Kārikā* 1.7)

Although he has utterly achieved the reality of independence, which is absolute freedom, he still must remain active for the whole of his life. This is a great task for such a yogī because for the remainder of his life, he has to remain absolutely active to realize the truth of reality again and again, again and again, so that in the end, he becomes one with Śiva.

So he says:

15. bījāvadhānam //

Maintain breakless awareness on that supreme energy which is the seed of the universe.

So *bīja*, Sanskrit for "seed" or "germ," is understood and realized in *samādhi* as the cause of this whole universe. That *bīja* is the supreme energy of Śiva, *svātantrya śakti*.

The Sanskrit word *avadhāna* means to be attentive, to put your mind and your intellect on a point that is to be meditated on, again and again, in continuity, without pause. Here, in this sūtra, you are told to maintain breakless awareness on that supreme *svātantrya śakti*. This is to be done in continuity after you realize it, not before. Why? Because before you have realized it, you won't have the strength of awareness to do it in continuity. At the time you realize it, that strength of meditating on it in continuation comes spontaneously.

Suppose you are given to the state of *samādhi* but you have not yet realized your real nature. Until then, you want to relax, to take life easy, to rest and be at ease. But after you realize the reality of the self, you will naturally become active and you will remain active. You will never remain inactive. After realization, the cause of your being always active comes from above and you will remain fully active for the remainder of your life.

It is said in *Mṛityujit (Netra Tantra)*:

> That germ, which is the cause of the entire organic world, the cause of all energies, the cause of all breath, both incoming and outgoing, is that supreme energy of Lord Śiva, the universal cause. (*Netra Tantra* 7.40)

Śiva Sūtra 3.15

This yogī has to put his mind and intellect on that point again and again, without any pause, in continuity.

Then, when such a yogī acts in this way:

16. āsanasthaḥ sukhaṁ hrade nimajjati //

Seated in that real posture, he effortlessly dives in the ocean of nectar.

Actually, the postures (*āsanas*) explained in the *yogadarśana* are not really *āsanas* at all. *Śivayoga* is the only posture that must be understood when you are seeking to understand the real posture for such a yogī. This real posture is the supreme energy of awareness. You are seated in that posture when you hold and possess the supreme energy of awareness. Then in each and every act of your life you are aware, you are seated in that posture. This is the real *āsana*. The physical postures called *āsanas* are not actually *āsanas*. These so-called *āsanas* are only imitations of the real *āsana*. They are only imagination. The real *āsana* actually exists when you are truly residing in the state of absolute awareness, the awareness of self.

The yogī who, leaving aside the effort of *āsana* (yogic exercises), *prāṇāyāma* (breathing exercises), *dhyāna* (contemplation), and *dhāraṇā* (meditation), simply remains in that posture with nothing left to do, aware of what he actually is. This is why the author has used the word *sukham* in the sūtra because "effortlessly" means that without exerting any effort in respect to breathing or yogic exercise, contemplation or meditation, he remains seated in that posture.

So in an internal, not external, way he perceives the reality of his embodiment of awareness[18] and without any effort finally

18. You must not be aware of your dress, your beauty, or charm, or your body. You must be aware of your nature, what you really are. That is, in the real sense, awareness.

immerses himself in the ocean from which the universe rises and expands. He dives and enters for good in that ocean, which is filled with real nectar.

What does diving mean? In diving into the ocean of nectar, he lets the impressions of the body (*deha*), of the breath *(prāṇa)*, of the eight constituents *(puryaṣṭaka)* and of the void *(śūnya)* sink into that ocean and he becomes one with that nectar. This is the real way of diving.

In *Mṛityujita Tantra (Netra Tantra),* it is said:

> You do not have to concentrate above on *sahasrārdha cakra* or below on *mūlādhāra cakra*. You have not to concentrate on the tip of the nose, on the backside, or on the nostrils—breathing and exercising *prāṇa* and *apāna*.
>
> Nor do you have to concentrate on someplace in your body or concentrate in a universal way. You do not have to put your concentration on ether nor do you have to concentrate downward.
>
> You do not have to close your eyes. You do not have to open your eyes and keep your eyes wide open. You do not have to take any support in meditation, nor do you have to have absence of support.
>
> You do not have to concentrate on your organic field, or on the universal elements, or on sensations of the five senses—sound *(śabda),* touch *(sparśa),* sight *(rūpa),* taste *(rasa)* and smell (*gandha).* You have to put all of these aside and enter into that universal being of awareness. This is what Śaivaite yogīs do successfully.
>
> Actually, this state of the Śaivaite yogī is the real state of Śiva. This state is not revealed to others; it is revealed only to the revealers. (*Netra Tantra* 8.41–45)

This state, which is the real nature of Śiva, is not revealed; this state is the revealer. This state is subjective, not objective. So the aspirant must be active in an interior way, not in an external way. He must be active in being aware of himself. That is real activity. Real activity is not moving about here and there. The revealed is not the point to be sought; it is the revealer that is to be striven for. And this state of the revealer is not separate from subjective consciousness. It is only subjective consciousness.

When, by adopting the means of *āṇavopāya*, this yogī's breathing movements end, then, because he gains entry into *suṣumnā*, the central path, he conquers the world of illusion and attains the power of *śāktopāya*. And when that yogī acquires the supreme nectar of the *śāmbhava* state, then . . .

17. svamātrānirmāṇamāpādayati //

Experiencing that this objective world
is the product of his subjective consciousness,
he can create anything he desires.

In this sūtra, the word *svamātra* means "the product of one's own consciousness." When one's own consciousness congeals in the shape of time and space, that is the measure for the creativity of consciousness. So he can create this universe according to his choice. He can create whatever he thinks, whatever he desires. He does it because he creates it.

This is said in *Svacchanda Tantra:*

> By taking the deception of grossness, he becomes gross in this universe and by taking the deception of subtleness, he becomes subtle. Therefore, existing in both, he alone is the player in the gross and subtle worlds. (*Svacchanda Tantra* 4.295)

In *Pratyabhijñā Kārikā,* it is also said:

> Because of his independent freedom of consciousness, he creates this universe directly from his own nature. So his reality of being becomes this universe, which is not separate from his being. This objective world is not created by the inherent power of this objectivity; it is created by subjective consciousness. (*Īśvarapratyabhijñā Kārikā* 1.5, 1.15)

It is because of subjective consciousness that this objective world is created. So subjective consciousness is the player and the creator of everything that is created in the objective or subjective field.

In Tantra, it is also said:

> O dear Pārvatī, the one who, by the grace of the master, realizes what reality lies in water and its solidified formation snow, nothing remains undone in this world. This is his last birth. Liberated while living *(jīvanmukta)*, he won't again enter into the wheel of repeated births and deaths.

There is a difference between water and snow. It is the formation of these two that is different—snow is snow and water is water. The substance of these two, however, is one. For the one who realizes this, nothing remains undone in this world.

The *Spanda Kārikā* expresses this same point of view in this verse:

> For the one who observes that there is no difference between the universe and its creator, the creator having become the universe and the universe having become the creator, this universe is not defective, but a playful amusement. Realizing this, he is always attached to his own reality of self-consciousness. There is no doubt he is liberated in this very life *(jīvanmukta)*. (*Spanda Kārikā* 2.5)

This yogī has created, by his own *svātantrya śakti,* a gross elementary body and a subtle body of emotions.[19] For him, there is no longer any bondage of birth and death. This is explained in the next sūtra.

18. vidyā 'vināśe janmavināśaḥ //

When his knowledge of the Self is permanently established, then birth (and death) are gone forever.

When knowledge of being is established in continuation, and is therefore permanent, then the reality of repeated births and deaths no longer exists. In this sūtra, the word *janma* includes both *janma* (birth) and *maraṇa* (death). So, he is never born and he does not die.

When this pure knowledge of consciousness is established in continuity, then birth *(janma)* is gone forever. For him, there is no more birth and there is also no more death. What is the cause of birth *(janma)*? Action attached with ignorance is the cause of birth. That action creates the organs, the body and all its limbs. Therefore, when that action which is the cause ends, then the effect, being created and being born, also ceases to exist.

About this, the *Śrī Kaṇṭhī Śāstra* says:

> For the one who has abandoned the world along with its diversity, including the perception of right and wrong, and who realizes that the blades of grass, leaves, rocks, both animate and

---

19. He has created *bhūta śarīra,* the elementary body and *bhāva śarīra,* the subtle body. The subtle body exists in the dreaming and the dreamless states. The elementary body exists in the waking state.

> inanimate from Śiva to the element earth (*pṛithvī*), all existent objects and nonexistent objects[20] are one with Lord Śiva. He is never born again in this world.

In *Svacchanda Tantra*, it is also said:

> When, through the successive teachings of the masters, one is established in one's own consciousness, which is supreme and pure, then one becomes liberated *(muktaḥ)* and never again comes into this universe. (*Svacchanda Tantra)*

About this, the *Netra Tantra* says:

> If, by adopting the divine path of yoga which is beyond the three-fold states of being, that supreme eternal stable state of being is experienced, then he does not again come into this world. (*Netra Tantra* 8.26–27)

---

20. Existent objects are what we feel. Nonexistent objects are what we imagine.

But when, however, this pure knowledge of his real being subsides, then,

19. kavargādiṣu māheśvaryādyāḥ paśumātaraḥ //

In the world of letters, words and sentences, the eight energies of the Lord, who are the mothers of beasts (take control and hold him).

In this sūtra, the word *kavargādiṣu* refers to the world of letters, words and sentences. First, there are letters, then words, and then sentences. Letters create words and words create sentences. In the world of these three, the eight energies of Lord Śiva *(māheśvaryādyāḥ)*—who are the mothers or rulers of beasts *(paśumātaraḥ)*—mothers of beasts. Who is the beast? The ignorant human being. What is the function of these eight mothers? The first five energies are the five senses: hearing *(śabda)*, touch *(sparśa)*, seeing *(rūpa)*, taste *(rasa)* and smell *(gandha)*. Then there are the three energies of mind *(manas)*, intellect *(buddhi)* and limited ego *(ahaṁkāra)*. These eight mothers—the five senses, along with mind, intellect and limited ego—take you away from your reality of consciousness. This is the objective field upon which the eight ladies govern those who are ignorant.

Kṣemarājā, in his commentary, says that the words *adiṣṭḥātryo bhavanti*, which mean "they take charge of holding them," must be added to this sūtra.

Now Kṣemarājā offers the following references from the Tantras to explain how the supreme energy of Lord Śiva, *svātantrya śakti*, seems to have descended to the level of the ignorant being. Actually, this supreme energy has not fallen at all but, for the ignorant, it seems as though it has.

> This *svātantrya śakti*, the supreme energy of absolute independence, is always one with the creator of the universe, Lord Śiva. (*Mālinī Vijaya Tantra* 3.5)

> When Lord Śiva desires to manifest himself in this world, then *svātantrya śakti* is transformed into the energy of will *(icchā śakti)*. (*Mālinī Vijaya Tantra* 3.6)

> O dear *Devi*, I will explain to you how that energy which is one with Lord Śiva, although she is only one, taking many formations becomes many. (*Mālinī Vijaya Tantra* 3.6)

> When that energy of will *(icchaśakti)* perceives that this is what is truly to be desired, then that energy of will is transformed into the energy of knowledge *(jñānaśakti)*. (*Mālinī Vijaya Tantra* 3.7)

When the energy of will perceives that this is to be desired and this is not to be desired, which means she distinguishes between what is to be desired and what is not to be desired, then for him the energy of will is transformed into the energy of knowledge *(jñānaśakti)*.

> And so, when that energy of knowledge actually wants this desire to be fulfilled, then that energy of knowledge becomes the energy of action *(kriyā śakti)*. (*Mālinī Vijaya Tantra* 3.8)

> This energy of will, which is the supreme energy of absolute independence of Lord Śiva *(svātantrya śakti)*, is just like the *cintāmaṇi* stone,[21] for although she has become two as the energy of knowledge and the energy of action, yet because of objective perception, whatever object he desires, she becomes like that and becoming one with that object, she becomes many. (*Mālinī Vijaya Tantra* 3.9)

> The first formation she takes is *mātṛikā cakra*, the wheel of the class of letters from "*a*" to "*kṣa*." And this garland of letters has become twofold, ninefold and fiftyfold. (*Mālinī Vijaya Tantra* 3.10)

21. The *cintāmaṇi* stone is a particular jewel that assumes the form of whatever is kept under it.

> There are two classes in the garland of letters: one is the class of vowels and the second is the class of consonants. The letters from *"a"* to *"ḥ" (visarga)* are the vowels and that is the germ *(bīja)*. The letters from "*ka*" to "*kṣa*" are the consonants and that is the womb *(yoni)*, the basis from which this *bīja* is expanded. When this class is explained as ninefold, because of the nine *vargas*,[22] then the first class is from the letter "*a*" to *"ḥ" (visarga)*. The second class is "*ka*" *varga*. The third class is "*ca*" *varga*. The fourth class is *"ṭa"* *varga*. The fifth class is "*ta*" *varga*, the sixth is "*pa*" *varga*, the seventh is "*ya*" *varga*, the eighth is "*śa*" *varga*, and the ninth is "*kṣa*" varga. The fifty-fold class comprises all the separate letters from *"a"* to "*kṣa*." All these classes, the fiftyfold class, the ninefold class and the twofold class of the garland of letters, are adopted by *svātantrya śakti*. (*Mālinī Vijaya Tantra* 3.11)

> This germ is Lord Śiva himself and the basis of this germ *(yoni)* is his energy of *svātantrya śakti*. These eight *vargas* are governed by the eight great mothers who command ignorant beings *(paśus)*. *(Mālinī Vijaya Tantra* 3.12)

> When each letter is taken separately, then there are fiftyfold letters. These fifty letters corresponds to the fifty *rūdras*. And by combining them together, along with the subjective field and the objective field, they become one hundred *rūdras*. (*Mālinī Vijaya Tantra* 3.13)

By the explanation given in the *Mālinī Vijaya Tantra*, you will understand that when the supreme energy of Lord Śiva (*pārameśvarī*), which is supreme transcendental speech (*parāvāk*),[23] descends to the field of the universe, she first be-

22. A *varga* is a division or class. Here, *varga* refers to the classes of letters that comprise the Sanskrit alphabet. In Sanskrit, the vowels are one class of letters. There are eight classes of consonants which are defined by where the letter is created.

23. *Parāvāk* is known as transcendental speech because it is speech not uttered through the lips, or through the mind, or through any other medium. This speech is automatic. *Parāvāk* is another name for that perfect independence *(svātantryam)*. It is soundless sound that resides in your own universal consciousness. It is the supreme sound that has no sound, the life of the other three kinds of speech that comprise the kingdom of speech—*paśyantī, madhyamā,* and *vaikharī.*

comes will, then knowledge and then action. Then she assumes the form of the vowels (*bija*), the consonants (*yoni*), then the classes of letters (*varga*), and the holders of the classes. These are Śiva—his energy and the eight great mothers.

There are two ways to observe this garland of letters—as *savikalpa* or as *nirvikalpa*. The Sanskrit word *savikalpa* means "with varieties of thoughts" and *nirvikalpa* means "without varieties of thoughts."

The *nirvikalpa* way of observing sounds, letters, and sentences is experienced by yogīs. For example, if you say, "Get me a bucket of water, I want a bucket of water," then when you examine this statement in a *nirvikalpa* way, you won't get that bucket of water. Rather, you will observe this is only the flow of consciousness in its own nature. The word "get" will have no meaning. It is only the letters "g," "e," "t" and nothing else. There is no meaning in the separate letters. To derive meaning, you have to attach your individual consciousness. When individual consciousness is not attached to these letters, words and sentences, then you will become one with Lord Śiva. This is the *nirvikalpa* reality of realization.

The *savikalpa* manner of observing these sounds is said to be existing when, in response to the request, "Get me a bucket of water," you actually go and fetch a bucket of water. This kind of observation is meant for ignorant beings. For those ignorant people, those beasts, these letters, words and sentences pierce their minds and make them weep, make than smile, make them laugh, make them joyous, make them happy and make them sad.

For example, when you hear the words "your father is dead," then, because you are a limited being (*paśu*), you begin to weep. But what is contained in these words "your father is dead" You hear "your" which are the letters "y," "o," "u," "r" and nothing else, and you hear "father" which are the letters "f," "a," "t," "h," "e," "r" and nothing else. What meaning has come out from these sounds? Nothing, it is all divine. This is the *nirvikalpa* way of understanding. With this understanding, you won't weep. But ignorant limited beings, who observe in the *savikalpa* way, are pierced through their senses and their minds.

They are governed by the eight mothers who are the mothers of beasts and who create in their minds sometimes wonder, sometimes joy, sometimes fear, sometimes attachment, sometimes detachment—all the things that happen in this universe in the realm of ignorance. And when they understand in this limited way, then that which is never limited by these letters, words and sentences, which is *(nirvikalpa),* always free and filled with consciousness, is covered by these energies and they become the object and are played by this limited way of being.

The *Timirodghāṭa Tantra* also says the same thing:

> In the center of *brahmarandhra*[24] is situated the supreme energy of Lord Śiva, the Divine Mother, surrounded by the eight divine mothers of beasts. In their hands, they hold the noose *(brahma pāśa)* which entangle and bind one with limitation, keeping one from the unlimited state. These supreme terrible *(mahāghorā) śaktis*, create disturbance and ignorance again and again, and are very difficult to conquer.

This topic has already been referred to in the fourth sūtra of the First Awakening which says, "The Universal Mother commands this triple knowledge." There this mother (*mātṛikā*) who governs all differentiated knowledge is explained in a general way. But here, in this eighteenth sūtra, she is clarified in a particular way. Here, we are told that if, through negligence, the yogī who has already perceived his own nature allows his awareness to ebb, then he becomes the object of those mothers of beasts (*paśumātaraḥ*). By the penetration of the sounds of letters, words and sentences, he is oppressed with the delusion (*moha*) created by those who rule limited beings (*paśus*). This is the essence of this sūtra.

24. The *brahmarandhra* is a subtle opening in the crown of head. Through this subtle opening, the *kuṇḍalinī* departs from the entanglements of this body.

Now the author explains that a yogī must remain fully aware in each and every state of life so that this state of pure knowledge of consciousness remains stable and does not decline.

20. triṣu caturthaṁ tailavadāsecyam //

The fourth state (turya) *must be expanded like oil so that it pervades the other three: waking, dreaming, and deep sleep.*

What are the three states? The three states are the waking state *(jāgrat),* the dreaming state *(svapna),* and the state of deep sleep *(suṣupti).* The fourth state *(turya),* which is filled with pure knowledge, pure light and the ecstasy and joy of *turya,* must be sprinkled and expanded just as oil expands when it is poured on a smooth surface like a piece of cloth. For just as oil spreads on this surface, adhering to it, so in this way a yogī must expand the state of *turya* into the other three states.

The state of *turya* is found in all these three at the moment of entry and at the moment of exit. So at the time of entering into the state of wakefulness, or the dreaming state, or the dreamless state, and at the time of coming out from any one of these three states, the yogī finds *turya* existing.

The yogī must prolong *turya* in such a way that its nectar becomes established and pervades not only in the beginning and the end but also in the middle of these three states. And the means to accomplishing this in all three states is to "hold it." Hold it at the time of entry and hold it at the time of exit. This nectar of *turya (turyarasa)* must be properly held with full awareness so that it is expanded in the center of these three states. Accomplishing this, the yogī becomes one with that nectar of *turya* in all three states.

The present sūtra is also explained in the seventh sūtra of the First Awakening, which states, "Such a heroic yogī experiences the expansive state of *turya* in the differentiated states of waking, dreaming and deep sleep." This sūtra explains that *turya* is already found in the states of waking, dreaming, and deep sleep. In addition, the eleventh sūtra of the First Awakening is very similar. This sūtra states, "The one who enjoys the oneness of the three states—waking, dreaming and deep sleep—in *turya* becomes the master of all organic energies." In this sūtra, it is explained that by utilizing *śāmbhavopāya* with force (*haṭhapākayuktyā*), *jāgrat, svapna,* and *suṣupti* subside and are melted in *turya*.

In the present sūtra of the Third Awakening, however, we are told that the three states—*jagrat, svapna,* and *suṣupti,* along with *turya*—are like a sword and its sheath. Here, the three states are said to be found in the sheath of *turya*. And although the three states are separated from *turya,* as a sword is separated from its sheath, they are united with each other. In the same manner, the yogī must be aware that *jagrat, svapna* and *suṣupti* are found as one with *turya*. This is the difference between these three sūtras. So these sūtras are not a repetition.

Now he indicates the means for attaining this end:

21. magnaḥ svacittena praviśet //

The yogī who is merged in his self must enter completely with his mind filled with great awareness.

> When he establishes and resides in the awareness of his God consciousness in the waking state (*jāgrat*), the dreaming state (*svapna*), and in the state of deep sleep (*suṣupti*), then the gross movement of his breath enters into the subtle movement of breath and the subtle movement of breath enters into that which is supreme, where he experiences the supreme motion *(spanda)* in his own nature. *(Netra Tantra* 8.12)

Here, the author Kṣemarāja begins his commentary by saying:

> . . . then you should enter with your mind fully aware of your God consciousness.

In the *Mṛityujit Bhaṭṭāraka Śāstra*, which is part of the *Netra Tantra*, this is explained by Lord Śiva to Pārvatī in this way.

> Set aside the gross means such as the holding of breath, concentration and contemplation, and by means of the thoughtless process, maintain one-pointed thought merged in the self *(svacitta).* And when his mind is merged in his own nature, then one must gain entry by that introverted knowledge *(antarmukha saṁvedanena)* where he finds the ecstasy *(camatkāra)* of internal awareness *(vimarśa).* This means one must be absorbed in and become one with that.

But how is this achieved? . . . by becoming merged in his being. What is the meaning of "being merged"? When you have developed I-ness on the body of wakefulness, on the body of dreaming and on the body of deep sleep, which means you have developed I-ness on the gross body, I-ness on *prāṇa,* and I-ness on *puryaṣṭaka,* then that I-ness is to be merged in the nectar of the ecstasy of consciousness *(citta camatkāra).* This is the meaning of "becoming merged in that."

This was said earlier in the *Svacchanda Tantra*:

> Keeping the activity of the mind apart, one must unite that activity in God consciousness. Then this bound limited being *(paśu)* will realize the state of Śiva and be liberated *(muktaḥ).* Thereupon, he is beyond the ocean of repeated births and deaths. (*Svacchanda Tantra* 4.437)

This is also said in the *Vijñānabhairava*:

> When mind (*mānasaṁ*), individual consciousness (*cetanā*), the energy of breathing (*śaktiḥ*), and ego (*ātmā*), disappear, then that formation of Bhairava is found existing there. (*Vijñānabhairava* 138)

This very point is explained in the *Jñānagarbha Stotra*:

> O Mother, "when, in ordinary daily life one repels the actions of the mind and shatters dependence on the senses, by which one is enslaved, causing one to follow them according to their every wish, and instead diverts his senses towards God consciousness, then by your grace he instantly achieves that supreme state of God consciousness, which floods him with the unparalleled nectar of bliss *(ānanda).*"

This is what is said by our great masters.

Now, for the one who is established in that supreme state of God consciousness, there is no mind, no breath, no thoughts, no senses. For him, nothing else exists, only God consciousness pervades everywhere. After a period of time, this yogī automatically comes out from the state of *samādhi*. So what happens to him when he comes out? This is explained in this next sūtra.

22. prāṇasamācāre samadarśanam //

When his breath begins to slowly move out toward the external state, then he also experiences the pervasion of God consciousness there.

When his breath slowly begins to move out to external *samādhi,* then he experiences that God Consciousness is also existing there, in the external world. He does not experience any difference between the waking state and *turya* or the dreaming state and *turya* or between the state of deep sleep and *turya*. For him, these three states are filled with the state of *turya*.

Filled with the fragrance of the supreme glittering (*sphuraṇa*) of God consciousness, that yogī, slowly coming out from *samādhi*, feels his breath is filled with a supreme fragrance. And although his breath is moving out, he feels his breath is not moving out. He feels his breath is established in his Supreme Being. Then after exhaling very slowly, he experiences that the three states of waking, dreaming and deep sleep are filled with the dense nectar of God consciousness and he comes out in the waking state with this fragrance. He is a king of yogīs. He never loses the fragrance of God consciousness. This means that his God consciousness endures in each and every state of his life, whether it be waking, dreaming, or deep sleep.

This has already been explained in *Ānanda Bhairava Śāstra*:

> When he has brought the daily active routine of his life to an end and holds the monistic state which bestows final liberation, then he is one with each and every deity. All castes *(varṇa)* and positions in life *(āśrama)*, whether it be *brāhmaṇa*, *kṣatriya*, *vaiśya* or *śūdra*, are equal to him. He does not discern any difference between what is to be eaten and what is not to be eaten, or what is forbidden and what is accepted. He is liberated *(muktaḥ)*, totally freed from all the various kinds of bondage of daily life.

In *Pratyabhijñā*, Utpaladeva has also explained:

> Although these great yogīs come out in the waking, dreaming, and deep sleep states, working and performing all actions, they do not have any limitation of owning and disowning, pure and impure, good and bad. These limitations have ended for them. These yogīs attain that supreme universal God consciousness.

But on the contrary, the yogī who cannot hold the nectar of *turya* in the waking, dreaming, and deep sleep states, as explained in the previous sūtra, remains and becomes satisfied in that nectar of *turya (turyarasa)*, which he experiences only during entry and exit of any of the three states. And even though he experiences this nectar while entering and exiting these three states, he does not experience it in the midst of wakefulness, dreaming, or dreamless deep sleep. For the one who is like that,

23. madhye 'varaprasavaḥ //

He does not experience the state of God consciousness in the center of these three states.

He only experiences the state of God consciousness in the beginning and in the end of these three states of waking, dreaming, and deep sleep.

Though he experiences and enjoys the nectar of supreme God consciousness in the beginning and the end of these three states, what happens to him in the center, when he is in the midst of any of these states? In the center, he flows out but not in the supreme way. That is, he experiences in wakefulness, in dreaming and in deep sleep just as we do. It is only in the beginning and in the end of these states that he is filled with God consciousness. In the center he is just like us.

But you must not conclude that *"although he is established in God consciousness in* samādhi, *not being able to maintain awareness, after a few minutes he enters into the dreaming state,"*[25] he is away from God consciousness.

25. Sūtra 2.10

He holds God consciousness in the beginning and in the end, but he is incapable of holding God consciousness in the center of these three states. So, he is not always covered with illusion. He is only covered with illusion in the middle of these three states.

About this, the *Mālinīvijaya Tantra* says:

> Due to the impressions he has of what others think of him or expect from him and of his wanting to help others, to satisfy them with boons, he may lose his temper and become careless and uneven-minded, blocking his flow of God consciousness from the center of the three states of waking, dreaming and deep sleep. So, although he is aware of God consciousness in the beginning and in the end, he is played by this universe in the center, played by hunger, played by thirst, played by every aspect of daily life. Therefore, the one who desires to achieve the highest being should not be attached to these outer impressions. (*Mālinīvijaya Tantra)*

These impressions are keeping him from the center. If he does not have these thoughts, then his God consciousness will flow throughout, in the beginning, in the end and in the center. This has already been explained in previous sūtras.

Previously, it was explained that some yogīs experience this inferior generation of the self where they experience the nature of the self only in *turya* and not in the other three states. Now the next sūtra explains what happens to that yogī when, even though the inferior generation (*avaraḥ prasavaḥ*) of his self has taken place, he again sprinkles the blissful nectar of *turya* in the other three states.

24. mātrāsvapratyayasaṁdhāne
naṣṭasya punarūtthānam //

When a yogī, in coming out from samādhi, also attempts
to maintain awareness of God consciousness
in the objective world, then,
even though his real nature of self is destroyed by the
inferior generation of self-consciousness,
he again rises in that supreme nature of the self.

The expression from the sūtra, "When a yogī also attempts to maintain awareness of God consciousness in the objective world . . . " is explained in the following two references:

> Supreme God consciousness should be sought with great effort in whatever is seen by the eyes, whatever is felt by speech, whatever is thought by the mind, whatever is perceived by the intellect, whatever is owned by limited ego, whatever is existing in the objective world, and whatever is not existing in the objective world. (*Svacchanda Tantra* 12.163–64)

It is explained in the *Svacchanda Tantra* that when a yogī, whose God consciousness was totally destroyed by the inferior means used to generate that God consciousness, which means that his nature was snatched away by an inferior type of trance, meditates thinking, "This whole universe is one with myself," and perceives the fullness of God consciousness in each and every object, then again he rises in his own nature. In other words, in this way, this yogī, whose nature was removed, again becomes one with the glory of God consciousness.

Again, in the *Svacchanda Tantra,* it is said:

> Due to God's energy of *māyā,* the minds of yogīs are diverted by force towards worldly pleasures and away from God consciousness. But, in those masses of yogīs, there exists some great yogī who is fully aware of his self. His state of God consciousness is fully established and totally complete and his mind is never diverted toward worldly pleasures. (*Svacchanda Tantra* 4.311–12)

Another thing that happens to this yogī:

> Whenever the mind flows out, he centers his consciousness on that one God consciousness. Because he feels the oneness of Śiva existing everywhere, if his mind moves here and there, even then it does not move at all because it moves in his own nature. Wherever he feels and experiences the existence of the objective world, he feels and experiences that the objective world is actually nothing but Śiva. (*Svacchanda Tantra* 4.313–14)

Therefore, when a yogī has attained the supreme intensity of God consciousness:

25. śivatulyo jāyate //

He becomes just like Śiva.

This yogī does not becomes one with Śiva, he becomes just like Śiva. Through the intensity of meditating on *turya,* this yogī has realized and achieved the state of *turyātīta.* He becomes like Lord Śiva who is completely filled with pure independent consciousness and independent bliss.

He becomes like Lord Śiva. Why is it said that he becomes like Lord Śiva? Why not say that he becomes one with Śiva? It cannot be said he becomes one with Śiva because he has a body, a physical frame. As long as his physical frame is existing, he is *just like Śiva,* he is not *one with Śiva.* His having a physical frame will divert him toward inferior states. For instance, he may cough, have headaches, experience muscle pain, stomach aches, ulcers, or fever. Śiva does not have these ailments or suffer these physical discomforts. So, as long as the yogī possesses a body, he can only be like Śiva, not one with Śiva. When he casts off this physical frame composed of the five elements, then he becomes one with Śiva.

In *Śrī Kalikākrama Śāstra,* it is said:

> So, without harboring the slightest doubt, you should learn from the mouth of your master this practical yoga for entering into God consciousness everywhere. You must consider his every word to be doubtless and true. Also, you should try to experience that state of God consciousness until you become one with that state. Lord Śiva himself has said this, so it is absolutely true. (*Śrī Kalikākrame Śāstra)*

Because his physical body is existing, even when he becomes like Śiva, that action (*karma*) that has brought his body into existence is ended by enjoying that action, not by casting it aside. *Prārabdha karma*[26] cannot be overcome unless it is enjoyed. For an embodied being, *prārabdha karma* is unavoidable. He may be just like Śiva or he may be an ordinary person; *prarabdha karma* must be overcome by being enjoyed. It cannot be cast aside or abandoned.

So, for the remainder of his life, he must continue to exist with this physical frame. He must welcome whatever comes to him, whether it be good or bad. Whatever he gets to eat, he must eat. It is not worthwhile to cast his body aside. For such a yogī, this body is to be maintained until the time of death.

This he explains in the next verse.

26. śarīravṛittirvratam //

His virtuous behavior is the maintenance of his body.

What is virtuous behavior? For ordinary beings, virtuous behavior may involve special ways of acting and being. For example, there is the special behavior that some people observe during the eclipse of the moon. These people fast and perform special ceremonies during the eclipse and continue these special actions until the eclipse has ended. For these people acting in this way during an eclipse is a virtuous act.

But for such a yogī, behaving virtuously is just to remain in his body as it is. For him, virtuous behavior involves getting up from bed at four o'clock in the morning, going to the bathroom, taking bed tea, going for a walk, having lunch, gardening, taking a nap, cleaning up his living quarters and so on. Other than these ordinary daily actions, there is no need for him to adopt any other virtuous behavior. So routine talk, taking tea, going for a walk, going to the cinema; these assorted actions comprise the virtuous behavior he adopts for the remaining period of his life.

This is what this sūtra says. For such a yogī, who is just like Śiva, which means whose I-consciousness is just like Śiva consciousness, existing in his physical frame is his virtuous behavior. Therefore, just to exist in his body is a virtuous act. This is because while he remains in his body, he is intent only on performing the supreme worship of Lord Śiva in each and every action of his life—while eating, while drinking, while talking, while taking tea, while eating lunch, and so forth. Although everyone around him experiences that he is acting just like an ordinary human being, he is not, he is somewhere else.

About this, the *Svacchandra Tantra* says:

> Whenever a fire is kindled on the ground, where are the flames seen? The flames are seen in the sky. In the same way, although this yogī's body is existing in the inferior field of individuality, this yogī is actually established in God consciousness. (*Svacchandra Tantra* 4.389)

The yogī is established in that God consciousness, just like a flame in the fire. Although he is residing in the inferior states of waking, dreaming, and deep sleep, he has already attained entry into Śiva. And yet because his actions are just like ours, you must not think he is not fully aware of his God consciousness and therefore he is just like us. Even if he does all the same things we do, he is somewhere else; he is above. There are no other virtuous actions for him to adopt except to remain in this physical frame and perform actions.

---

26. *Prārabdha karma* is *karma* that has brought your body into being and is based on the actions of your past lives.

It is said in the *Trika Śāstra*:

> The one who is always stamped by the various poses associated with the body, such as taking tea, going to bed, resting, talking, joking, having lunch, walking and resting, is the real holder of all the postures *(mudras)* of yoga. All other yogīs, who are not like him, only hold a bundle of bones.

The yogī's body has no flesh, no bones. You must not think that he is in a body with flesh and bones. Being one with God consciousness, he is supreme.

The energies of Lord Śiva are classified in three ways: the supreme class of energies, the medium class of energies, and the inferior class of energies. The inferior class of energies, known as *ghoratarī* energies, are determined to cause an individual to enter into the depths of the darkness of ignorance. The medium class of energies, known as *ghorā* energies, cause one to stand still. These energies will not allow the individual to enter into the state of God consciousness. The supreme class of energies are known as *aghora* energies. In the next verse from the *Kulapañcāśikā Śāstra,* the *aghora* class of energies are clarified and explained.

> The supreme *aghorā* energies of God consciousness always embrace that yogī who lives in such a way that he remains absolutely unknown as a yogī. They carry him to God consciousness, where he is forever established. This is the secret of rising because this state of God consciousness has come forth from a secret point and he is residing in a secret way of life. That yogī, on the other hand, who is known to everyone as an elevated yogī, is not embraced by these *aghora* energies. They shun him and consequently, he is carried away from God consciousness.

In talking about the yogī who is hidden and embraced by the supreme energies of Lord Śiva, everyone says that because he walks and talks just as they do and seems to be an enjoyer of sensual pleasures, he is an ordinary person. It is worthwhile, therefore, for a yogī to behave in such a way that he is not known as a yogī by the outside world. He must keep it a secret and not publicize it. He must be known to the world as an ordinary person. As long as he does not publicize his spiritual state, he is there. Otherwise, he is carried away from God consciousness. This is the secret of rising.

Even the disciple must not know the depth of his master's realization. The master must also hide his power of spirituality from the disciple. He must absolutely conceal his spirituality within his nature and not expose it to anyone. The disciple must possess and maintain blind faith. This is the manner of the *Śiva Sūtras*.

For this kind of yogī,

27. kathā japaḥ ///

Ordinary talk of life is the recitation of mantra.

He recites mantra when he laughs with you, when he embraces you and talks to you, when he goes with you to the theater. All of this is, for him, the real recitation *(japaḥ)* of mantra. So, for him, the ordinary talk of daily life is recitation of mantra because,

> In talking, he experiences and is aware of his fullness of I-consciousness of God.[27] (*Svacchanda Tantra*)

This is explained in *Svacchanda Tantra* in this way:

> He is always merged in that supreme I-consciousness of God.

It is also said in the *Kālikākrama Śāstra:*

> For him, who is one with that supreme cognitive state of the Lord, that supreme energy is awareness *(vimarśaḥ)* and it is filled and shining with all knowledge.

It is explained in the *Śri Kālikākrama* that the daily conversations of the yogī, who is established in that unartificial awareness *(vimarśaḥ)*, which is self-generated and spontaneous, become the recitation *(japaḥ)* of the real mantra of the self.

It is also said in the *Vijñānabhairava Tantra*:

> Establishing the state of awareness in the state of God consciousness repeatedly without break or pause is real recitation of man-

tra. From this recitation which is full of universal "I", real "I" consciousness automatically flows forth. (*Vijñānabhairava Tantra* 145)

Again, it is said,

By going out he utters "*sa*," by coming in he utters "*ha*," in this way he recites the mantra *haṁsa,* repeating *so'haṁ, so'haṁ, so'haṁ* day and night. This sacred recitation is always existing for him. (*Vijñānabhairava Tantra* 155)

And again, it is said in the *Vijñānabhairava Tantra*:

He recites this mantra with breath twenty-one thousand six hundred times in a day and a night. This recitation, which is of that supreme energy of God consciousness, is very easy for those who are aware and very difficult for those who are not. (*Vijñānabhairava Tantra* 156)

---

27. In this verse from the *Svacchanda Tantra,* it is the "I-consciousness of God," not individual "I-consciousness," that is referred to. Therefore, we cannot call it "I-consciousness" because "I-consciousness" can also be individual consciousness. It is not individual "I-consciousness"; it is "I God consciousness."

The daily routine of the yogī who is immersed in this kind of automatic recitation *(ajāpa gāyatrī)* is as follows:

28. dānamātmajñānam //

His only purpose for remaining in his body is to impart his knowledge to others.

During the remainder of his life, his reason for living is giving his real knowledge of God consciousness to others. This is the meaning of this sūtra.

The Sanskrit word *dāna* found in the sūtra has many meanings. Whatever this yogī, who has become one with God consciousness, experiences, which means whatever he sees in his own self, that is *dāna* for him. The word *dāna* can also mean that which gives him fullness of consciousness. Moreover, *dāna* can mean that which destroys the differentiated perception of the universe. *Dāna* can also be referring to that which remains when illusion ends. And, it is that state where the nature of his God consciousness is completely protected. This is how he acts during the remainder of his life.

The definitions of *dāna* given above are in reference to his own person. There is another meaning of *dāna.* In this case, *dāna* is explained in reference to another and it means "whatever is given to another." So, those who are his devoted disciples get the knowledge of the self from him. This same thing is said in some tantras.

> Those yogic heroes who are established in the *Kula* system reveal the reality of God consciousness to others by merely looking *(darśana)* or touching. By this revelation, all of their disciples cross over to the other side of the bondage *(saṁsāra)* of repeated births and deaths and are liberated.

In fact, only that person who has become just like Śiva,[28] being always busy in his daily routine with internal recitation *(ajapa)* and ruling his own wheel of energies, can be helpful in illuminating others. He explains this in the next sūtra:

29. yo'vipastho jñāhetuśca //

The one who rules the wheel of energies becomes the cause of inserting knowledge in others.

The master who has established sovereignty over the wheel of energies *(śakticakra)* is not played by these energies but is instead the player. The wheel of energies is classified in two segments: the energies pertaining to cognition *(jñānendriyas)*, and the energies pertaining to action *(karmendriyas)*. This master is the player of both these kind of energies. They do not play with him as they do with us. Whatever our sensual energies ask for or demand, we are bound to obey them. But he is not like that. He maintains dominion over these energies and so he becomes the cause of inserting real knowledge into others. This is the meaning of this sūtra.

Those who are ignorant are protected in their own way by this wheel of energies. These *śakti cakras* protect these ignorant souls by providing them with taste, with form, with touch, with smell, and with whatever else they need. This so-called protection is not really protection because it provides them with these sensual pleasures.

28. As we've seen above in sūtra 25, this yogī is not one with Śiva; he is "just like Śiva." He will become one with Śiva immediately upon leaving his physical body.

In sūtra 19 of this Third Awakening of the *Śiva Sūtras,* these energies are said to be the mothers of these ignorant people. In that sūtra, these energies are called *māheśvaryādi śakticakraṁ,* which means those energies, *māheśvarī, khecarī, gocarī, dikcarī, bhūcarī,* etc., concerned with the organic field.

To say that a master has sovereignty over these energies is to say he is not played by them. On the contrary, he is the player and he becomes the cause of inserting knowledge into others.

In the present sūtra, the Sanskrit word *jñā* means the energy of knowledge *(jñānaśakti).* For those who are his disciples, this master becomes the source of knowledge and by the energy of that knowledge, he becomes successful in inserting knowledge into his disciples.

The person who is influenced by the wheel of energies, which means who is dependent on his senses, is not able to protect himself, so how could he possibly protect others? He is constrained to follow the demand of his senses, so how could he possibly elevate others? He could not. It is impossible.

In this sūtra, you will also find the Sanskrit word *yo* which is derived from the Sanskrit pronoun *yat* (who). In Sanskrit, whenever *yat* is found, then the pronoun *tat* must also be added to complete the sentence. Therefore, *Yo'yam avipasthaḥ,* "the one who governs this wheel of energies" . . . *sa,* "that master" . . *jñānaprabodhanahetu,* "becomes the cause of inserting knowledge into others." So it is well said in sūtra 28 of this Third Awakening, *dānamātmajñānam,* "he gives knowledge of the self to others."

Some commentators explain this sūtra in another way. They say this sūtra must be explained according to the words and letters as follows. Take the first word *yo'vipastho.* Because of the *yo* sound in *yogīndra, yo* indicates *yogīndra,* the foremost yogī. *Vi* indicates *vijñānam* "knowledge," *pa* indicates "state," *stha* refers to "the one who is established in that state." Now the last word *jñāhetuśca. Jña* means "who knows that." *He* indicates *heyaḥ,* "what is to be abandoned." *Tu* indicates *tucchatā,* "that which is abandoned is differentiated perception." And the *visargaḥ* (*ḥ*) refers to *visargaśaktiḥ,* creative energy. The word *ca* does not mean "and" here but rather indicates "one who does this."

So with this in mind, this meaning now emerges from this sūtra:

> That *yogīndra* who *(vimarśaśaktyā)*, by the energy of his awareness *(svarūpātmavijñānapadasthaḥ)* is established in his own nature of God consciousness becomes the knower and the doer. He can perceive and differentiate what is to be achieved and what is to be discarded and he does not own that which is to be discarded.

We, however, do not accept this explanation. So, if we do not accept this explanation then why include it? From my point of view, *Kṣemarāja* should not have included it. After all, if one begins including incorrect explanations then they could be introduced for every sūtra. I am only including it because it is part of *Kṣemarāja's* commentary.

30. śvaśaktipracayo'sya viśvam //

For him, this universe is the embodiment of his collective energies

For such a master, this universe is the collection of his own energies. He perceives that this universe is the embodiment of, and not separate from, his innumerable collective energies. So just as that master is said to be just like Śiva, this whole universe is his own collective energy. And by saying this whole universe is nothing but Śiva's energy, so then, in the same way, this universe is not only the collection of Śiva's energies but also for the yogī, because he is one with that God consciousness, this universe is the collection and expansion of his energies. It is said in *Mṛityujitabhaṭṭāraka*:

> This Lord Śiva is filled with knowledge and that knowledge is the innumerable[29] knowledge found in the universe. Real knowledge is universal knowledge. The knowledge that frees you from the limited knowledge of the universe is called *netra*. By holding and possessing only one class of this limitless universe of knowledge, and by not possessing universal knowledge, you are bound with limitation. When your master reveals the universal truth to you, then you emerge from limitation and the whole universe becomes your possession. To possess the whole universe as your own self is real knowledge and that is *netra* and that is liberation. (*Netra Tantra* 9.12)

If you pick only one class of knowledge out of this universe and

29. This knowledge is said to be innumerable because it is the endlessly divisible knowledge of the particular. It is knowledge of a tree, a rock, a person, a second person, a third person, etc.

hold and possess only that one class, that is ignorance. But if you possess this whole universe as your own self, then you are liberated. This is what is meant by this verse of the *Netra Tantra.*

It is also said in the *Kālikākrama:*

> This knowledge is found everywhere, inside and outside, because without knowledge, an object cannot exist. This entire universe is, therefore, filled with that knowledge. And that knowledge, which may be objective knowledge, is, in fact, knowledge of God consciousness.
>
> No one has ever perceived an object without that knowledge. That knowledge, which is the real knowledge of God consciousness, has taken the form of the object. Objective knowledge is not separate from that knowledge of God consciousness. It is by that knowledge of God consciousness that this knowledge of objects takes place.
>
> If you think that in practicing yoga, God consciousness is to be possessed and that which is other than God consciousness is to be discarded, that is not the proper understanding. The correct understanding is that you must unite these two together. God consciousness must be united with objective consciousness and objective consciousness must be united with God consciousness. This reality of knowledge, this reality of God consciousness, is established in the objective world because through meditation all these objects are found as one with God consciousness. As long as you meditate upon and are aware that this objective world is not separate from God consciousness, it will be just like God consciousness. And so, you will not find any difference between God consciousness and objective consciousness.
>
> When you simultaneously possess this kind of knowledge, then knowledge and the known will be not separated. Known will become knowledge and knowledge will become known. (*Krama Strotra)*

Not only is this universe the expansion of his energies in the created sphere of the world, but it is also the expansion of his energies in impressions and in the void state (*laya*).

31. sthitilayau //

This universe is the expansion of his energy in objective impressions and in the dissolution of those impressions.

Not only is this universe the expansion of his energy in its creation, it is also the expansion of his energy in the impressions of the objective world left in your mind *(sthiti)* and in the void state where these impressions are absorbed *(laya).*

When this objective world is shining vividly in your sphere of organs, that is the state of creation *(sṛiṣṭi daśā).* But it is not only in the state of creation that this universe is one with his real energies of God consciousness. This universe is also one with his energies when only impressions of this objective world remain *(sthitidaśā)* or when these impressions melt in voidness *(layadaśā)* at the time of death or deep sleep, or when one is rendered unconscious. When only impressions remain, in those impressions you will find God consciousness prevailing. And in the state of dissolution when there is no impression, when the impression is dissolved in voidness, pure God consciousness prevails. God consciousness is never in any way absent from being.

Initially, this universe is revealed to you by the energy of action. And after this universe shines before you, the knowledge of the universe remains for some time as an impression in your objective consciousness. That is what is meant by the word *sthiti.*

Then the impression of this universe in your objective consciousness also melts away and all that is left is the void state where there is nothing. That is what is meant by the word *layaḥ*. And this state where there is nothing is also held in consciousness.

For such an elevated soul, these two states are only the expansion of His energies and nothing else. For him, this objective world may be created in his sensual world, or it may be stored in his impressions, or it may be taken away from his impressions; but this threefold world is nothing more than the expansion of his God consciousness everywhere. Otherwise, if this threefold world was not existing in his God consciousness, then the impressions would not arise from that nothingness and from those impressions, this objective world would not arise. For example, when you go to sleep and enter the dreaming state and after dreaming, you enter the dreamless state and after some time, you wake up, throughout all of these states God consciousness is existing. If God consciousness were not existing throughout, then how would you be able to travel from one state to the next, from the dreaming state to the state of deep sleep, and from the state of deep sleep to the waking state? Between each of these states, there is a gap, a point where one state has ceased to exist and the next state has yet to begin. When you direct your consciousness from waking state to the dreaming state and from the dreaming state to the dreamless state, there is a point, a gap, when your consciousness, having left one world, has not yet entered the next world. How could you travel through that gap if God consciousness did not exist in that gap? So God consciousness must exist throughout. It is why the commentator Kṣemarāja says "there would be disconnection of your consciousness."

As an example, consider that I am staying with you and before going to bed, I give you some money to keep for me. I then go to bed and enter the dreaming state and after that, I enter the state of dreamless sleep and after that, I wake up and again enter the waking state. And after waking, I ask you for the money I gave you to keep for me. If God consciousness did not persist in every moment, did not travel throughout all three states, then the continuity of memory would not be possible and I would not remember to ask you for the money or even that I had given you this money to hold for me. It is God consciousness existing in all states that maintains the continuity of awareness and memory.

It is said in the *Śri Kālikākrama*:

> That which exists, that which does not exist; this differentiation of existence and nonexistence and their connection [is only maintained by God consciousness].
>
> This whole universe is absolutely pure, without any support, and one with the knowledge of the consciousness of self. If that consciousness of self is revealed and perceived, then at that very moment, he is without a doubt liberated in this very life. (*Kālikākrama Śāstra)*

The previous sūtras state that this whole universe is the expansion of his own glory, not only in creation (*sṛiṣṭi*), but also in protection (*sthiti*) and destruction (*saṁhāra*). But now the question can be asked, "If this yogī feels that the universe, in creation, in protection, and in destruction, is the expansion of his own nature, then would not his nature be changeable? It would definitely change. In creation it would be one way, in protection another way, and in destruction another way. Therefore, as his original state of being would occasionally change, the essential nature of the self would not remain unchangeable. The next sūtra answers this question.

32. tatpravṛitāvapyanirāsaḥ saṁvettṛibhāvāt //

Although he is determined in creating, protecting, and destroying the universe, even then he is not separated from the real state of his subjectivity.

Although he creates, protects and destroys this universe, for him the reality of the self remains the same in creation, protection and destruction. This yogī is never separated from the state of the knower, which is that state where he holds the bliss of *turya* (*camatkāra*). This subjectivity is the real state of being of the knower. In these threefold actions of creation, protection, and destruction, he is always one with that state.

If in these actions, he was separated from the reality of the self, then the state of creation, the state of protection and the state of destruction would not exist. The existence of these three states comes from the power of the reality of the knower.

It is said in the *Kālikākrama Śāstra*:

Although the expansion of ignorance is destroyed, the being of the self is never destroyed because that self is beyond creation

> and destruction. There is no creation and there is no destruction of that self. Therefore, if that being is one with this universe, then in reality, nothing is destroyed.
>
> It is imagined that ignorance is created and ignorance is destroyed but ignorance itself cannot exist without the knowledge of truth. So ignorance cannot be created or destroyed because it is one with the real nature of the self. When it is the nature of the self that it is never destroyed, then how can it be destroyed in creation, protection and destruction? (*Kālikākrama Śāstra*)

This is written in *Spanda*:

> In the two states which are termed "doer" and "done," the aspect known as done is destroyed while the aspect known as doer always remains and can never be destroyed.
>
> Only that force, which is the effort to create that which is to be done, is destroyed. But when that force is destroyed, ignorant people cry, saying, "we too are also destroyed." (*Spanda Kārikā* 1.14–15)

For example, a young woman gives birth. That baby is the outcome of your effort towards objectivity. If that baby is destroyed, why should that woman say that she is destroyed? She is never destroyed. But at that time, ignorant people think that they are also destroyed.

> In the absence of the other agency, you can't say the introverted state is destroyed. If in the state of ignorance you are not aware of your reality of self, you cannot say that the self is destroyed. It is not destroyed but, because you are not aware of it, you remain away from it. (*Spanda Kārikā* 1.16)

For such a yogī:

33. sukhaduḥkhayorbahirmananam //

He experiences his joy and his sadness just like an object, with "this-consciousness" separate from his being.

Such a yogī experiences the state of pleasure *(sukha)* and pain *(duḥkha)* with "this-consciousness," not "I-consciousness." For example, he does not experience joy thinking "I am joyous" and sadness thinking "I am sad." Rather, he experiences "this is sadness" and "this is joy," just as an ordinary person experiences external objects in his daily life. He experiences "this-consciousness" not "I-consciousness," thinking "this is a pot" or "this is a bottle." So, this yogī experiences his joy and sadness just like an object, separate from his being.

For this yogī, these two states of pleasure and pain, though touched by the known, are without the touch of the knower. He experiences his pleasure and pain just like other objects such as stoves or pots. He experiences pleasure and pain with "this-consciousness." He does not experience pleasure and pain like ignorant people do, by putting their I-consciousness in that experience, saying, "I am happy," "I am sad," or "I am never happy," "I am never sad." On the contrary, this yogī experiences, "I am always in myself, the same in happiness and sadness."

As explained in sūtra 30 of this Third Awakening, "For him, this universe is the embodiment of his collective energies," so for such a yogī, this universe is the expansion of his own energy. This explanation reveals to us that he experiences this whole universe with I-consciousness and he experiences his individuality with this-consciousness. Because he is never individual being, he is always universal being, he experiences his nature as universal being and not as individual being. If he were to experience his nature as individual being, then he would become sad and happy.

The present sūtra is not concerned only with pleasure and pain. Here, "pleasure and pain" is a metaphor for everything that exists in this world. This yogī experiences whatever exists in this world in the individual mode as this-consciousness and when he remains in the universal mode he experiences everything with I-consciousness. "I am everything." Because this yogī has destroyed the attachment of his state of I-ness with *puryaṣṭaka,*[30] found in the waking state, dreaming state, and the state of deep sleep, how can he be touched by the two states of pleasure and pain?

In the commentary of *Śrī Pratyabhijñā,* it is also said,

> Those yogis who have crossed the boundary of individuality, who have achieved the real state of universal being and are established in the state of universality, although in their daily lives they experience pleasure and pain, these experiences do not affect them at all. There is no apprehension that pain and pleasure will rise in them because the cause of the rise of pain and pleasure is individuality and they have destroyed individuality. They are apart from that and so, in the experience of pleasure and pain, they experience the real state of supreme beatitude, supreme bliss *(ānanda),* which is actually more than bliss. *(Pratyabhijñā)*

This is explained in *Spanda* in this verse:

> Reality exists in that universal state where there is no pain, no pleasure, no object, no subject and not even the negation of these. (*Spanda Kārikā* 1.5)

---

30. Here, the word *puryaṣṭaka* does not only refer to the eightfold subtle body, consisting of mind, intellect, ego, and the five *tanmātras* (subtle elements) which exists in the dreaming state *(svapna).* Here, the word *puryaṣṭaka* is meant to include the body *(deha)* existing in the state of wakefulness *(jagrat)* and the void state *(śūnya)* existing in the state of deep sleep *(suṣupti).*

The yogī who has crossed the individual state of I-consciousness is never touched by pleasure and pain. So,

34. tadvimuktastu kevalī //

Separated from pleasure and pain, he is established in real seclusion.

What is real seclusion? Real seclusion is actually the state of I-consciousness where this-consciousness (as the opposite of I-consciousness) does not arise. When you are established in I-consciousness, this-consciousness is absent. As long as I-consciousness prevails, this-consciousness is excluded. Where this-consciousness is not excluded, then this-consciousness is also absorbed in I-consciousness. That is the state of seclusion (*kevalī bhāva*) where there is nothing.

It is rightly said in *Upaniṣads*:

> In the beginning, there was only one Lord, and because he was only one, there being no other, he became afraid.

The *Upaniṣads* is telling us that this is the reason why those who are alone become afraid. They become frightened because in that state of being alone, this-ness is excluded. This is the state of *divtīya brahma*. When this-ness is not excluded, then you are only one and there is nothing to fear. That is what is delineated by the word "seclusion" (*kevalī*). This is the state of seclusion (*kevalī bhāva*).

The one who is absolutely freed from pleasure and pain is solely established (*kevalī*) in the formation of God consciousness. In *Kālikākrama,* it is said:

> All those states, like the perception of pleasure and pain and the thoughts associated with them, have arisen by imagination. That differentiation is actually the great illusion of duality. Herein one distinguishes between two opposites, such as the differentiation between pleasure and pain, thinking pleasure is welcome and pain is to be avoided. The yogī who has destroyed this kind of illusion actually attains the real fruit of yoga. *(Kālikākrama Stotra)*

In the present sūtra the word *tu* is not meant to indicate separation, but to indicate supremacy, to indicate that he is above the state of individuality.

And now, contrarily, the author will, in the next sūtra, explain the state of individuality that is absolutely the opposite of this state.

35. mohapratisaṁhatastu karmātmā //

The yogī whose God consciousness is destroyed by this state of illusion is dependent on his action.

On the contrary, the yogī whose God consciousness is destroyed by this state of illusion is dependent on his action. The past, present and future actions *(karmas)* of this yogī, whose God consciousness has been destroyed by the illusion of duality, will control him and make him their plaything. He is just an ordinary human being. He is not capable as a yogī. Having his state of being destroyed by this illusion of duality, he thinks, "This is pain and it is not good. This is pleasure and it is better than pain. I have a good job which is very nice. I have been fired and I am very sad!" This is the state of individual being.

The Sanskrit word *moha* means ignorance *(ajñāna)*. The words *prati saṁhataḥ* mean "who is constricted by this ignorance, this illusion" *(moha)*. He is not the player of pain and pleasure as a yogī is. Being shrunk by illusion, he is pain and pleasure's plaything. He is said to be the embodiment of action *(karmātmā)* and as such, he is dependent upon action. Actions will control him. He is always stained *(kalaṅkita)* by good and bad actions.

This is well said in the *Kālikākrama Śāstra*:

> When this yogī does not maintain the awareness of God consciousness, having his God consciousness covered by ignorance, then because of his differentiated perception of the world, he does not experience the thirty-six elementary states of the universe, beginning with the element Śiva and ending with the ele-

ment earth, in a supreme or universal manner. Only the states of good and bad appear to him, which are unfortunate and which, when experienced, cause supreme pain to shine within him. Because of this, he has become an absolutely unfortunate being. (*Kālikākrama Śāstra*)

So, although such a yogī has become dependent on his past actions, as ignorant persons are, when, by the means of the absolutely independent grace of Lord Śiva, his state of perfect independence again shines, then,

36. bhedatiraskāre sargāntarakarmatvaṁ //

He drives away the field of differentiated perceptions and enters into a new world of God consciousness.

In this verse we are told, "He drives away the field of differentiated perception." This means the differentiated perceptions of that subjective being are kept apart from his self. This subjective being is that individual who is residing in the *sakala* and *pralayākala* states because he has defined his ego in relation to the body *(śarīra),* the vital breath *(prāṇa),* the self of the dreaming state *(puryaṣṭaka),* and the self of deep sleep *(śūnya),* and not in relation to his own real nature of God consciousness.

The Sanskrit word *tiraskāre,* which I am rendering as "drives away," does not mean he totally ignores this differentiated perception. Here, "drives away" indicates that he ignores it through the mind. Although internally he does everything that other individuals do, he is not attached to those differentiated perceptions. So, although he lives in these differentiated perceptions, the nature of his God consciousness shines forth and these perceptions subside.

Then, successively, he enters into the world of *mantra pramātā, mantreśvara pramātā* and *mantramaheśvara pramātā,* which are, consecutively, the states of *śuddha vidyā, īśvara,* and *sadāśiva.*[31] Here he attains his own real glory of God consciousness.

31. In any experience, there is the known, the object of perception, the means of experiencing, and the experiencer. The Sanskrit word for the object

Then, ignoring the previous state of degraded individual consciousness, he *(sargāntara karmatvaṁ)* enters into a new world of God consciousness wherein whatever he thinks, whatever he desires, comes true. This is already illustrated in *Svacchanda Tantra*:

> When you fix your awareness not only in two, but in three, you are carried to God consciousness and you become one with *Svacchanda.*[32] *(Svacchanda Tantra)*

What is the meaning of "triple awareness"? The verse tells us there must be triple awareness, not just awareness of two. Awareness of two is the awareness of two actions, such as inhaling and exhaling. Triple awareness includes the junction, the gap, between any two actions, between inhaling and exhaling and between exhaling and inhaling. It is the junction between one step and another step, between one thought and another thought, between one sensation and another sensation, etc. When you are aware of the three centers, then you are carried to *Svacchanda*, to God-consciousness.

And so it is explained in this verse in the *Svacchanda Tantra*, as he becomes one with *Svacchanda* (with *Bhairavanātha*), then differentiated perceptions do not exist. In another verse in the same Tantra, we are told:

> He becomes so great he terrifies *Brahma*, *Viṣṇu*, and *Indra*, the *Siddhas*, *Daityas*, and those who rule the great deities, *garuḍa*,

---

of perception is *prameya*. The word for the means of experience is *pramāṇa*, and the word for the subject of the experience is *pramātṛi* or *pramātā*. To further clarify, the *pramātṛi* is the state of the knower where the knower is attached to the known—to the object. In *śuddhavidyā tattva*, you find the state of *mantra pramātā*, which is also called *śuddhavidyā pramātṛi*. In *īśvara tattva*, you find the state of *mantreśvara pramātā*, which is also called *īśvara pramātṛi*. And in *sadāśiva tattva*, you experience the state of *mantra maheśvara pramātā*. In the above three states, you find that both the state and the state holder—the state and the experiencer of that state—exist together simultaneously.

32. *Svacchanda* is that *Bhairava* who is absolutely filled with free will.

etc. He causes them to be fearful, or if he is satisfied with them, drives fear away from them. He is the bestower of boons and curses. Even the Lord of Death cannot stand before him. By the power of his will, he can level great mountains. (*Svacchanda Tantra* 6.54–55)

This is not difficult for him to attain, because:

37. karaṇa śaktiḥ svato'nubhavāt //

The power of creation is the experience of every individual.

It is the experience of each and every individual being that while they are in the dreaming state or using their imagination, they have the power to create and destroy as they will *(karaṇaśakti)*. When you are intoxicated with alcohol, you can think that you are the Lord and that no power can weaken you. That is your conception in that state. Or, when you enter the dreaming state, you can create a motorcar to drive, the road to drive on and the fields and vegetation to drive through. In this dream, the road is created by you, the motorcar is created by you, the trees on the sides of the road are created by you, and it is you who are seated in the car and you are you. Everything in this dream is you. If somebody comes in front of you and stops your car, that is also you. In this dream, you create the entire universe yourself because in dreams no one else is created except your own glory. So in this way, the power of creation is experienced by every individual, and in the same way, the power of creation of this yogī is universal.

It is your own experience that in the world of imagination or in the world of dreaming, you have the power of doing and undoing, enabling you to create a world by your own power of thinking, a world you are unable to create in the waking state.

In this respect, it is said in the *Pratibhijñā Kārikā*:

> So according to the thoughts he chooses, every individual being has the power of knowing and acting. (*Īśvarapratyabhijñā Kārikā* 1.6.11)

So, when it is proven that the power (*karaṇa śakti*) to create and destroy already exists, then when he desires with an intense force of awareness, that desire will come true not only in the dreaming state or world of imagination, but also in the waking state. He can also create worlds of his own in the waking state. In fact, he can create whatever he desires in the outside world and these worlds which he has created can also be perceived by others.

It is also said in *Tattvagarbha*:

> When those individuals, who are masters of the dreaming state and the world of imagination, discard the absence of the establishment of awareness and secure and strengthen the power of their awareness, then their desire becomes just like the heavenly wish-fulfilling tree *(kalpataru)*.[33]

They become just like Lord Śiva and being just like Lord Śiva, whatever they desire, whatever they think, that becomes true.

33. The *kalpataru* tree is one of the five trees of heaven, fabled to fulfill all desires.

And so, it is proved that the essence of this power of doing and undoing is *svātantrya śakti,* which is the essence of *pramātā,* the subject, and which is one with *turya.* It is only the power of absolute independence that carries you to that supreme summit. Now the author tells us what we must do to regain that power which has been diminished by the power of illusion.

38. tripadādyanuprāṇanam //

Emerging from the state of turya,
insert the absolute bliss of that state into the waking,
dreaming, and deep sleep states,
and they will become one with that state of turya.

Just as soon as you emerge from *samādhi,* coming out from the state of *turya,* insert the absolute bliss of that state into the other three states of consciousness—waking, dreaming and deep sleep—and in time, these four states will become one without distinction.

There are three states of creation; *(sṛiṣṭi),* protection *(sthiti),* and reabsorption *(layaḥ).* The state of *creation* exists when you are just about to direct your consciousness towards an object *(bhāvaunmukhya).* In the creative state, you have not yet directed your consciousness, but you are going to direct it. When your consciousness is positively directed towards that object *(bhāvābhiṣvaṅga),* that is the *protective* state. And, when your consciousness is carried away from that object and is going to be inserted into another object, that is the state of *reabsorption.* In this state of reabsorption, your consciousness is being withdrawn from the object you are presently perceiving and is about to be inserted into a new object. Being inserted into another object is the creative state for that new object you are about to perceive. But at this moment, in the state of reabsorption, your attention is not on either object. It has entered internal consciousness *(āntarmukhabhāvā)*.

Take the example of the perception of a pair of reading glasses. When you are going to perceive these glasses, that is the first state, the creative state. Next, when you are perceiving these glasses, that is the protective state. And when you have perceived these glasses, what happens next? You lose curiosity to perceive these glasses. When you lose curiosity to perceive them then you become curious to perceive another object, such as a book. In relation to your perception of the glasses, this is the third state, the state of reabsorption. But in your relation to your perception of the book, it is the first state, the creative state. In the third state, the state of reabsorption, your consciousness has entered into your God consciousness in the state of absolute voidness *(śūnya)*. This is the way of perception in this world. First, you are about to perceive an object. Then you perceive that object. Then after some time, you tire of perceiving that object and redirect your consciousness to perceive another object, and so on. In this world, perception continues in this chainlike fashion. This is why we agree with the Buddhists in this regard. They also recognize that perception is the flux of knowledge moving from one state to another state.

That which is residing in each and every point of these three states is the state of *turya*. This *turya* is filled with bliss and enjoys the ecstasy of all these three states. Although it is covered by the energy of illusion still when you are relishing these enjoyments of the senses in the beginning of enjoyment, in the center of enjoyment and in the end of enjoyment, when the curiosity has ended, that *turya* is felt for just one moment like a flash of lightning. It is revealed there for one instant. How is that point, that instantaneous flash, to be held, to be maintained? The technique of holding this point is only the trick of the master.

For example, when you take an ear of corn, which is well cooked and you taste that corn, at the time of tasting, even though this tasting is covered by the energy of illusion—just like lightning—God consciousness is found. If, by the grace of your Master, you have the power and the capacity to hold that moment, then you will gain entry into God consciousness. That God consciousness is found in the beginning of that tasting. How to hold it is just a trick. You do not have to move here and there with breath. That will not accomplish it. It is a trick to hold that awareness. You cannot hold God consciousness with prayer, weeping, or worship, or by any other means. It can only be held by the trick of awareness which can be taught to you by your master.

So, even if your sense perceptions are covered by the energy of illusion, at the time when you enjoy any sensation, God consciousness is momentarily shining like a flash of lightning. What must be done in these moments where God consciousness shines is to be absolutely aware. If you do not maintain awareness, then you are finished; you are just like an ordinary human being.

Although this God consciousness rises for only one moment, you have to give life to it and sustain it with awareness. To accomplish this, just hold it internally by keeping your consciousness introverted, not extroverted. It is with introverted consciousness that you will be successful. With introverted successive unbroken consciousness, you must give life to that God consciousness which is held only momentarily. In these moments, you must give rise to that God consciousness again and again. It is said in *Vijñānabhairava Tantra*:

> You must perceive the reality of that state which is filled with your own bliss of God consciousness, which is without differentiated thought and which is always full of the *śakti* of *Bhairava*. This state, which is absolutely pure and filled with universal consciousness, fills the whole universe with bliss. (*Vijñānabhairava Tantra* 15)

> The experience of joy which rises at the moment you are united with and are absolutely embracing your life partner is actually the joy of *brahman*. This joy can only be known by a trick. If, however, you do not know this trick, then it is just the union of two beasts. (*Vijñānabhairava Tantra* 69)

> O Devi, it is not only in the union of two partners where you will get entry in God consciousness but, if you possess the trick, then

> also at the time of remembering that sexual union you will gain entry into God consciousness. (*Vijñānabhairava Tantra* 70)

It is not only in the matter of sex. Appearance will also carry you to that God consciousness.

> By employing the trick of awareness, you will enter God consciousness at the very moment the joy, from seeing a desired thing after a long time, arises in your mind. (*Vijñānabhairava Tantra* 71)

For instance, your son, who has lived in a foreign country for twenty years, returns unexpectedly and you see him with great surprise. You didn't know he was coming. You had not received any communication from him informing you of his coming. He just arrives. So you were not prepared to see him, and then, suddenly, you see him. If you know the trick of awareness for gaining entry into God consciousness, then, at that very moment, when the joy of seeing you son arises in your mind and fills your being, you will enter God consciousness. That is meaning of this verse.

If you know the trick, you can also enter God consciousness through taste.

> If at the time you experience the joy that arises in your consciousness when you eat a nicely prepared feast or taste a delicious drink you have the trick to attain the awareness of Bhairava, then you will enter in that bliss of God consciousness while eating or drinking. (*Vijñānabhairava Tantra* 72)

> If, upon hearing a melodious song, he inserts his awareness into the sound of that song, he will, at that very moment in one flash, enter into and become one with Bhairava. (*Vijñānabhairava Tantra* 73)

This whole universe has come into existence just to carry you to God consciousness. It is not meant to push you down. This universe is meant for your upliftment.

In these verses in the *Spanda Kārikā,* it is said:

> If, in those moments when you are completely overcome with rage, overwhelmed with happiness, filled with indecision or wracked with fear caused by being pursued by a fierce lion, you adopt the trick of awareness, you will, in those very moments, attain entry into God consciousness. (*Spanda Kārikā* 1.22)

So, it is not only in the experience of joy that you can play this trick. It can also be utilized in the experience of grief and sadness.

> It is only the player of tricks who is always without any covering. There is nothing that can conceal his God consciousness. He is always present. (*Spanda Kārikā* 1.25)

Kṣemarāja now tells us that in *Spanda Nirṇaya* he has, with great authority, explained this and we would be well advised to examine that clarification.

In the Third Awakening, verse 20 said, "The fourth state *(turya)* must be expanded so that it pervades the other three—waking *(jāgrat),* dreaming *(svapna)* and deep sleep *(suṣupti)*"—just as oil falling on a sheet expands and spreads.

What is the difference between this sūtra 20 and our present sūtra 38? There must be a difference even though Lord Śiva has given us two sūtras that seem to have the same meaning. In sūtra 38, we are told that in three states, you must give life to that fourth state and in sūtra 20, we are told that in three states, you must insert the fourth state. This seems to give essentially the same meaning to both of these verses.

But there is a difference of understanding in these two sūtras. In sūtra 20, we are to understand that ultimately we have to insert the state of *turya* into the waking state, the dreaming state and the dreamless state, so that these three states become one with the fourth state *turya.* In the present sūtra 38, we are told that by using the trick of awareness, we have to insert *turya* into each and every act of our daily life. This is the difference between these two sūtras.

A yogī should not only be satisfied to infuse the awareness of God consciousness into these three states—waking, dreaming, and deep sleep but also:

39. citta sthitivaccharīra karaṇabāhyeṣu //

The awareness of God consciousness
should not only be infused in that state where
one's mind is established in one-pointedness,
but it should also be infused in the
establishment of his body,
in his organic actions,
and in the external objective world.

He should also find the state of *turya* in the objective world. You must infuse *turya*—which gives life to the three states, waking, dreaming and deep sleep—in each and every action of the universe. When one is introverted and his mind is established in one-pointedness, that is the state of *turya*. In the same way, when his conciousness is directed toward the objective world, when he is extroverted and not introverted, then in the action of the body, in the action of the organs, and in the action of the external objective world, he should hold the awareness of internal consciousness. Then in time, he should also infuse the life of *turya* into that state.

It is said in *Vijñāna Bhairava:*

> You must infuse your consciousness with the awareness that this whole universe or your own body has been simultaneously filled with your own state of bliss. Through this bliss, you will become melted in supreme bliss. (*Vijñāna Bhairava* 65)

Infuse consciousness in the beginning and also in the center of these three states and you will become one with that blissful state. There will be no difference between you and that blissful state.

In this way, in each and every state of life, the energy of absolute independence *(svātantrya śakti)*, which is filled with supreme bliss, gives you whatever you desire.

And conversely, when this internal state of *turya* is not constantly maintained with awareness, then I-consciousness on body, I-consciousness on *puryaṣṭaka,* and I-consciousness on *prāṇa* and *śūnya* exists and he feels he is absolutely incomplete. Then desire appears in him.

40. abhilāṣādbahirgatiḥ saṁbāhyasya //

Due to the insatiable and insistent desire to fill that gap (in his nature), his flow and movement are toward the objective world, not subjective consciousness, and so he is carried from one birth to another.

This yogī feels there is a gap in his nature of being. Because of this feeling of incompletion, a desire arises within him to fill his nature of being. And so to accomplish the fulfillment of this desire, he directs his attention toward the objective world and not subjective consciousness. And so, just like a beast, he is carried from one birth to another birth, from one death to another.

By whom is he carried? He is carried by those energies governed by the supreme wheel of the energies of God *(śakticakra).* And those energies are the six coverings *(kañcuka): kalā, vidyā, rāga, kāla, niyati,* along with *māyā*; the internal organs *(antaḥkaraṇa),* mind, intellect, and ego; the five organs of actions, the five organs of the senses, and the five *tantmātrās*: sound *(śabda),* touch *(sparśa),* form *(rūpa),* taste *(rasa),* and smell (*gandha*). By these energies, he is carried from one state to another state, from one life to another life, from one womb to another womb. And so he is not a carrier; he is being carried. In brief, he is just like a beast *(paśu),* dependent upon his past and future actions. And this insatiable and insistent desire is dirt, impurity *(mala).*

In this quote from the *Svacchanda Tantra,* we are told:

> *Āṇava mala,* which has appeared by perceiving one's own self as incomplete, is ignorance *(avidyā).* Because of this *āṇavamala,* desire *(abhilāsā)* arises and one is carried outside to the external world and not to the internal world of spirituality. *(Svacchanda Tantra)*

Thus his consciousness is diverted toward worldly pleasures. He does not maintain awareness to become established internally in his own nature *(antarmukharūpā).* That internal awareness is lost.

It is said in *Kālikākrama Śāstra:*

> When, by means of differentiated thought *(vikalpa),* that self is covered by ignorance, then he is unable to perceive this whole universe, beginning from earth and ending in Śiva, as one with God consciousness.
>
> And so he becomes the object of the two states, good and bad, and this causes him to experience only pain in his own nature. Thus even pleasure is experienced as that pain. When his consciousness is established on that which is not real, then he becomes the object of hells, not heaven.
>
> So, just like bamboo trees, which are burned by their own internal fire,[34] he destroys himself by his own impurities and limitations.
>
> Those who integrate into their nature those objects which are not beyond illusion, take the form of *māyā* and cherish the nature of ignorance, not the nature of spirituality. In the end, they experience only pain *(kleśās)* and sadness.

---

34. This fire is produced by the bamboo trees themselves when they are subjected to strong winds. The bamboo canes rub against one another and the resulting friction ignites a fire.

On the contrary, when the grace of Lord Śiva is infused into his consciousness, this causes him to contemplate and realize his own nature in its true sense. He then destroys all desires in himself, refrains from moving toward the outside world, and is constantly centered in his own God consciousness.

That is what is explained in this next sūtra.

41. tadārūḍhapramitestatkṣayājjīva saṁkṣayaḥ //

All desire vanishes in that fortunate person whose consciousness is established in his own real nature. For him, the state of being a limited individual has ended.

In this sūtra, the Sanskrit word *tat* means "real nature." In previous sūtras, it was explained that this real nature, which is the state of *turya,* is only the state of the knower, not knowledge or the known. When his consciousness is established, which means his consciousness is fully aware in the state of supreme God consciousness, then desire, which seemed to be existing there, vanishes and individuality ends.

What is the meaning of the Sanskrit word *jīva* (individuality) used in this sūtra? The word *jīva* refers to the state of being wherein the awareness exists that "I am the body," "I am the sense organs and organs of action," "I am the mind, the intellect, and the ego." This state of individuality (*jīva*) comes to an end and is alleviated when the yogī's consciousness shines in his own nature.

It is said in that *Kālikākrama:*

> When one is experiencing in the dreaming state, he perceives many different dreams. And yet when he awakens, these dreams completely vanish and are not existing at all. In the same way, when a fortunate yogī puts his awareness on this objective world, thinking in this way, "This universe is not the objective world, it is only subjective consciousness," then, the more he puts his awareness in continuity on subjective consciousness, the more he becomes one with that subjective consciousness. (*Kālikākrama)*

Here, for this yogī, this imagination has become true. If you, with continuous awareness, imagine this universe is nothing but your own self, your own nature, then by continuing to meditate in this way, a time will come when you will become one with God consciousness.

> Avoid those states which are existing and those states which are not existing and by the oneness of God consciousness, eliminate all the classes of imagination and hold that state which is established internally in your own nature.
>
> That yogī, who is always established in his own nature and who is determined to destroy the sphere of time (*kāla*)[35] by fixing his consciousness on the timeless point, will in the near future find that time has ceased to exist. He is established in the final beautification of God consciousness and has achieved the state of final liberation. (*Kālikākrama)*

When your consciousness is resolute in finding the timeless point, then you are said to be *kālagrāsaikatatparaḥ,* "determined to destroy the sphere of time." Where is this timeless point to be found? It is found between two breaths, between one step and another step, between one word and another word.

In this verse, what is the meaning of *kaivalyapadabhāg*? It means "final liberation." This yogī does not become the object of "being carried." He is not carried by anybody. He becomes

35. Here, the Sanskrit word *kāla* does not mean "death," but "the sphere of time."

the carrier. He carries everyone from one state to another state. The question can now be asked, when this yogī's individuality vanishes, will he not have to immediately leave his physical body? But actually, we don't experience his leaving his physical body. Even after realization of God consciousness, he still maintains the body. But if he is still living in his physical body, which is filled entirely with individuality, how can it be said that he is established in God consciousness? This yogī, who is said to be established in God consciousness, continues to suffer from the limitations of the body. Sometimes he has to spit and sometimes he has to blow his nose. He may experience headaches, toothaches, or stomach aches. In short, he experiences all of the physical problems associated with a body. But, these physical problems are the concerns of the individual, not of God, so how can you say he is established in God consciousness? Therefore, this theory of yours is incorrect.

In the next sūtra, this criticism is answered.

42. bhūtakañcukī tadā vimukto bhūyaḥ patisamaḥ paraḥ //

For him, the five elements are only coverings. At that very moment, he is absolutely liberated, supreme and just like Śiva.

In this sūtra, he is said to be *bhūtakañcukī*—covered by the five elements. This means he maintains his physical frame externally and not in his internal consciousness. From the point of view of his internal consciousness, he is above the physical body. He does not insert ego or I-consciousness into the physical body nor does he say, "I am this body." He thinks, "This body is the frame, let it remain like this, what do I care?"

He is absolutely liberated from the misery of repeated births and deaths *(vimuktaḥ)*. He is supreme *(paraḥ)* and just like Lord Śiva *(patisamaḥ)*. And as I explained earlier,[36] when he leaves this physical frame, he becomes one with Lord Śiva.

In this sūtra, the Sanskrit word *tadā* (then) means "when all desires disappear in him." This is the destruction of the state of the individual. This takes place when the attachment of his I-consciousness to his physical body disappears. When this occurs, he is said to be *bhūtakañcukī*, "covered by the five elements," not *bhūtadhārin*, "holding the five elements." The person who is covered by the five elements (*bhūtakañcukī*) thinks, "I can take off this physical body at any time I like." This body is just a case covering him. He does not insert his I-consciousness into that body, which covers him, so he is absolutely free

36. See the commentary for sūtra 3.25

from that covering. As such, he is completely liberated *(vimuktaḥ).* He actually is just like Lord Śiva. He is supreme.

For him, this physical frame is like a different covering, such as a blanket. Limited beings *(jīva)* insert I-consciousness into their physical bodies thinking, "this is my body, I am this body." When they go to the doctor, they say, "Please check my pulse." In fact, they have no pulse. In the true sense, the pulse is the pulse of the body. But they say to the doctor, "Please check my pulse. I don't feel well." Actually, it is the body that is unwell; they are always the same.

And, so, he is said to be absolutely liberated *(vimuktaḥ),* one with *nirvaṇa* (blowing out or extinquishing). He is said to be exactly the same as Lord Śiva. Having entered into the state of supreme God consciousness, he is supreme, full, and complete.

In sūtra 26 of this Third Awakening, it was explained that his body is just like a sheath, the casing for a sword *(śarīravṛittirvratam).* This yogī does not infuse his I-consciousness into that sheath. Like the sword, he remains separate from the sheath.

It is said in *Kularatnamālā Tantra*:

> When a supreme master reveals to him the ultimate reality, then, from that very moment, he is said to be absolutely liberated. For him, the remaining portion of his life is just like a machine. *(Kularatnamālā Tantra)*

After he is liberated, he lives in his body, which is just like a machine, without any awareness of that living. He is eternally centered in his God consciousness.

What can we say about that wise person who is established for only one second in that supreme Brahman? He becomes liberated and he liberates the whole universe.

It is also said in the *Netra Tantra*:

> If one realizes the state of supreme God consciousness for only a fraction of the time it takes to blink one's eyes, then from that very moment, he is said to be completely liberated and will not come again into this world. (*Netra Tantra* 8.8)

In *Kulasāra Śastra* it is also said,

> O beautiful Goddess, the glory and greatness of the real nature of God consciousness is a wonder. If the word of that real nature of God consciousness travels only in sound from one ear to another, not in actual existence, then when the sound of that word has entered the other ear, that word will liberate him instantaneously. This is the greatness of that supreme state of God consciousness. *(Kulasāra Śastrā)*

In previous sūtras, the author explained how this yogī was covered by the five elements. These five elements are not the elements of ignorance *(deha kañcukatād) deha, prāṇa, puryaṣṭaka,* and *śūnya;* they are the five elements of the elementary world *(pañca mahābhūtas).* And so it is that this body, covered with these five elements, does not produce fruit. So, what causes this covering of five elements to continue to exist after he has realized the real truth of his being? Why is it that this fivefold covering does not instantaneously disappear at the time of the realization of one's own reality of being? To this question, he answers,

43. naisargikaḥ prāṇasambandhaḥ //

This connection with breathing in and breathing out is his nature.

Upon returning from the eternal state of God consciousness the connection with breathing in and breathing out occurs naturally. It is his nature to travel with the breathing movement. So just as soon as he descends from the state of God consciousness he begins the journey of breathing in and breathing out. This has already been said by Kallaṭṭa, *prāksaṁvit prāṇe pariṇatā,* "The first change of God consciousness takes place in the breath." Therefore, as long as he continues to breathe his body must also continue to exist so that breathing is possible. And so he maintains this body of five elements.

The word *naisargikaḥ* (this is his nature) explains that his connection with breath comes about due to the nature of his energy of absolute independence *(svātantrya śakti),* because whenever this supreme Goddess of consciousness intends to create this differentiated universe, she first creates limitation in her being by entering the state of the first breath, the breathless breath, *prāṇana*. When this *prāṇana* is existing, this body does not become lifeless and even though the body may not breathe in and out, it is not rigid. It is alive. Take your hand as an example. It is not breathing in and breathing out and yet it is not rigid. So there is the breath of life in your hand.

When a woman conceives a child in her womb, that child is initially produced with *prāṇana*. In that child, there is no breathing, there is only life. This breathless breath is the breath of life. At the first movement of that energy, this supreme Goddess is transformed into this kind of breath. And then that breath (*prāṇana*) is transformed into the second movement of breath, which is breathing in and breathing out (*prāṇa*). This breath of life (*prāṇana*) is the seed of breathing in and breathing out. And here she holds the state of limited being and then also enters into the objective field. So this attachment with the breath that appeared at the beginning is the glory of her *svātantrya*.

In *Vājasaneyā Saṁhitā,* it is said:

> That supreme and subtle energy is all-pervading, without impurities, always blissful, creating the entire class of energies of Lord Śiva and filled with supreme bliss. This supreme energy *Mahāghoreśvarī*, fearful for the ignorant, is creative for those who are blissful and destructive for those who are unaware. *Mahāghoreśvarī* destroys the sphere of time, which flows in three ways as *īḍā, piṅgalā,* and *suṣumnā,* which is existing in *prāṇa, apāna,* and *samāna*[37] and which is found in present, past, and future. *(Vājasaneyā Saṁhitā)*

This energy of Lord Śiva, which is not other than his consciousness, creates and destroys the sphere of time by entering the path of breath, and the three states of *soma, sūrya,* and *vahni*

37. *Prāṇa, apāna* and *samāna* are three of the five states of the vital life force, which are *prāṇa, apāna, samāna, udāna,* and *vyāna*. *Prāṇa* is breathing in and out; *apāna* exists when you go to the bathroom and push out your excrement or urine. *Samāna* is the breath that keeps your nerves in tune and all vital channels in balance. *Udāna* is the breath used to digest food in your body. *Vyāna* is the breath that stimulates all this and directs it with vibrating force.

(fire). There, she first carries the three veins (*nāḍi*), *īdā, piṅgalā,* and *suṣumnā*[38] (*trivahaṁ).* And she is filled in the three states of *soma nāḍi, sūrya nāḍi,* and *vahni nādi* (*trividhaṁ).* And she carries three times, past, present, and future *(tristhaṁ).* Not only does she carry time, she also destroys time. She destroys time and she creates it. She creates time for those who are ignorant and destroys time for those who are elevated.

In *Svacchanda Tantra,* it is said:

> He is manifested first in the initial movement of that breath, which is only filled with life *(prāṇamayaḥ)* and then in breathing in and breathing out *(prāṇa),* which in exhaling, creates and in inhaling, destroys. In reality, this breath is residing in the heart of beings. (*Svacchanda Tantra* 7.25)

> This second breath *(prāṇa)* is represented by the Sanskrit letter "*ha,*" which is (in *Śārada* script) shaped like a plough. The directing of creation and destruction is attributed to this breath. (*Svacchanda Tantra* 4.275)

So it is well said in the present sūtra *(naisargikaḥ praṇasaṁbandhaḥ)* "this connection to breath is Lord Śiva's natural way."

And so as I said earlier, Bhaṭṭakallaṭa in his book *Tattvārtha Cintāmaṇi* has also explained this in this sūtra:

> Entering in breath *(prāṇa)* is the first change of God consciousness. This is the initial step towards manifestation. *(Tattvārtha-cintāmaṇi)*

---

38. *Iḍā, piṅgalā,* and *suṣumnā nāḍi* are three predominant subtle veins or channels that function as "the path of breath." The first vein in the left side is called *īḍā*, the predominant vein on the right side is called *piṅgalā*, and the particular artery between these two veins is called *suṣumnā.* These three veins pertain to the states of perceived *(prameya)*, perceiving *(pramāṇa)* and perceiver *(pramātṛi).* The state of the perceived *(prameya)* is the function of *īḍā* vein *(nāḍi).* The state of perceiving *(pramāṇa)* is the function of *piṅgalā* vein, and the state of the perceiver *(pramātṛi)* is the function of *suṣumnā.* They are represented by the moon, the sun, and fire. The moon is *īḍā* vein *(nāḍi)*, the perceived *(prameya).* The sun is *piṅgalā* vein, state of perceiving *(pramāṇa).* Fire is *suṣumnā nāḍi*, the state of the perceiver *(pramātṛi).*

So, although this yogī breathes in and out just like an ordinary person, yet even in breathing, he is constantly aware of the supreme state of the internal being of consciousness. This yogī is exceptional. He is beyond the state of ordinary people.

44. nāsikāntarmadhyasaṁyamāt,
kimatra, savyāpasavyasauṣumneṣu //

If his consciousness is established in the central vein in that force, which is the energy of life (prāṇan), then he remains always the same.
For him, there is no difference in traveling in prāṇa, apāna, or suṣumnā.

If his consciousness is attached to the life force (force of *kuṇḍalinī),* then it does not matter to him how he journeys in this world. He may travel in any of the three veins, yet he always remains the same. He may travel in ordinary breathing in the right vein *(dakṣiṇā nāḍi)* or in the left vein *(vāmanāḍī),* or he may travel in *prāṇana śakti* the central vein *(madhya-nāḍī).* These three veins *īḍa, piṅgalā,* and *suṣumā* are predominent in all seventy-two thousand veins.[39]

In this sūtra, the word *nāsikā* means "that energy of breath that gives life and removes the stiffness in your body." When

39. The first start manifestation of *prāṇana,* the vibrating breath of life, is *cit* (consciousness). The second start is *spanda* (vibration). The third start is *prāṇa.* When that movement (flux) of *prāṇa (prāṇa vṛitti)* enters into the grossness of a body, then it moves through the many subtle channels existing in the body. There are 72,000 principal veins and these are gross. Actually, there are more than 72,000 veins.

In the *Svacchanda Tantra,* these 72,000 veins are compared to the veins in the leaf of the Chinār Tree. Just like the veins in that leaf, so also in your body dies and you leave this physical frame, your body becomes rigid. The flexibility it used to have no longer exists. The arms and legs can no longer be easily moved. This is because the life force *(prāṇaśakti)* has left this body.

But for he whose consciousness is established in the center of that internal consciousness *(āntarī saṁvit)*, and in the center of that central breath *(madhyaṁ prāṇa)*, which is predominent in the whole of the body in each and every being,

> the supreme energy of that being, who is Lord of Lords and who is one with the supreme cognition, is only the energy of awareness. It is all-knowing, all-acting, and completely glorious. (*Kālikākrama*)

When he puts his consciousness into the formation of that awareness *(tat saṁyamāt)* by being aware in the continuity of his being, then what can we say about him? This person is established in, and glorified by, that supreme *samādhi* where, for him, there is no external state of dualistic consciousness *(vyutthānaḥ)*. This is also said in *Vijñānabhairava*:

> Subjective knowledge and objective knowledge is the same for all living beings, except there is one difference for yogīs. In both kinds of knowing, yogīs always remain aware. (*Vijñānabhairava* 106)

This is the difference between yogīs and ordinary people.

---

the body of *prāṇa* there is only one central vein, from which are projected thousands of smaller secondary channels. As the threadlike veins in the leaf of a Palāśa tree completely pervade that leaf, so do those innumerable subtle channels completely pervade (*vyāptaṁ*) this body.

Now, the author tells us what the fruit of this yoga is for such a yogī. This sūtra ends this scripture containing the theory of the *Śiva Sūtras.*

45. bhūyaḥ syātpratimīlanam //

This yogī simultaneously and repeatedly experiences the revealing state and the concealing state of the objective world.

When this universe has arisen from the state of God consciousness, then the yogī experiences the destruction of all differentiated impressions and this whole world enters into his own nature. Traveling toward the state of consciousness, it is eclipsed *(nimīlana).* And again, repeatedly, he feels this universe has emerged from God consciousness afresh. This is what the yogī who is established on the supreme path of yoga repeatedly experiences.

This is well said in *Svacchanda Tantra:*

> O Goddess, there is one state which is beyond the state of *unmanā,* into which one should direct his consciousness. And when one's self is absolutely directed into that state, he becomes one with that state. (*Svacchanda Tantra* 6.332)

> When fire, which has arisen from wood, has become absolutely pure, filled with glamour and shining with flames, it does not again enter into that wood. In the same way, when the self (*ātmā*) has separated itself from the differentiated perception of the universe, it does not again get entry into that differentiated universe. (*Svacchanda Tantra* 10.371)

भट्टश्रीकल्लटाद्येषु सच्छिष्येषु प्रकाशितवान् स्पन्दकारिकाभिश्च संगृहीतवान् । तत्पारम्पर्यप्राप्तानि स्पन्दसूत्राणि अस्माभिः स्पन्दनिर्णये सम्यक् निर्णीतानि । शिवसूत्राणि तु निर्णीयन्ते ॥ तत्र प्रथमं नरेश्वरभेदवादि-प्रातिपक्ष्येण चैतन्यपरमार्थतः शिव एव विश्वस्य आत्मा इति आदिशति-

चैतन्यमात्मा ॥१॥

इह अचेतितस्य कस्यापि सत्त्वाभावात्, चितिक्रिया सर्वसामान्यरुपा इति, चेतयते इति चेतनः सर्वज्ञानक्रियास्वतन्त्रः, तस्य भावः चैतन्यं सर्वज्ञानक्रियासंबन्धमयं परिपूर्ण स्वातन्त्र्यम् उच्यते । तच्च परमशिवस्यैव भगवतः अस्ति; अनाश्रितान्तानां तत्परतन्त्रवृत्तित्वात् । स च यद्यपि नित्यत्व-व्यापकत्वामूर्तत्वाद्यनन्तधर्मात्मा, तथापि नित्यत्वादीनाम् अन्य-त्रापि संभाव्यत्वात्, अन्यासंभविनः स्वातन्त्र्यस्यैव उद्धुरीकारप्रदर्शनमिदम् । इत्थं धर्मान्तरप्रतिक्षेपतश्च, चैतन्यमिति भावप्रत्ययेन दर्शितम् । तदेतत् आत्मा, न पुनरन्यः को ऽपि भेदवाद्यभ्युपगतो भिन्नभिन्नस्वभावः । तस्य अचैतन्ये जडतया अनात्मत्वात् । चिदात्मत्वे भेदानुपपत्तेः, चितो देशकालाकारैः चिद्व्यतिरेकात् अचेत्यमानत्वेन असद्भिः, चेत्यमानत्वेन तु चिदात्मभिः, भेदस्य आधातुम् अशक्यत्वात्, चिन्मात्रत्वे तु आत्मनां स्वभावभेदस्य अघटनात्; वक्ष्यमाणनीत्या अव्यतिरिक्तमलसंबन्ध-योगेनापि भेदस्य अनुपपत्तेः; प्राक् मलस्य सत्तवेऽपि मुक्तिदशायां तदुपशमनात् नानात्मवादस्य वक्तुम् अशक्यत्वात्, मलसंस्कार-संभवे वा, अनादिशिवात् कथंचित् अपकर्षे वा,मुक्तशिवाः संसारिण एव स्युरिति । यथोक्तम्

`चैतन्यमे क एवात्मा ...`

इति नानात्मवादस्य अनुपपत्तिः सूचिता ।

अथ च `आत्मा क` इति जिज्ञासून् उपदेश्याम् प्रति बोधयितुं, न शरीर-प्राणबुद्धिशून्यानि लौकिकचार्वाकवैदिकयोगाचारमाध्यमिकाद्यभ्युपगतानि आत्मा, अपि तु यथोक्तं चैतन्यमेव । तस्यैव शरीरादि-कल्पितप्रमातृपदेऽपि अकल्पिताहंविमर्शमय-सत्यप्रमानृत्वेन स्फुरणात् ।

तदुक्तं श्रीमृत्युजिद्भट्टारके

`परमात्मस्वरूपं तु सर्वोपाधिविवर्जितम् ।
चैतन्यमात्मनो रूपं सर्वशास्त्रेषु पठ्यते ।`
इति । श्रीविज्ञानभैरवेऽपि
`चिद्धर्मा सर्वदेहेषु विशेषो नास्ति कुत्रचित् ।
अतश्च तन्मयं सर्वं भावयन् भवजिज्जनः ॥`
इति । एतदेव
`यतः करणवर्गोऽयं ...।`

इति कारिकाद्वयेन संगृह्य उपदेश्यान् प्रति साभिज्ञानं गुरुणा उपदिष्टं श्रीस्पन्दे । किंच यदेतत् चैतन्यम् उक्तं स एव आत्मा, स्वभावः, विशेषाचोदनात् भावाभावरूपस्य विश्वस्य जगतः । नहि अचेत्यमानः कोऽपि कस्यापि कदाचिदपि स्वभावो भवति । चेत्यमानस्तु स्वप्रकाशचिदेकीभूतत्वात् चैतन्यात्मैव । तदुक्तं श्रीमदुच्छुष्मभैरवे

`यावन्न वेदका एते तावद्वेद्याः कथं प्रिये ।
वेदकं वेद्यमेकं तु तत्त्वं नास्त्यशुचिस्ततः ॥`

इति । एतदेव

`यस्मात्सर्वमयो जीवः ...।`

इति कारिकाद्वयेन संगृहीतम् ।

यतः चैतन्यं विश्वस्य स्वभावः तत एव तत्साधनाय प्रमाणादि वराकम्

अनुपयुक्तं; तस्यापि स्वप्रकाशचैतन्याधीन सिद्धिकत्वात, चैतन्यस्य च प्रोक्तयुक्त्या केनापि आवरीतुम् अशक्यत्वात् सदाप्रकाशमानत्वात् । यदुक्तं श्रीत्रिकहृदये

`स्वपदा स्वशिरश्छायां यद्वल्लङ्घितुमीहते ।
पादोद्देशे शिरो न स्यात्तथेयं बैन्दवी कला ॥`

इति । यो लङ्घितुम् ईहते तस्य यथा पादोद्देशे शिरो न स्यात् तथा इयमिति अत्र संबन्धः । अनेनैव आशयेन स्पन्दे

`यत्र स्थितम् ...।`
इत्यादि उपक्रम्य
` ... तदस्ति परमार्थतः ॥`

इत्यन्तेन महता ग्रन्थेन शङ्करात्मक-स्पन्दतत्त्वरूपं चैतन्यं सर्वदा स्वप्रकाशं परमार्थसत् अस्ति इति प्रमाणीकृतम् ॥१॥

यदि जीवजडात्मनो विश्वस्य परमशिवरूपं चैतन्यमेव स्वभावः तत् कथम् अयं बन्ध इत्याशङ्काशान्तये संहितया इतरथा च अकारप्रश्लेषाप्रश्लेषपाठतः सूत्रम् आह-

ज्ञानं बन्धः ॥२॥

इह उक्तयुक्त्या चित्प्रकाशव्यतिरिक्तं न किञ्चद् उपपद्यत इति मलस्यापि का सत्ता कीदृग् वा तन्निरोधकत्वं स्यादिति भेदवादोक्तप्रक्रिया-परिहारेण

`मलमज्ञानमिच्छन्ति संसाराङ्कुरकारणम् ॥`

इति ।

`अज्ञानाद्बध्यते लोकस्ततः सृष्टिश्च संहृतिः ॥`

इति श्रीमालिनीविजय-श्रीसर्वाचारोक्तस्थित्या यः परमेश्वरेण

स्वस्वातन्त्र्यशक्त्याभासितस्वरूपगोपना-रूपया महामाया-शक्त्या स्वात्मन्याकाश-कल्पेऽनाश्रितात्-प्रभृति मायाप्रमात्रन्तं संकोचोऽवभासितः स एव शिवाभेदाख्यात्यात्मका- ज्ञानस्वभावोऽपूर्णम्मन्यत्तात्मकाणवमल सतत्त्वसंकुचितज्ञानात्मा बन्धः। यथा च व्यतिरिक्तस्य मलस्यानुपपन्नत्वं तथा अस्माभिः श्रीस्वच्छन्दोद्योते पञ्चमपटलान्ते दीक्षाविचारे वितत्य दर्शितम् । एष च सूत्रार्थः

`निजाशुद्ध्या ासमर्थस्य ...।`

इति कारिकाभागेन संगृहीतः। एवमात्मनि अनात्मताभि-मानरूपाख्यातिलक्षणाज्ञानात्मकं ज्ञान नं केवलं बन्धो यावद् अनात्मनि शरीरादौ आत्मताभिमानत्मकम् अज्ञानमूलं ज्ञानमपि बन्ध एव । एतच्च

`परामृतरसापाय ...।`

इति कारिकाया संगृहीतम् ।

एवं चैतन्यशब्देनोक्तं यत्किञ्चित् स्वातन्त्र्यात्मकं रूपं, तत्र चिदात्मन्यपि स्वातन्त्र्याप्रथात्मविज्ञानाकलवद् अपूर्णम्मन्य-तामात्रात्मना रूपेण, स्वातन्त्र्येऽपि देहादौ अबोधरूपेण अनात्मन्यात्मताभिमानात्मना रूपेण, द्विप्रकारमाणवमलम् अनेन सूत्रेण सूत्रितम् । तदुक्तं श्रीप्रत्यभिज्ञायाम्

`स्वातन्त्र्यहानिर्बोधस्य स्वातन्त्र्यस्याप्यबोधता ।
द्विधाणवं मलमिदं स्वस्वरूपापहानितः ॥`

इति ॥२॥

किम् ईदृगाणवमलात्मैव बन्धः ? न इत्याह-

योनिवर्गः कलाशरीरम् ॥३॥

बन्ध इत्यनुवर्तते, योऽयं योनेर्विश्वकारणस्य मायायाः संबन्धी वर्गः साक्षात् पारम्पर्येण च, तद्धेतुको देहभुवनाद्यारम्भी किञ्चित्कर्तृत्वाद्यात्मककलादिक्षित्यन्तस्तत्त्वसमूहः, तद्रूपं मायीयम्, तथा कलयति स्वस्वरूपावेशेन तत्तद् वस्तु परिच्छिनत्तीति कला व्यापारः, शरीरं स्वरूपं यस्य तत् कलाशरीरं कार्मं मलमपि बन्ध इत्यर्थः । एतदपि

`निजाशुद्ध्यासमर्थस्य कर्तव्येष्वभिलाषिणः ।`

इत्यनेनैव संगृहीतम् । यथा चैतत् तथा अस्मदीयात् स्पन्दनिर्णयादवबोद्धव्यम् । एषां च कलादीनां किञ्चित्कर्तृ-त्वादिलक्षणं स्वरूपमाणवमलभित्तिलग्नं पुंसामावरकतया मलत्वेन सिद्धमेव । यदुक्तं श्रीमत्स्वच्छन्दे

`मल प्रध्वस्तचैतन्यं कलाविद्यासमाश्रितम् ।
रागेण रञ्जितात्मानं कालेन कलितं तथा ॥
नियत्या यमितं भूयः पुंभावेनोपबृंहितम् ।
प्रधानाशयसंपन्नं गुणत्रयसमन्वितम् ॥
बुद्धितत्त्वसमासीनमहङ्कारसमावृतम् ।
मनसा बुद्धिकर्माक्षैस्तन्मात्रैः स्थूलभूतकैः ।`

इति । कार्म-मलस्याप्यावरकत्वं श्रीमालिनीविजये प्रदर्शितम्

`धर्माधर्मात्मकं कर्म सुखदुःखादिलक्षणम् ।`

इति । तदेतत् मायीयं कार्मं च मलम्

`भिन्नवेद्य प्रथात्रैव मायाख्यं जन्मभोगदम् ।
कर्तर्यबोधे कार्मं च मायशक्त्यैव तत्त्रयम् ॥`

इति

श्रीप्रत्यभिज्ञायाम् आणवमलभित्तिकं संकुचित विशिष्टज्ञानतयैवोक्तम् ॥३॥

अथ कथमस्याज्ञानात्मकज्ञान-योनिवर्ग-कलाशरीररूपस्य त्रिविधस्य मलस्य बन्धकत्वमित्याह-

ज्ञानाधिष्ठानं मातृका ।।४।।

यदेतत् त्रिविधमलस्वरूपम् अपूर्णम्मन्यताभिन्नवेद्यप्रथाशुभाशुभवासनात्मक-विविधंज्ञानरूपमुक्तम्, तस्य आदिक्षान्तरूपा अज्ञाता माता मातृका विश्वजननी तत्तत्संकुचीतवेद्याभासात्मनो ज्ञानस्य `अपूर्णोऽस्मि, क्षामः स्थूलो वास्मि, अग्निष्टोमयाज्यस्मि, इत्यादितत्तदविकल्पकसविकल्प-कावभासपरामर्शमयस्यतत्तद्वाचकशब्दानुवेधद्वारेण शोक-स्मय-हर्ष-रागादिरूपतामादधाना

`करन्ध्रचितिमध्यस्था ब्रह्मपाशावलम्बिकाः ।
पीठेश्वर्यो महाघोरा मोहयन्ति मुहुर्मुहुः ॥`

इति श्रीतिमिरोद्घाटप्रोक्तनीत्या वर्गकलाद्यधिष्ठातृब्राह् म्यादि-शक्तिश्रेणी-शोभिनी श्रीसर्ववीराद्यागमप्रसिद्धलिपिक्रमसंनिवेशो-त्थापिका अम्बा-ज्येष्ठा-रौद्री-वामा-ख्यशक्तिचक्रचुम्बिता शक्तिरधिष्टात्री, तदधिष्टानादेव हि अन्तर-भेदानुसंधिवन्ध्यत्वात क्षणमपि अलब्धविश्रान्तीनि बहिर्मुखान्येव ज्ञानानि, इति युक्तैव एषां बन्धकत्वोक्तिः । एतच्च

`शब्दराशिसमुत्थस्य ...।`

इति कारिकया,

`स्वरूपावरणे चास्य शक्तयः सततोत्थिताः ।`

इति च कारिकया संगृहीतम् ।।४।।

अथ एतद्बन्धप्रशमोपायमुपेयविश्रान्तिसतत्त्वमादिशाति-

उद्यमो भैरवः ।।५।।

योऽयं प्रसरद्रूपाया विमर्शमय्याः संविदो झगिति उच्छलनात्मकपरप्रति-भोन्मज्जनरूप उद्यमः स एव सर्वशक्तसामरस्येन अशेषविश्वभरितत्वात् सकलकल्पनाकुलालंकवलनमयत्वाच्च भैरवो भैरवात्मकस्वस्वरूपा-भिव्यक्तिहेतुत्वात् भक्तिभाजाम् अन्तर्मुखैतत्तत्त्वावधानधनानां जायते, इत्युपदिष्टं भवति । उक्तं च श्रीमालिनीविजये

`अकिंचिच्चिन्तकस्यैव गुरूणा प्रतिबोधतः ।
जायते यः समावेशः शाम्भवोऽसावुदीरितः ॥

इति । अत्र हि `गुरूणा प्रतिबोधताः` इत्यत्र गुरूतः स्वस्मात् प्रतिबोधतः इत्यस्यार्थो गुरुभिरादिष्टः । श्रीस्वच्छन्देऽपि उक्तम्

`आत्मनो भैरवं रूपं भावयेद्यस्तु पूरुषः ।
तस्य मन्त्राः प्रसद्ध्यन्ति नित्ययुक्तस्य सुन्दरि ॥`

इति । भावनं हि अत्र अन्तर्मुखोद्यन्तृतापदविमर्शनमेव । एतच्च

`एकचिन्ताप्रसक्तस्य यतः स्यादपरोदयः ।
उन्मेषः स तु विज्ञेयः स्वयं तमुपलक्षयेत् ॥`

इत्यनेन संगृहीतम् ॥५॥

एवं झगिति परप्रतिभोन्मेषावष्टम्भोपायिकां भैरवसमापत्तिम् अज्ञानबन्धप्रशमैकहेतुं प्रदर्श्य, एतत्परामर्शप्रकर्षाद् व्यु त्थानमपि प्रशान्तभेदावभासं भवतीत्याह-

शक्तिचक्रसंधाने विश्वसंहारः ॥६॥

योऽयं परप्रतिभोन्मज्जनात्मोद्यन्तृतास्वभावो भैरव उक्तः अस्यैव अन्त-र्लक्ष्यबहिर्दृष्ट्यात्मतया निःशेषशक्तिचक्रक्रमाक्रमाक्रामिणी अतिक्रान्तक्रमा-क्रमाति- रिक्तारिक्ततदुभयात्मतयापि अभिधीयमानापि अनेतद्रूपा अनुत्तरा

परा स्वातन्त्र्यशक्तिः काप्यस्ति यया स्वभित्तौ मह्युल्लासात् प्रभृति परप्रमातृविश्रान्त्यन्तं श्रीमत्सृष्ट्यादिशक्तिचक्रस्फारणात्मा क्रीडेयमादर्शिता । तस्यैतदाभासितस्य शाक्तिचक्रस्य रहस्याम्नायाम्नातनीत्या यत्संधानं यथोचितक्रमविमर्शनं तस्मिन् सति, कालाग्न्यदेश्चरमकलान्तस्य विश्वस्य संहारो, देहात्मतया बाह्यतया च अवस्थितस्यापि सतः परसंविदग्निसाद्भावो भवतीत्यर्थः । उक्तं च श्रीभर्गशिखायाम्

`मृत्युं च कालं च कलाकलापं
विकारजालं प्रतिपत्तिसात्म्यम् ।
ऐकात्म्य नानात्म्यविकल्पजातं
तदा स सर्वं कवलीकरोति ॥`

इति । श्रीरीमद्वीरावलावपि

`यत्र सर्वे लयं यानति दह्यन्ते तत्त्वसंचयाः ।
तां चितिं पश्य कायस्थां कालानलसमत्विषम् ॥`

इति श्रीमन्मालिनीविजयेऽपि

`उच्चाररहितं वस्तु चेतसैव विचिन्तयन् ।
यं समावेशमाप्नोति शाक्तः सोऽत्राभिधीयते ॥`

इत्युक्त्या एतदेव भङ्ग्या निरूपितम् । एतच्च सद्गुरुचरणोपासनया अभिव्यक्तिमायातीति नाधिकमुन्मीलितम् ।

एतदेव

`यस्योन्मेषनिमेषाभ्यां ... ।`

इति

`यदा त्वेकत्र संरूढः ... ।`

इति च प्रथमचरमश्लोकाभ्यां संगृहीतम् ॥६॥

एवमुपसंहृतविश्वस्य न समाधिव्युत्थानभेदः कोऽपि इत्याह-

जाग्रत्स्वप्नसुषुप्तभेदे तुर्याभोगसंभवः ॥७॥

समनन्तरनिरूपयिष्यमाणानां जाग्रत्स्वप्नसुषुप्तानां भेदे नानारूपे पृथक्त्वावभासे `उद्यमो भैरवः` (१-५) इति लक्षितस्य स्फुरत्तात्मनः सर्वदशानुस्यूतस्य तुर्यस्य य आभोगश्चमत्कारः तस्य संभवो नित्यमेव तुर्यचमत्कारमयतवं प्रोक्तमहायोगयुक्तस्य भवतीत्यर्थः । केचित् संभव इत्यत्र संविदिति स्पष्टार्थं पठन्ति । एतच्च

`ययेन्दुः पुष्पसंकाशः समन्तादवभासते ।
आह्लादनसमूहेन जगदाह्लादयेत्क्षणात् ॥
तद्वद्देवि महायोगी यदा पर्यटते महीम् ।
ज्ञानेन्दुकिरणैः सर्वैर्जगच्चित्रं समस्तकम् ॥
आह्लादयेत्समन्तात्तदवीच्यादशिवान्तकम् ।`

इत्यदिना श्रिचन्द्रज्ञाने जागरादौ तुर्याभोगमयत्वं महायोगिनोदर्शितम् । स्पन्दे तु

`जागरादिविभेदेऽपि ...।`

इति कारिकया संगृहीतम् ॥७॥

एतज्जाग्रदादित्रयं सूत्रत्रयेण लक्षयति-

ज्ञानं जाग्रत् ॥८॥

स्वप्नो निकल्पाः ॥९॥

अविवेको मायासौषुप्तम् ॥१०॥

सर्वसाधारणार्थविषयं बाह्येन्द्रियजं ज्ञानं लोकस्य जाग्रत् जागरावस्था ।

ये तु मनोमात्रजन्या असाधारणार्थविषया विकल्पाः स एव स्वप्नः स्वाप्नावस्था, तस्य एवंविधविकल्पप्रधानत्वात् । यस्तु अविवेको विवेचनाभावोऽख्यातिः, अतदेव मायारूपं मोहमयं सौषुप्तम । सौषुप्तं लक्षयता प्रसङ्गात् उच्छेद्याया मायाया अपि स्वरूपमुक्तम् । इत्थमपि च ईदृशेनाप्यनेन लक्षणेन तिसृष्वपि जागरादिदशासु त्रैरूप्यमस्तीति दर्शितम् । तथा चात्र यद्यत् स्वप्नदशोचितं प्रथममविकल्पकं ज्ञानं सा जागरा । ये तु तत्र विकल्पाः स स्वप्नः । तत्त्वाविवेचनं सौषुप्तम् । सौषुप्ते यद्यपि विकल्पा न संचेत्यन्ते, तथापि तत्प्रविविक्षायां तथोचितजाग्रज्ज्ञानमिव तदनन्तरं संस्कारकल्पविकल्परूपस्तदुचितः स्वप्नोऽप्यस्त्येव । किं च योग्यभिप्रायेण प्रथमं तत्तद्धारणारूपं ज्ञानं जाग्रत, ततः तत्प्रत्ययप्रवाहरूपा विकल्पाः स्वप्नः, ग्राह्यग्राहकभेदासंचेतनरूपश्च समाधीः सौषुप्तम्, इत्यनया वचोयुक्त्या दर्शितम् । अत एव च श्रीपूर्वशास्त्रे जागरा दीनां परस्परानुवेधकृतो योग्यभिप्रायेणापि

`.................. अबुद्धं बुद्धमे व च ।
प्रबुद्धं सुप्रबुद्धं च .... ॥`

इत्यादिना भेदो निरूपितः ॥८॥९॥१०॥

एवं लोकयोग्यनुसारेण व्याख्याते जागरादित्रये शक्तिचक्रसंघानाद्विश्व-संहारेण यस्य तुर्याभोगमयत्वमभेदव्याप्त्यात्मकं स्फुरति, स तद्धाराधिरोहेण तुर्यातीतं पूर्वोक्तं चैतन्यमाविशन्-

त्रितयभोक्ता वीरेशः ॥११॥

एतज्जागरादित्रयं शक्तिचक्रानुसंधानयुक्त्या तुर्यानन्दाच्छुरितं यः तत्परामर्शनुप्रवेशप्रकर्षाद्विगलितभेदसंस्कारमानन्दरसप्रवाहमयमेव

पश्यति स त्रितयस्यास्य भोक्ता चमत्कर्ता । तत एव

`त्रिषु धामसु यद्भोग्यं भोक्ता यश्च प्रकीर्तितः ।
वेदैतदुभयं यस्तु स भुञ्जानो न लिप्यते ॥`

इति नीत्या निःसपत्नस्वात्मसाम्राज्योऽयं परमानन्दपरिपूर्णो भवभेदग्रसन-प्रवणानां वीराणामिन्द्रियाणामीश्वरः स्वामी, श्रिमन्थानभैरवसत्तानुप्रविष्टो महाम्नायेषूच्यते । यस्तु एवंविधो न भवति स जागराद्यवस्थाभिर्भुज्यमानो-लौकिकः पशुरेव । योग्यपि इमां धारामनधरूढो न वीरेश्वरः, अपि तु मूढ एवेत्युक्तं भवति । एतच्च

`योगी स्वच्छन्दयोगेन स्वच्छन्द गतिचारिणा ।
स स्वच्छन्दपदे युक्तः स्वच्छन्दसमतां व्रजेत् ॥`

इत्यादिना श्रीस्वच्छन्दादिशास्त्रेषु वितत्य दर्शितम् । स्पन्देऽपि

`तस्योपलब्धिः सततं त्रिपदाव्यभिचारिणी ।`

इति कारिकया संगृहीतमेतत् ॥११॥

किमस्य महायोगिनः काश्चित् तत्त्वाधिरोहप्रत्यासन्ना भूमिकाः सन्ति? याभिस्तत्त्बोर्ध्ववर्तिनी भूमिर्लक्ष्यते । सन्ति, इत्याह-

विस्मयो योगभूमिका ॥१२॥

यथा सातिशयवस्तुदर्शने कस्यचित् विस्मयो भवति तथा अस्य महायोगिनो नित्यं तत्तद्वेद्यावभासामर्शाभोगेषु निःसामान्यातिशयनवनवचमत्कार-चिद्घनस्वात्मावेशवशात् स्मेरस्मेरस्तिमितविकसितसमस्तकरणचक्रस्य यो विस्मयोऽनवच्छिन्नानन्दे स्वात्मनि अपरितृप्तत्वेन मुहुर्मुहुराश्चर्यायमाणता, ता एव योगस्य परतत्त्वैक्यस्य संबन्धिन्यो भूमिकाः, तदध्यारोहविश्रान्ति-सूचिकाः परिमिता भूमयो, न तु कन्दबिन्द्वाद्यनुभववृत्तयः ।

तदुक्तं श्रिकुलयुक्तौ

`आत्मा चैवात्मना ज्ञातो यदा भवति साधकैः ।
तदा विस्मयमात्मा वै आत्मन्येव प्रपश्यति ॥`

इति । एतच्च

`तमधिष्ठातृभावेन स्वभावमवलोकयन् ।
स्वयमान इवास्ते यस्तस्येयं कुसृतिः कुतः ॥`

इति कारिकया संगृहीतम् ॥१२॥

ईदृग्योगिनः भूमिकासमापन्नस्यास्य

इच्छा शक्तिरुमा कुमारी ॥१३॥

योगिनः परभैरवतां सभापन्नस्य या इच्छा सा शक्तिरुमा, परैव पारमेश्वरी स्वातन्त्र्यरूपा, सा च कुमारी विश्वसर्गसंहाराक्रीडापरा `कुमार क्रीडायाम्` इति पाठात् । अथ च कुं भेदोत्थापिकां मायाभूमिं मारयति अनुद्भिन्नप्रसरां करोति तच्छीला । कुमारी च परानुपभोग्य भोक्त्रैकात्म्येन स्फुरन्ती ।

अथवा यथा उमा कुमारी परीहृतसर्वासङ्गा महेश्वरैकात्म्यसाधनाराधनाय नित्योद्युक्ता तथैव अस्येच्छा, इत्यस्मद्गुरुभिरित्थमेव पाठो दृष्टो व्याख्यातश्च । अन्यैस्तु `शक्तितमा` इति पठित्वा ज्ञानक्रियापेक्षोऽस्याः प्रकर्षो व्याख्यातः । एवं न लौकिकवत् अस्य योगिनः स्थूलेच्छा, अपि तु परा शक्तिरूपैव सर्वत्राप्रतिहता । तदुक्तं श्रिमत्स्वच्छन्दे

`सा देवी सर्वदेवीनां नामरूपैश्च तिष्ठति ।
योगमायाप्रतिच्छन्ना कुमारी लोकभाविनी ॥`

इति । श्रीमृत्युञ्जयभट्टारकेऽपि

`सा ममेच्छा पराशक्तिरवियुक्ता स्वभावजा ।
वह्नेरूष्मेव विज्ञेया रश्मिरूपा रवेरिव ॥
सर्वस्य जगतो वापि सा शक्तिः कारणात्मिका ॥`

इति । तदेतत्

`नहीच्छानोदनस्यायं प्रेरकत्वेन वर्तते ।
अपि त्वात्मबलस्पर्शत्पुरुषस्तत्समो भवेत् ॥`

इति कारिकया भङ्ग्या प्रतिपादितम् ॥१३॥

ईदृशस्य महेच्छस्य-

दृश्यं शरीरम् ॥१४॥

यद्यद् दृश्यं बाह्यमाभ्यन्तरं वा, तत्तत् सर्वम् `अहमिदम्` इति-सदाशिव-वन्महासमापत्त्या स्वाङ्गकल्पमस्य स्फुरति, न भेदेन ।
शरीरं च देहधीप्राणशून्यरूपं नीलादिवद् दृश्यं, न तु पशुवद्द्रष्टृतया भाति ।
एवं देहे बाह्ये च सर्वत्रास्य मयूराण्डरसवदविभक्तैव प्रतिपत्तिर्भवति ।
यथोक्तं श्रीविज्ञानभैरवे

`जलस्येवोर्मयो वह्नेर्ज्वालाभङ्ग्यः प्रभा रवेः ।
ममैव भैरवस्यैता विश्वभङ्ग्यो विनिर्गताः ॥`

इति । एतच्च

`भोक्तैव भोग्यभावेन सदा सर्वत्र संस्थितः ।`

इत्यनेन संगृहीतम् ॥१४॥
यच्चेदं सर्वस्य दृश्यस्य शरीरतया, शून्यान्तस्य च दृश्यतया, एकरूपं प्रकाशनमुक्तं नैतत् दुर्घटम्, अपि तु-

हृदये चित्तसंघट्टाद्दृश्यस्वापदर्शनम् ॥१५॥

विश्वप्रतिष्ठास्थानत्वात् चित्प्रकाशो हृदयं, तत्र [चित्त] संघट्टात् चलतश्चलतः तदेकाग्रभावनात् दृश्यस्य, नीलदेहप्राणबुद्ध्यात्मनः, स्वापस्य च, एतदभाव-रूपस्य शून्यस्य, दर्शनं, त्यक्तग्राह्यग्राहकविभेदेन यथावस्तु स्वाङ्गकल्पतया प्रकाशनं भवति । चित्प्रकाशतामभिनिविशमानं हि चित्तं तदाच्छुरितमेव विश्वं पश्यति । तदुक्तं श्रीविज्ञानभैरवे

`हृद्याकाशे निलीनाक्षः पद्मसंपुटमध्यगः ।
अनन्यचेताः सुभगे परं सौभाग्यमाप्नुयात् ॥`

इति । परं हि अत्र सौभाग्यं विश्वेश्वरतापत्तिः ।
तत्त्ववृत्तिसमापन्नं महायोगिनमुद्दिश्य श्रीमत्स्वच्छन्देऽपि

`स च सर्वेषु भूतेषु भावतत्त्वेन्द्रियेषु च ।
स्थावरं जङ्गमं चैव चेतनाचेतनं स्थितम् ॥
अध्वानं व्याप्य सर्वं सु सामरस्येन संस्थितः ।`

इति । स्पन्दे तु

`तथा स्वात्मन्यधिष्ठानात्सर्वत्रैवं भविष्यति ॥`

इत्यनेनैव एतत्संगृहीतम् ॥ १५॥

अत्रैव उपायान्तरमाह-

शुद्धतत्त्वसंधानाद्वाऽपशुशक्ति ॥१६॥

शुद्धं तत्त्वं परमशिवाख्यं, तत्र यदा विश्वमनुसंधत्ते `तन्मयमेव एतत्` इति, तदा अविद्यमाना पश्वाख्या बन्धशक्तिर्यस्य तादृगयं सदाशिववत् विश्वस्य जगतः पतिर्भवति । तदुक्तं श्रीमल्लक्ष्मीकौलार्णवे

`दीक्षासिद्धौ तु ये प्रोक्ताः प्रत्ययाः स्तोभपूर्वकाः ।
संधानस्यैव ते देवि कलां नार्हन्ति षोडशीम् ॥`

इति । श्रीविज्ञानभैरवे तु

`सर्वं देहं चिन्मयं हि जगद्वा परिभावयेत् ।

युगपन्निर्विकल्पेन मनसा परमोद्भवः ॥`

इति । तदेतत्

`इति वा यस्य संवित्तिः क्रीडात्वेनाखिलं जगत् ।

स पश्यन्सततं युक्तो जीवन्मुक्तो न संशयः ॥`

इति कारिकया संगृहीतम् ॥१६॥

ईदृग्ज्ञानरूपस्य अस्य योगिनः -

वितर्क आत्मज्ञानम् ॥१७॥

`विश्वात्मा शिव एवास्मि` इति यो वितर्को विचारः, एतदेव अस्य आत्मज्ञानम् । तदुक्तं श्रीविज्ञानभैरवे

`सर्वज्ञः सर्वकर्ता च व्यापकः परमेश्वरः ।`

स एवाहं शैवधर्मा इति दार्ढ्याच्छिवो भवेत् ॥`

इति । स्पन्देऽपि

` ........................... अयमेवात्मनो ग्रहः ।`

इत्यनेन एतदुक्तम् । तत्र ही आत्मनो ग्रहणं ग्रहो ज्ञानम् एतदेव, यद्विश्वात्मकशिवाभिन्नत्वम्, एषोऽपि अर्थो विवक्षितः ॥१७॥

किं च अस्य-

लोकानन्दः समाधिसुखम् ॥१८॥

लोक्यते इति लोको, वस्तुग्रामः, लोकयति इति च लोको, ग्राहकवर्गः, तस्मिन्स्फुरति सति

`ग्राह्य ग्राहकसंवित्तिः सामान्या सर्वदेहिनाम् ।
योगिनां तु विशेषोऽयं संबन्धे सावधानता ॥`

इति श्रीविज्ञानभट्टारकनिरूपितनीत्या प्रमातृपदविश्रान्त्यवधानतश्चमत्कार-मयो य आनन्द एतदेव अस्य समाधिसुखम् । तदुक्तं तत्रैव

`सर्वं जगत्स्वदेहं वा स्वानन्दभरितं स्मरेत् ।
युगपत्स्वामृतेनैव परानन्दमयो भवेत् ॥`

इति । एतच्च

`इय मेवामृतप्राप्तिः ....................।` ३२ (कारिका)

इत्यनेन संगृहीतम् ।

अथ च यत् अस्य स्वात्मारामस्य समाधिसुखं, तदेव तत्तादृशम् अवलो-कयतां लोकानाम् आनन्दसंक्रमणयुक्त्या स्वानन्दाभिव्यक्तिपर्यवसायि भवति। एतदपि श्रीचन्द्रज्ञानग्रन्थेन प्रागुक्तेन (सू० ७) सुसंवादम् ॥१८॥

अथ ईदृशस्य अस्य योगिनो विभुतियोगं दर्शयति-

शक्तिसन्धाने शरीरोत्पत्तिः ॥१९॥

`इच्छा शक्तिरुमा कुमारी` (१-१३) इति सूत्रेण या अस्य शक्तिरुक्ता, तामेव यदा अनुसंधत्ते, दार्ढ्येन तन्मयीभवति, तदा तद्वशेन अस्य यथाभिमतं शरीरमुत्पद्यते । तदुक्तं श्रीमृत्युञ्जयभट्टारके

`ततः प्रवर्तते शक्तिर्लक्ष्य हीना निरामया ।
इच्छा सा तु विनिर्दिष्टा ज्ञानरूपा क्रियात्मिका ॥`

इत्युपक्रम्य

`सा योनिः सर्वदेवानां शक्तीनां चाप्यनेकधा ।
अग्नीषोमात्मिका योनिस्तस्यां सर्वं प्रवर्तते ॥`

इति । शक्तिसंधानमाहात्म्यं लक्ष्मीकौलार्णवे

`न संधानं विना दीक्षा न सिद्धीनां च साधनम् ।
न मन्त्रो मन्त्रयुक्तिश्च न योगाकर्षणं तथा ॥`

इत्यादिना प्रतिपादितम् । एतच्च

`यथेच्छाभ्यर्थितो धाता जाग्रतोऽर्थान्हृदिस्थितान् ।
सोमसूर्योदयं कृत्वा संपादयति देहिनः ॥`

इत्यनेन संगृहीतम् । देहिनः अत्यक्तदेहवासनस्य योगिनो हृदि स्थितान् अर्थान् तत्तदपूर्वनिर्माणादिरूपान् धाता महेश्वरः प्रकाशानन्दात्मतया सोमसूर्यरूपवाहोन्मीलनेन सोमसूर्यसामरस्यात्मनश्च शक्तेरुदयं कृत्वा बहिर्मुखवाहित्वेन तामासाद्य संपादयति, इति हि अस्यार्थः

`तथा स्वप्नेऽप्यभीष्टार्थान् ...।`

इत्येतच्छ्लोकप्रतिपादितस्वप्नस्वातन्त्र्यं प्रति दृष्टान्ते योजितः, इति स्पन्दनिर्णये मयैव दर्शितम् ॥१९॥

अन्या अपि अस्य यथाभिलषिताः सिद्धय एतन्माहात्म्येनैव घटन्ते इत्याह-

भूतसंधानभूतपृथक्त्वविश्वसंघट्टाः ॥२०॥

भूतानि शरीरप्राणभावाद्यात्मकानि, तेषां क्वचित् आप्यायनादौ संधानं, परिपोषणं, व्याध्याद्युपशमादौ पृथक्त्वं, शरीरादेर्विश्लेषणं, देशकालादि-विप्रकृष्टस्य च विश्वस्य संघट्टो, ज्ञानविषयीकार्यत्वादिकः, अस्य पूर्वोक्त-शक्तिसंधाने सति जायते । एतच्च सर्वागमेषु साधनाधिकारेषु अस्ति । तदेव स्पन्दे

`दुर्बलोऽपि तदाक्रम्य यतः कार्ये प्रवर्तते ।
आच्छादयेद्बुभुक्षां च तथा योऽतिबुभुक्षितः ॥`

इति ।

`ग्लानिर्विलुण्ठिका देहे तस्याश्चाज्ञानतः सृतिः ।
तदुन्मेष विलुप्तं चेत्कुतः सा स्यादहेतुका ॥`

इति ।

`यथा ह्यर्थोऽस्फुटो दृष्टः सावधानेऽपि चेतसि ।
भूयः स्फुटतरो भाति स्व बलोद्योगभावितः ॥
तथा यत्परमार्थेन येन यत्र यथा स्थितम् ।
तत्तथा बलमाक्रम्य न चिरात्संप्रवर्तते ॥`

इत्यादिना विभूतिस्पन्दे सोपपत्तिकं दर्शितम् ॥२०॥

यदा तु मितसिद्धीरनभिलष्यन् विश्वात्मप्रथामिच्छति तदा अस्य-

शुद्धविद्योदयाच्चक्रेशत्वसिद्धिः ॥२१॥

वैश्वात्म्यप्रथावाञ्छया यदा शक्तिसंधत्ते तदा `अहमेव सर्वम्` इति शुद्धविद्याया उदयात् विश्वात्मकस्वशक्तिचक्रेशत्वरूपं माहेश्वर्यमस्य सिद्ध्यति । तदुक्तं स्वच्छन्दे

`तस्मात्सा तु परा विद्या यस्मादन्या न विद्यते ।
विन्दते ह्यत्र युगपत्सार्वज्ञ्यादिगुणान्परान् ॥

वेद नानादिधर्मस्य परमात्मत्वबोधना ।
वर्जनापरमात्मत्वे तस्माद्विद्येति सोच्यते ॥

तत्रस्थो व्यञ्जयेत्तेजः परं परमकारणम् ।

परस्मिंस्तेजसि व्यक्ते तत्रस्थः शिवतां व्रजेत् ॥`

इति । तदेतत्

`दिदृक्षयेव सर्वार्थान्यदा व्याप्यावतिष्ठते ।

तदा किं बहुनोक्तेन स्वयमेवावभोत्स्यते ॥`

इत्यनेनैव संगृहीतम् ॥२१॥

यदा तु स्वात्मारामतामेव इच्छति तदा अस्य-

महाह्लदानुसंधानान्मन्त्रवीर्यानुभवः ॥२२॥

पराभट्टारिका संवित् इच्छाशक्तिप्रमुखं स्थूलमेयपर्यन्तं विश्वं वमन्ती, खेचरीचक्राद्यशेषवाहप्रवर्तकत्व-स्वच्छत्वानावृतत्व-गभीरत्वादि-धर्मयोगान्महा-ह्लदः, तस्यानुसंधानात्, अन्तर्मुखतया अनारतं तत्तादात्म्यविमर्शनात्, वक्ष्यमाणस्य शब्दराशिस्फारात्मकपराहन्ता-विमर्शमयस्य मन्त्रवीर्यस्यानुभवः, स्वात्मरूपतया स्फुरणं भवति । अत एव श्रीमालिनीविजये

`या सा शक्तिर्जगद्धातुः ...।`

इत्युपक्रम्य इच्छादिप्रमुखपञ्चाशद्भेदरूपतया मातृका-मालिनीरूपताम् अशेषविश्वमयीं शक्तेः प्रदर्श्य, तत एव मन्त्रोद्धारो दर्शितः, इति परैव शक्ति-र्महाह्लदः, ततः तदनुसंधानात् मातृका-मालिनीसतत्त्वमन्त्रवीर्यानुभव इति युक्तमुक्तम् । एतदेव

`तदाक्रम्य बलं मन्त्राः ...,`

इत्याद्युक्त्या भङ्ग्या प्रतिपादितम् ।

तदेवं `चैतन्यमात्मा` (१-१) इत्युपक्रम्य तत्स्वातन्त्र्यावभासिततदख्याति-मयं सर्वमेव बन्धं यथोक्तोद्यमात्मकभैरवसमापत्तिः प्रशमयन्ती, विश्वं स्वानन्दामृतमयं करोति, सर्वाश्च सिद्धीः मन्त्रवीर्यानुप्रवेशान्ता ददाति, इति

शाम्भवोपायप्रथनात्मा अयं प्रथम उन्मेष उक्तः । अत्र तु मध्ये शक्ति-स्वरूपमुक्तं, तत् शाम्भवरूपस्य शक्तिमत्ताप्रदर्शनाभिप्रायेण

इति शिवम् ॥२२॥

इति श्रीमन्महामाहेश्वराचार्याभिनवगुप्तपादपाद्मोपजीवि-श्रीक्षेमरज-विरचितायां शिवसूत्रविमर्शिन्यां शाम्भवोपायप्रकाशनं नाम प्रथम उन्मेषः ॥१॥

—:०:—

शिवसूत्रविमर्वशिनी

अथ द्वितीय उन्मेषः

इदानीं शाक्तोपायः प्रदर्श्यते । तत्र शक्तिः मन्त्रवीर्यस्फाररूपा, इति प्रथमोन्मेषान्तसूत्रिततत्स्वरूपविवेचनपुरःसरमुन्मेषान्तरमारभमाणो मन्त्रस्वरूपं तावत् निरूपयति-

चित्तं मन्त्रः ॥१॥

चेत्यते विमृश्यते अनेन परं तत्त्वम् इति चित्तं, पूर्णस्फुरत्तासतत्त्वप्रासाद-प्रणवादिविमर्शरूपं संवेदनम्, तदेव मन्त्र्यते गुप्तम्, अन्तर् अभेदेन विमृश्यते परमेश्वररूपम् अनेन, इति कृत्वा मन्त्रः । अत एव च परस्फुरत्तात्मकमनन-धर्मात्मता, भेदमयसंसारप्रशमनात्मक-त्राणधर्मता च अस्य निरुच्यते । अथ च मन्त्रदेवताविमर्शपरत्वेन प्राप्ततत्सामरस्यम् आराधकचित्तमेव मन्त्रः न तु विचित्रवर्णसंघट्टनामात्रकम् । यदुक्तं श्रीमत्सर्वज्ञानोत्तरे

`उच्चार्यमाणा ये मन्त्रा न मंत्रांश्चापि तान्विदुः ।
मोहिता देवगन्धर्वा मिथ्याज्ञानेन गर्विताः ॥`

इति । श्रीतन्त्रसद्भावेऽपि

`मन्त्राणां जीवभूता तु या स्मृता शक्तिरव्यया ।
तया हीना वरारोहे निष्फलाः शरदभ्रवत् ॥`

इति । श्रीश्रीकण्ठीसंहितायां तु

`पृथङ्मन्त्रः पृथङ्मन्त्री न सिद्ध्यति कदाचन ।
ज्ञानमूलमिदं सर्वमन्यथा नैव सिद्ध्यति ॥`

इत्युक्तम् । एतच्च स्पन्दे

`सहाराधकचित्तेन तेनैते शिवधर्मिणः ॥`

इति भङ्ग्या प्रतिपादितम् ॥१॥

अस्य च-

प्रयत्नः साधकः ॥२॥

यथोक्तरूपस्य मन्त्रस्य अनुसंधित्सा प्रथमोन्मेषावष्टम्भप्रयतनात्मा अकृतको यः प्रयत्नः स एव साधको, मन्त्रयितुर्मन्त्रदेवतातादात्म्यप्रदः ।

तदुक्तं श्रीतन्त्रसद्भावे

`आमिषं तु यथा खस्थः संपश्यञ्शकुनिः प्रिये ।
क्षिप्रमाकर्षयेद्यद्वद्वेगेन सहजेन तु ॥
तद्वदेव हि योगीन्द्रो मनो बिन्दुं विकर्षयेत् ।
यथा शरो धनुःसंस्थो यत्नेनाताड्य धावति ॥
तथा बिन्दुर्वरारोहे उच्चारेणैव धावति ॥`

इति । अन्यत्रापि

`तद्ग्रहो मन्त्रसद्भावः ...।`

इति । अत्र हि तद्वत्, इति अकृतकनिजोद्योगबलेन योगीन्द्रो मनः (कर्म),

बिन्दुं विकर्षयेत् परप्रकाशात्मतां प्रापयेम् इति । तथा बिन्दुः परप्रकाशः अकृतकोद्यन्तृतात्मना उच्चारेण धावति, प्रसरति इत्यर्थः । एतच्च स्पन्दे

`अयमेवोदयस्तस्य ध्येयस्य ध्यायिचेतसि ।
तदात्मतासमापत्तिरिच्छतः साधकस्य या ॥`

इत्यनेनोक्तम् ॥२॥

ईदृशसाधकसाध्यस्य मन्त्रस्य पूर्वोपक्षिप्तं वीर्यं लक्षयति—

विद्याशरीरसत्ता मन्त्ररहस्यम् ॥३॥

विद्या पराद्वयप्रथा, शरीरं स्वरूपं, यस्य स विद्याशरीरो भगवान् शब्दराशिः, तस्य या सत्ता, अशेषविश्वाभेदमयपूर्णाहंविमर्शनात्मा स्फुरत्ता, सा मन्त्राणां रहस्यम्, उपनिषत् । यदुक्तं श्रीतन्त्रसद्भावे

`सर्वे चर्णात्मका मन्त्रास्ते च शक्त्यात्मकाः प्रिये ।
शक्तिस्तु मातृका ज्ञेया सा च ज्ञेया शिवात्मिका ॥`

इति । तत्रैव च अयमर्थः अतिरहस्योऽपि वितत्य स्फुटीकृतः । तथा च

`न जानन्ति गुरू देवं शास्त्रोक्तान्समयांस्तथा ।
दम्भकौटिल्यनिरता लौल्यार्थाः क्रिययोज्झिताः ॥
अस्मात्तु कारणाद्देवि मया विर्यं प्रगोपितम् ।
तेन गुप्तेन ते गुप्ताः शेषा वर्णास्तु केवलाः ॥`

इति पीठिकाबन्धं कृत्वा

`या सा तु मातृका देवि परतेजः समन्विता ।
तया व्याप्तमिदं विश्वं सब्रह्मभुवनान्तकम् ॥
तत्रस्थं च यदा देवि व्यापितं च सुरार्चिते ।
अवर्णस्थो यथा वर्णः स्थितः सर्वगतः प्रिये ॥

तथाहं कथयिष्यामि निर्णयार्थं स्फुटं तव ।`

इत्युपक्रम्य

`या सा शक्तिः परा सुक्ष्मा निराचारेति कीर्तिता ॥
हृद्बिन्दुं वेष्टयित्वान्तः सुषुप्तभुजगाकृतिः ।
तत्र सुप्ता महाभागे न किञ्चिन्मन्यते उमे ॥
चन्द्राग्निरविनक्षत्रैर्भुवनानि चतुर्दश ।
क्षिप्त्वोतरे तु या देवी विषमूढेव सा गता ॥
प्रबुद्धा सा नानादेन परेण ज्ञानरूपिणा ।
मथिता चोदरस्थेन विन्दुना वरवर्णिनि ॥
तावद्वै, भ्रमवेगेन मथनं शक्तिविग्रहे ।
भेदात्तु प्रथमोत्पन्ना विन्दवस्तेऽतिवर्चसः ॥
उत्थिता तु यदा तेन कला सूक्ष्मा तु कुण्डली ।
चतुष्कलमयो विन्दुः शक्तेरूदरगः प्रभुः ॥
मथ्यमन्थनयोगेन ऋजुत्वं जायते प्रिये ।
ज्येष्ठाशक्तिः स्मृता सा तु विन्दुद्वयसुमध्यगा ॥
बिन्दुना क्षोभमायाता रेखैवामृतकुण्डली ।
रेखिणी नाम सा ज्ञेया उभौ बिन्दू यदन्तगौ ॥
त्रिपथा सा समाख्याता रौद्री नाम्ना तु गीयते ।
रोधिनी सा समुद्दिष्टा मोक्षमार्गनिरोधनात् ॥
शशाङ्कशकलाकारा अम्बिका चार्धचन्द्रिका ।
एकैवेत्थं परा शक्तिस्त्रिधा सा तु प्रजायते ॥
आभ्यो युक्तवियुक्ताभ्यः संजातो नववर्गकः ।
नवधा च स्मृता सा तु नववर्गोपलक्षिता ॥
पञ्चमन्त्रगता देवि सद्य आदिरनुक्रमात् ।

तेन पञ्चविधा प्रोक्ता ज्ञातव्या सुरनायिके ॥
स्वरद्वादशगा देवि द्वादशस्था उदाहृता ।
अकारादिक्षकारान्ता स्थिता पञ्चाशता भिदा ॥
हृत्स्था एकाणवा प्रोक्ता कण्ठे प्रोक्ता द्वितीयका ।
त्रिराणवा तु ज्ञातव्या जिह्वामूले सदा श्रिता ॥
जिह्वाग्रे वर्णनिष्पत्तिर्भवत्यत्र न संशयः ।
एवं शब्दस्य निष्पत्तिः शब्दव्याप्तं चराचरम् ॥`

इत्यादिना ग्रन्थेन परभैरवीयपरवाक्शक्त्यात्मकमातृका, अत एव ज्येष्टा-रौद्री-अम्बाख्यशक्तिप्रसरसंभेदवैचित्र्येण सर्ववर्णोदयस्य उक्तत्वात्, वर्णसंघट्टनाशरीराणां मन्त्राणां सैव भगवती व्याख्यातरूपा विद्याशरीरसत्ता रहस्यम्— इति प्रदर्शितम् ।

प्रत्यागमं च मातृकामालिनीप्रस्तारपूर्वकं मन्त्रोद्धारकथनस्य अयमेव आशयः ।
रहस्यागमसारसंग्रहरूपत्वात् शिवसूत्राणाम् आगमसंवादे भरः अस्माभिः कृत इति नास्मभ्यम् असूयितव्यम् ।

एवमपि संवादिते आगमे यदि रहस्यार्थो न बुध्यते, तस्मात् सद्गुरुसपर्या कार्या । एष च सूत्रार्थः

`तदाक्रम्य बलं मन्त्राः ...।`

इत्यनेन कारिकाद्वयेन स्पन्दे दर्शितः ॥३॥

येषां तु एवं विधमेतन्मन्त्रवीर्यं प्रोक्तमहाह्लदानुसंधानौपयिकमपि परमेश्वरेच्छात एव न हृदयङ्गमीभवति, अपि तु आनुषङ्गिकमात्रविन्दुनादादिकलाजनितासु मितसिद्धिषु चित्तं रोहति, तेषाम्—

गर्भे चित्तविकासोऽविशिष्टविद्यास्वप्नः ॥४॥

गर्भः अख्यातिर्महामाया, तत्र तदात्मके मितमन्त्रसिद्धिप्रपञ्चे यश्चित्तस्य विकासः, तावन्मात्रे प्रपञ्चे संतोषः असावेव अविशिष्टा, सर्वजनसाधारण-रूपाः विद्या, किञ्चिज्ज्ञत्वरूपा अशुद्धविद्या, सैव स्वप्नो, भेदनिष्ठो विचित्रो विकल्पात्मा भ्रमः। तदुक्तं पातञ्जले

`ते समाधावुपसर्गा व्युत्थाने सिद्धयः` (३-३७)

इति । तदेतत्

`अतो विन्दुरतो नादो रूपमस्मततो रसः ।
प्रवर्तन्तेऽचिरेणैव क्षोभकत्वेन देहिनाः ॥`

इत्यनेन दर्शितम् ॥४॥

यदां तु आगतामपि मितसिद्धिं खिलीकृत्य परामेव स्थिति-मवष्टभ्नाति योगी तदाः—

विद्यासमुत्थाने स्वाभाविके खेचरी शिवावस्था ॥५॥

प्राङ्निर्दिष्टसतत्त्वाया विद्यायाः स्वाभाविके समुत्थाने, मरमेशेच्छामात्र-घटिते मितसिद्धिन्यग्भाविनि सहजे समुन्मज्जने, खे बोधगगने चरति इति खेचरी मुद्रा अभिव्यज्यते । कीदृशी खेचरी, शिवस्य चिन्नाथस्य अवस्थातुः संबन्धिनी अवस्था, स्वानन्दोच्छलत्तारूपा । न तु

`बद्ध्वा प द्मासनं योगी नाभावक्षेश्वरं न्यसेत् ।
दण्डाकारं तु तावत्तन्नयेद्यावत्कखत्रयम् ॥
निगृह्य तत्र तत्तूर्णं प्रेरयेत् खत्रयेण तु ।
एतां बद्ध्वा महायोगी खे गतिं प्रतिपद्यते ॥`

इत्येवं संस्थानविशेषानुसरणरूपा, अपि तु

` .... पराम् ।

गतिमेत्यर्थभावेन कुल मार्गेण नित्यशः ॥

चरते सर्वजन्तूनां खेचरी नाम सा स्मृता ।`

इति श्रीतन्त्रसद्भावनिरूपितपरसंवित्तिस्वरूपा । एवमिह भेदात्मकमायीयसमस्तक्षोभप्रशान्त्या चिदात्मकस्वरूपोन्मज्जनैकरूपं मन्त्रवीर्यं मुद्रावीर्यं च आदिष्टम् । तदुक्तं कुलचूडामणौ

`एकं सृष्टिमयं बीजमेका मुद्रा च खेचरी ।

द्वावेतौ यस्य जायेते सोऽतिशान्तपदे स्थितः ॥`

इति । स्पन्दे तु मन्त्रवीर्यस्वरूपनिरूपणेनैव मुद्रावीर्यं संगृहीतम्।

`यदा क्षोभः प्रलोयेत तदा स्यात्परमं पदम् ।`

इत्यर्धेन अन्यपरेणापि चूडामण्युक्तं खेचरीस्वरूपं भङ्ग्या सूचितम् ॥५॥

तदत्र मुद्रामन्त्रवीर्यासादनेऽपि—

गुरूरुपायः ॥६॥

गृणाति उपदिशति तात्त्विकमर्थमिति गुरुः, सोऽत्र व्याप्तिप्रदर्शकत्वेन उपायः । तदुक्तं श्रीमालिनीविजये

`स गुरूर्मत्समः प्रोक्तो मन्त्रवीर्यप्रकाशकः ।`

इति । स्पन्दे तु एवमादिप्रसिद्धत्वात् न संगृहीतम् ।

`अगाधसं शयाम्भोधिसमुत्तरणतारिणीम् ।

वन्दे विचित्रार्थपदां चित्रां तां गुरुभारतीम् ॥`

इति पार्यन्तिकोक्त्या च एतदपि संगृहीतमेव ।

गुरुर्वा पारमेश्वरी अनुग्राहिका शक्तिः । यथोक्तं श्रीमालिनीविजये

`शक्तिचक्रं तदेवोक्तं गुरुवक्त्रं तदुच्यते ।`

इति । श्रीमन्त्रिशिरोभैरवेऽपि

`गुरोर्गुरुतरा शक्तिर्गुरुवक्त्रगता भवेत् ।`

इति । सैव अवकाशं ददती उपायः ॥६॥

तस्माद्गुरोः प्रसन्नात्—

मातृकाचक्रसम्बोधः ॥७॥

शिष्यस्य भवतीति शेषः। श्रीपरात्रिंशकादिनिर्दिष्टनीत्या अहंविमर्शप्रथम-कला अनुत्तराकुलस्वरूपा, प्रसरन्ती आनन्दस्वरूपा सती, इच्छेशनभूमिका-भासनपुरःसरं, ज्ञानात्मिकामुन्मेषदशां ज्ञेयाभासासूत्रेणाधिक्येन च ऊनतां प्रदर्श्य, इच्छामेव द्विरूपां विद्युद्विद्योतनकल्पतेजोमात्ररूपेण, स्थैर्यात्मना च एषणीयेन रञ्जितत्वात् र-लश्रुत्या आरूषितेन, अत एव स्वप्रकाशात्मीकृत-मेयाभासत्वतः अमृतरूपेण, मेयाभासारूषणमात्रतश्च बीजान्तरप्रसवासमर्थ-तया, षण्ढाख्यबीजचतुष्टयात्मना रूपेण प्रपञ्च्य, प्रोक्तानुत्तरानन्देच्छासंघट्टेन त्रिकोणबीजम्, अनुत्तरानन्दोन्मेषयोजनया च क्रियाशक्त्युपगमरूपमोकारं, प्रोक्तैतद्बीजद्वयसंघट्टेन षट्कोणं शूलबीजं च, इच्छाज्ञानशक्तिव्याप्तपूर्णक्रिया शक्तिप्रधानत्वात् शक्तित्रयसंघट्टनमयं प्रदर्श्य, इयत्पर्यन्तविश्वैकवेदनरूपं बिन्दुमुन्मील्य, युगपदन्तर्बहिर्विसर्जनममयविन्दुद्वयात्मानं विसर्गभूमि-मुद्दर्शितवती, अत एव अन्तर्विमर्शनेन अनुत्तरे एव एतद्विश्वं विश्रान्तं दर्शयति, बहिर्विमर्शेन तु कादि-मान्तं पञ्चकपञ्चकम् अ-इ-उ-ऋ-लृशक्तिभ्यः पुरुषान्तं समस्तं प्रपञ्चयति । एकैकस्याश्च शक्तेः पञ्चशक्तित्वमस्ति, इत्येकैकतः पञ्चकोदयः । आभ्य एव शक्तिभ्यः शिक्षोक्तसंज्ञानुसारेण अन्तः-पुंभूमौ नियत्यातिकञ्चुकत्वेन अवस्थानात् अन्तःस्थाख्यान्प्रमातृभूमिधारणेन विश्वधारणात् धारणाशब्देन आम्नायेषु उक्तान्, तदुपरि भेदविगलनेन अभोदापत्त्या उन्मिषितत्वात् ऊष्माभिधानान् चतुरो वर्णानाभासितवती ।

अत्र च अन्ते सर्वसृष्टिपर्यन्तवर्ति परिपूर्णममृतवर्णं प्रदर्श्य, तदन्ते प्राणबीज-प्रदर्शनं कृतम, तत् अनुत्तरशक्त्याप्यायितानाहतमयम्, इयद्वाच्यवाचकरूपं षडध्वस्फारमयं विश्वम्, इति प्रत्यभिज्ञापयितुम् । अत एव प्रत्याहारयुक्त्या अनुत्तरानाहताभ्यामेव शिवशक्तिभ्यां गर्भीकृतम् एतदात्मकमेव विश्वम्, इति महामन्त्रवीर्यात्मनोऽहंविमर्शस्य तत्त्वम् । यथोक्तमस्मत्परमेष्ठ श्रीमदुत्पलदेवपादैः

`प्र काशस्यात्मविश्रान्तिरहंभावो हि कीर्तितः ।
उक्ता सैव च विश्रान्तिः सर्वापेक्षानिरोधतः ॥
स्वातन्त्र्यमथ कर्तृत्वं मुख्यमीश्वरतापि च ।`

इति । तदियत्पर्यनतं यन्मातृकायास्तत्त्वं तदेव ककार- सकारप्रत्याहारेण अनुत्तरविसर्गसंघट्टसारेण कूटबीजेन प्रदर्शितमन्ते, इत्यलं रहस्यप्रकटनेन । एवंविधायाः

` ........................ न विद्या मातृकापरा ।`

इत्याम्नायसूचितप्रभावाया मातृकायाः संबन्धिनश्चक्रस्य प्रोक्तानु-त्तरानन्देच्छादिशक्तिसमूहस्य चिदानन्दघनस्वस्वरूपसमावेशमयः सम्यक् बोधो भवति । एतच्चेह दिङ्मात्रेणोट्टङ्कितम् । विततं तु अस्मत्-प्रभुपादैः श्रीपरात्रिंशकाविवरण-तन्त्रालोकादौ प्रकाशितम् । उक्तं च श्रीसिद्धामृते

`सात्र कुण्डलिनी बीजजीवभूता चिदात्मका ।
तज्जं ध्रुवेच्चोन्मेषाख्यं त्रिकं वर्णास्ततः पुनः ॥
आ इत्यवर्णादित्यादि यावद्वैसर्गिकी कला ।
ककारादिसकारान्ता विसर्गात्पञ्चधा स च ॥
बहिश्चान्तश्च हृदये नादेऽथ परमे पदे ।
बिन्दुरात्मनि मूर्धान्ते हृदयाद्व्यापको हि सः ॥

आदिमान्त्यविहीनास्तू मन्त्राः स्युः शरदभ्रवत् ।
गुरोर्लक्षणमेतावदादिमान्त्यं च वेदयेत् ॥
पूज्यः सोऽहमिव ज्ञानी भैरवो देवतात्मकः ।
श्लोकगाथादि यत्किञ्चिदादिमान्त्ययुतं यतः ॥
तस्माद्विदंस्तथा सर्वं मन्त्रत्वेनैव पश्यति ।`

इति । एतच्च स्पन्दे

`सेयं क्रियात्मिका शक्तिः शिवस्य पशुवर्तिनी ।
बन्धयित्री ....`

इत्युपक्रम्य

`स्वमार्गस्था ज्ञाता सिद्ध्युपपादिका ॥`

इत्यनेनैव भङ्ग्या सूचितम् ॥७॥

ईदृशस्य अस्य मातृकाचक्रसंबोधवतः —

शरीरं हविः ॥८॥

सर्वैश्वर्यप्रमातृत्वेन अभिषिक्तं स्थूलसूक्ष्मादिस्वरूपं शरीरं तत् महायोगिनः परस्मिन् चिदग्नौ हूयमानं हविः, शरीरप्रमातृताप्रशमनेन सदैव चिन्मातृताभिनिविष्टत्वात् । यदुक्तं श्रीविज्ञानभैरवे

`महाशून्यालये वह्नौ भूताक्षविषयादिकम् ।
हूयते मनसा साकं स होमः स्रुक्च चेतना ॥`

इति । श्रीतिमिरोद्धाटेऽपि

`यः प्रियो यः सुहृद्बन्धुर्यो दाता योऽतिवल्लभः ।
तदङ्ग भक्षणाद्देवि ह्युत्पतेद्गगनाङ्गना ॥`

इति । अत्र हि देहप्रमातृताप्रशमनमेव पिण्डार्थः । श्रीमद्भगवद्गीतास्वपि

`सर्वाणीन्द्रियकर्माणि प्राणकर्माणि चापरे ।
आत्मसंयमयोगाग्नौ जुह्वति ज्ञानदीपिते ॥`

इति । स्पन्दे तु

`यदा क्षोभः प्रलीयेत तदा स्यात्परमं पदम् ।`

इत्यनेनैव संगृहीतम् । क्षोभो देहाद्यहंप्रत्ययरूपः, इति हि तद्वृत्तौभट्टश्रीकल्लटः ॥८॥

अस्य च-

ज्ञानमन्नम् ॥९॥

यत्पूर्व `ज्ञानं बन्धः` (१-२) इत्युक्तं तत अद्यमानत्वात्, ग्रस्यमानत्वात् योगिनामन्नम् । यत्संवादितं प्राक्

`मृत्युं च कालं च कलाकलापं
विकारजातं प्रतिपत्तिसात्म्यम् ।
ऐकात्म्य-नानात्म्यवितर्कजातं
तदा स सर्वं कवलीकरोति ॥`

इति ।

अथ च यत्स्वरूपविमर्शात्मकं ज्ञानं तत् अस्य अन्नं, पूर्णपरितृप्तिकारितया स्वात्मविश्रान्तिहेतुः । तदुक्तं श्रीविज्ञानभैरवे

`अत्रैकतम युक्तिस्थे योत्पद्येत दिनाद्दिनम् ।
भरिताकारिता सात्र तृप्तिरत्यन्तपूर्णता ॥`

इति । युक्तिर्हि तत्र द्वादशोत्तरशतभूमिकाज्ञानरूपैव । एतच्च स्पन्दे

`प्रबुद्धः सर्वदा तिष्ठेत् ...।`

इत्यनया कारिकया संगृहीतम् ॥९॥

यदा तु एवं सततावहितो न भवति,
तदा ज्ञानवतोऽपि अस्य अवधानावलेपात्-

विद्यासंहारे तदुत्थस्वप्नदर्शनम् ॥१०॥

प्रोक्तज्ञानस्फाररूपायाः शुद्धविद्यायाः संहारे, निमज्जने, तदुत्थस्य, क्रमात्क्रमन्यक्कृतविद्यासंस्कारस्य स्वप्नस्य, भेदमयस्य विकल्पप्रपञ्चरूपस्य दर्शनं, स्फुटम् उन्मज्जनं भवति । तदुक्तं श्रीमालिनीविजये

`न चैतदप्रसन्नेन शङ्करेणोपदिश्यते ।
कथञ्चिदुपदिष्टेऽपि वासना नैव जायते ॥`

इत्युपक्रम्य

`वासनामात्रलाभेऽपि योऽप्रमत्तो न जायते ।
तमनित्येषु भोगेषु योजयन्ति विनायकाः ॥`

इति । तदेतत्

`अन्यथा तु स्वतन्त्रा स्यात्सृष्टिस्तद्धर्मकत्वतः ।
सततं लौकिकस्येव जाग्रत्स्वप्नपदद्वये ॥`

इत्यनेन स्पन्दे संगृहीतम् । अतश्च नित्यं शुद्धविद्याविमर्शन-परेणैव योगिना भाव्यम इत्युपदिष्टं भवति । यथोक्तम्

`तस्मान्न तेषु संसक्तिं कुर्वीतोत्तमवाञ्छया ।`

इति श्रीपूर्वे । श्रीस्पन्देऽपि

`अतः सततमुद्युक्तः स्पन्दतत्त्वविविक्तये ।
जाग्रदेव निजं भावमचिरेणाधिगच्छति ॥`

इति । एवं `चित्तं मन्त्रः` (२-१)

इत्यतः प्रभृति मन्त्रवीर्य-मुद्रावीर्यानुसंधिप्रधानम्

`उच्चाररहितं वस्तु चेतसैव विचिन्तयन् ।
यं समावेशमाप्नोति शाक्तः सोऽत्राभिधीयते ॥`

इत्याम्नातं शाक्तोपायं विविच्य, अवधानावलिप्तं प्रति `विद्यासंहारे तदुत्थ-स्वप्नदर्शनम्` (२-१०) इति सूत्रेण एतदनुषङ्गेण आणवोपायप्रतिपादनस्य अवकाशो दत्तः । इति शिवम् ॥१०॥

शिवसूत्रविमर्शिनी

अथ

तृतीय उन्मेषः

—:०:—

इदानीमाणवोपायं प्रतिपिपादयिषुः, अणोः तावात्स्वरूपं दर्शयति-

आत्मा चित्तम् ॥१॥

यदेतत् विषयवासनाच्छुरितत्वात् नित्यं तदध्यवसायादिव्यापारबुद्ध्य-हङ्कृन्मनोरूपं चित्तं, तदेव अतति, चिदात्मकस्वस्वरूपाख्यात्या सत्त्वा-दिवृत्त्यवलम्बनेन योनीः संचरति, इति आत्मा अणुरित्यर्थः । न तु चिदेकरूपस्य अस्य अतनमस्ति । अत एव `चैतन्यमात्मा` (१-१) इति-स्वभावभूततात्त्विकैतत्स्वरूपप्रतिपादनाशयेन पूर्वमात्मा लक्षितः । इदानीं तु एतदीयसंकोचावभासप्रधानाणवदशौचित्येन, इति न पूर्वापरवैषम्यम् ॥१॥

अस्य चित्तस्वरूपस्य अण्वात्मनः—

ज्ञानं बन्धः ।।२।।

सुखदुःखमोहमयाध्यवसायादिवृत्तिरूपं तदुचितभेदावभासनात्मकं यत् ज्ञानं, तत्बन्धः । तत्पाशितत्वादेव हि अयं संसरति ।

तदुक्तं श्रीतन्त्रसद्भावे

`सत्त्वस्थो राजसस्थश्च तमस्थो गुण वेदकः ।
एवं पर्यटते देही स्थानात्स्थानान्तरं व्रजेत् ।।`

इति । एतदेव

`तन्मात्रो दयरूपे ण मनोऽहंबुद्धिवर्तिना ।
पुर्यष्टकेन संरूद्धस्तदुत्थं प्रत्ययोद्भवम् ।।
भुङ्क्ते परवशो भोगं तद्भावात्संसरेत् ... ।`

इत्यनेनानूदितम् ।

` ....अतः ।
संसृतिप्रलयस्यास्य कारणं संप्रचक्ष्महे ।।`

इत्येतत्प्रतिविधानाय स्पन्दशास्त्रे ।।२।।

ननु च

`ज्ञानं प्रकाशकं लोके आत्मा चैव प्रकाशकः ।
अनयोरपृथग्भावाज्ज्ञाने ज्ञानी प्रकाशते ।`

इति-श्रीविज्ञानभैरवोक्तदृष्ट्या ज्ञानमपि प्रकाशमयमेव, इतिकथमस्य बन्धरूपत्वम् । सत्यमेतत् यदि परमेश्वरप्रसादादेवं प्रत्यभिज्ञायेत, यदा तु तन्मायाशक्तितो नैवं विमर्शस्तदा-

कलादीनां तत्त्वानामविवेको माया ।।३।।

किञ्चित्कर्तृतादिरूपकलादिक्षित्यन्तानां तत्त्वानां कञ्चुक-पुर्यष्टक-स्थूलदेहत्वेन अवस्थितानां योऽयमविवेकः, पृथक्त्वाभिमतानामेव

अपृथगात्मत्वेन प्रतिपत्तिः, सा माया तत्त्वाख्यातिमयः प्रपञ्चः ।
तदुक्तं श्रीतन्त्रसद्भावे

`कालोद्वलितचैतन्यो विद्याद शितगोचरः ।
रागेण रञ्जितात्मासौ बुद्ध्यादिकरणैर्युतः ॥
एवं मायात्मको बन्धः प्रोक्तस्तस्य दरात्मकः ।
तदाश्रयगुणो धर्मोऽधर्मश्चैव समासतः ॥
तत्रासौ संस्थितः पाश्यःपाशितस्तैस्तु तिष्ठति ।`

इति । स्पन्दे तु

`अप्र बुद्धधियस्त्वेते स्वस्थितिस्थगनोद्यताः ।`

इत्यनेन एतत् भङ्ग्या उक्तम् ॥३॥

अतश्च एतत्प्र-शमाय—

शरीरे संहारः कलानाम् ॥४॥

महाभूतात्मकं, पुर्यष्टकरूपं, समनान्तं यत स्थूलं, सूक्ष्मं, परं शरीरं, तत्र याः पृथिव्यादिशिवान्ततत्त्वरूपाः कला भागाः, तासां संहारः, स्वकारणे लयभावनया दाहादिचिन्तनयुक्त्या वा ध्यातव्यः, इति शेषः ।
यदुक्तं श्रीविज्ञानभैरवे

`भुवनाध्वादिरू पेण चिन्तयेत्क्रमशोऽखिलम् ।
स्थूलसूक्ष्मपरस्थित्या यावदन्ते मनोलयः ॥`

इति । तथा

`कालाग्निना कालपदादुत्थितेन स्वकं पुरम् ।
प्लुष्टं विचिन्तयेदन्ते शान्ताभासः प्रजायते ॥`

इति । एवमादि च सर्वागमेष्वस्ति । अत एव

`उच्चार करणध्यानवर्णस्थानप्रकल्पनैः ।

यो भवेत्स समावेशः सम्यगाणव उच्यते ॥`

इति श्रीपूर्वशास्त्रे ध्यानादि एव आणवत्वेन उक्तम् । एतच्च स्थूलत्वात् शाक्तोपायप्रकाशात्मनि स्पन्दशास्त्रे न संगृहीतम् । यत्तु अत्र पर्यवसानभङ्ग्या शाक्तादि अस्ति, तत् अस्माभिः अत्रापि स्पन्दग्रन्थात् संवादितं, संवादयिष्यते च किंचित् ॥ ४॥

एवं ध्यानाख्यमाणवमुपायं प्रदर्श्य, तदेकयोगक्षेमान् प्राणायाम-धारणा-प्रत्याहार-समाधीन् प्रदर्शयति—

नाडीसंहार-भूतजय-भूतकैवल्य-भूतपृथक्त्वानि ॥५॥

योगिना भावनीयानि इति शेषः । नाडीनां प्राणापानादिवाहीनीनां सुषीणां संहारः, प्राणापानयुक्त्या एकत्र उदानवह्न्यात्मनि मध्यनाड्यां विलीनतापादनम् । यदुक्तं श्रीमत्स्वच्छन्दे

`अपसव्येन रेच्येत सव्येनैव तु पूरयेत् ।

नाडीनां शोधनं ह्यतन्मोक्षमार्गपथस्य च ॥

रेचनात्पूरणाद्रोधात्प्राणायामा स्त्रिधा स्मृताः ।

सामान्या बहिरेते तु पुनश्चाभ्यन्तरे त्रयः ॥

आभ्यन्तरेण रेच्येत पूर्येताभ्यन्तरेण तु ।

निःस्पन्दं कुम्भकं कृत्वा कार्याश्चाभ्यन्तरास्त्रयः ॥`

इति । भूतानां पृथिव्यादीनां जयो धारणाभिर्वशीकारः। यथोक्तं तत्रैव

`वायवी धारणाङ्गुष्ठे आग्नेयी नाभिमध्यतः ।

माहेयी कण्ठदेशे तु वारुणी घण्टिकाश्रिता ॥

आकाशधारणा मूर्ध्नि सर्वसिद्धिकरी स्मृता ।`

इति । भूतेभ्यः कैवल्यं, चित्तस्यततः प्रत्याहरणम् । यदुक्तं तत्रैव

`नाभ्यां हृदयसंचारान्मनश्चेन्द्रियगोचरात् ।
प्राणायामश्चतुर्थम्तु सुशान्त इति स्मृतः ॥`

इति । हृदयान्नाभौ प्राणस्य, विषयेभ्यो मनसश्च तत्रैव संचारणादित्यर्थः । भूतेभ्यः पृथक्त्वं, तदनुपरक्तस्वच्छन्दचिदात्मता । यदुक्तं तत्रैव

`भित्त्वा क्रमेण सर्वाणि उन्मनान्तानि यानि च ।
पूर्वोक्तलक्षणैर्देवि त्यक्त्वा स्वच्छन्दतां व्रजेत् ॥`

इति । `भूतसंधानभूतपृथक्त्वविश्वसंघट्टाः` (१-२०) इति यत् पुर्वमुक्तम्, तत् शाम्भवोपायसमाविष्टस्य अयत्नतो भवति ।
इतं तु आणवोपायप्रयत्नसाध्यमिति विशेषः ॥५॥

एवं देहशुद्धि-भूतशुद्धि-प्राणायाम-प्रत्याहार-धारणा-ध्यान समाधिभिर्या तत्तत्तत्त्वरूपा सिद्धिर्भवति सा मोहावरणात्, न तु तत्त्वज्ञानादित्याह—

मोहावरणात्सिद्धिः ॥६॥

मोहयति इति मोहो, माया, तत्कृतादावरणात् प्रोक्तधारणा-दिक्रमसमासादिता तत्तत्तत्त्वभोगरूपा सिद्धिर्भवति ।
न तु परतत्त्वप्रकाशः । यदुक्तं श्रीलक्ष्मीकौलार्णवे

`स्वयम्भूर्भगवान्देवो जन्मसंस्कारवर्जितः ।
निर्विकल्पं परं धाम अनादिनिधनं शिवम् ॥
प्रत्यक्षं सर्वजन्तूनां न च पश्यति मोहितः ।`

इति । विगलितमोहस्य तु

`मध्यमं प्राणमाश्रित्य प्राणापानपथान्तरम् ।
आलम्ब्य ज्ञानशक्तिं च तत्स्थं चैवासनं लभेत् ॥

प्राणादिस्थूलभावं तु त्यक्त्वा सूक्ष्ममथान्तरम् ।
सूक्ष्मातीतं तु परमं स्पन्दनं लभ्यते यतः ॥
प्राणायामः स निर्दिष्टो यस्मान्न च्यवते पुनः ।
शब्दादिगुणवृत्तिर्या चेतसा ह्यनुभूयते ॥
त्यक्त्वा तां परमं धाम प्रविशेत्तत्स्वचेतसा ।
प्रत्याहार इति प्रोक्तो भवपाशनिकृन्तनः ॥
धीगुणान्समतिक्रम्य निर्ध्येयं परमं विभुम् ।
ध्यात्वा ध्येयं स्वसंवेद्यं ध्यानं तच्च विदुर्बुधाः ॥
धारणा परमात्मत्वं धार्यते येन सर्वदा ।
धारणा सा विनिर्दिष्टा भवपाशनिवारिणी ॥
शिवोऽहमद्वितीयोऽहं समाधिः स परः स्मृतः ॥`

इति श्रीमन्मृत्युजिद्भट्टारकनिरूपितनीत्या धारणदिभिरपि परतत्त्व-समावेश एव भवति, न तु मितसिद्धिः ॥६॥

तदाह—

मोहजयादनन्ताभोगात्सहजविद्याजयः ॥७॥

मोहस्य, अख्यात्यात्मकसमनान्तपाशात्मनो मायाया जयाद्, अभिभवात् ।
कीदृशात्? अनन्तः, संस्कारप्रशमपर्यन्तः आभोगो विस्तारो यस्य तादृशात्

`वेदनानादिधर्मस्य ............।`

इत्यादिना निरूपितरूपायाः सहजविद्याया जयो, लाभो भवति ।
आणवोपायस्यापि शाक्तोपायपर्यवसानादित्युक्तत्वात् ।
तथा च श्रीस्वच्छन्दे

`समनान्तं वरारो हे पाशजालमनन्तकम् ।`

इत्युपक्रम्य

`पाशावलोकनं त्यक्त्वा स्वरूपालोकनं हि यत् ।
आत्मव्याप्तिर्भवत्येषा शिवव्याप्तिस्ततोऽन्यथा ॥
सर्वज्ञादिगुणा येऽर्था व्यापकान्भावयेद्यदा ।
शिवव्याप्तिर्भवत्येषा चैतन्ये हेतुरूपिणी ॥`

इति ग्रन्थेन आत्मव्याप्त्यन्तस्य मोहस्य जयात् उन्मनाशिवव्याप्त्यात्मनः सहजविद्यायाः प्राप्तिरुक्ता । यदुक्तं तत्रैव

`आत्मतत्त्वं ततस्त्यक्त्वा विद्यातत्त्वे नियोज येत् ।
उन्मना सा तु विज्ञेया मनः संकल्प उच्यते ॥
संकल्पात्क्रमतो ज्ञानमुन्मनं युगपत्स्थितम् ।
तस्मात्सा च परा विद्या यस्मादन्या न विद्यते ॥
विन्दते ह्यत्र युगपत् सर्वज्ञादि गुणान्परान् ।
वेदनानादिधर्मस्य परमात्मत्वबोधना ॥
वर्जनापरमात्मत्वे तस्माद्विद्येति चोच्यते ।
तत्रस्थो व्यञ्जयेत्तेजः परं परमकारणम् ॥`

इति ॥७॥

एवमयमासादितसहजविद्यः-

जाग्रद्द्वितीयकरः ॥८॥

लब्ध्वापि शुद्धविद्यां तदैकध्यव्याप्तौ जागरूकः, पूर्णविमर्शात्मकस्वाहन्तापेक्षया यत् द्वितीयमिदन्तावमृश्यं वेद्यावभासात्मकं जगत्, तत् करो रश्मिर्यस्य तथाविधो भवति । विश्वमस्य स्वदीधितिकल्पं स्फुरति इत्यःर्थ । यथोक्तं श्रीविज्ञानभैरवे

`यत्र यत्राक्षमर्गेण चैतन्यं व्यज्यते विभोः ।
तस्य तन्मात्रधर्मित्वाच्चिल्लयाद्भरितात्मता ॥`

इति । श्रीसर्वमङ्गलायामपि

`शक्तिश्च शक्तिमांश्चैव पदार्थद्वयमुच्यते ।
शक्तयोऽस्य जगत्कृत्स्नं शक्तिमांस्तु महेश्वरः ॥`

इति ॥८॥

ईदृशश्चायं सर्वदा स्वस्वरूपविमर्शाविष्टः—

नर्तक आत्मा ॥९॥

नृत्यति, अन्तर्निगूहितस्वस्वरूपावष्टम्भमूलं तत्तज्जागरादिनानाभूमिकाप्रपञ्चं स्वपरिस्पन्दलीलयैव स्वभित्तौ प्रकटयति इति नर्तक आत्मा । तदुक्तं श्रीनैश्वासदेवीमहेश्वरनर्तकाख्ये सप्तमपटले देवीकृतस्तवे

`त्वमेकांशेनान्तरात्मा नर्तकः कोशरक्षिता ॥`

इति । भट्टश्रीनारायणेनापि

`विसृष्टाशेषसद्बीजगर्भं त्रैलोक्यनाटकम् ।
प्रस्ताव्य हर संहर्तुं त्वत्तः कोऽन्यः कविः क्षमः ॥`

इति । सर्वागमोपनिषदि श्रीप्रत्यभिज्ञायाम्

`संसारनाट्यप्रवर्तयिता सुप्ते जगति जागरूक एक एव परमेश्वरः ॥`

इति ॥९॥

एवं-विधस्य अस्य जगन्नाट्यनर्तकस्य भूमिकाग्रहण-पदबन्ध-स्थानरङ्गमा ह-

रङ्गोऽन्तरात्मा ॥१०॥

रज्यतेऽस्मिन् जगन्नाट्यक्रीडाप्रदर्शनाशयेनात्मना इति रङ्गः, तत्तद्भूमिकाग्रहणस्थानम् अन्तरात्मा, संकोचावभाससतत्त्वः शून्यप्रधानः प्राणप्रधानो वा पुर्यष्टकरूपो देहापेक्षया अन्तरो जीवः । तत्रा हि अयं कृतपदः स्वकरणपरिस्पन्दक्रमेण जगन्नाट्यमाभासयति ।

उक्तं च श्रीस्वच्छन्दे

> `पुर्यष्टकसमा वेशाद्विच रन्सर्वयोनिषु ।
> अन्तरात्मा स विज्ञेयः ....।।

इति ।।१०।।

इत्थमन्तरात्मरङ्गे नृत्यतोऽस्य-

प्रेक्षकाणीन्द्रियाणि ।।११।।

योगिनश्चक्षुरादीनि इन्द्रियाणि हि संसारनाट्यप्रकटनप्रमोदनिर्भनं स्वस्वरूपम् अन्तर्मुखतया साक्षात्कुर्वन्ति, तत्प्रयोगप्ररूढ्या विगलितविभागां चमत्काररससंपूर्णतामापाद यन्ति । यच्छ्रुतिः

> `कश्चिद्धीरः प्रत्यगात्मानमैक्षद् आवृत्तचक्षुरमृतत्वमश्नन् ।।`
> (कठोपनिषदि अ०२ । व०४ । मं०१) ।

इति ।।११।।

धीवशात्सत्त्वसिद्धिः ।।१२।।

धीः, तात्त्विकस्वरूपविमर्शनविशदा विशदा धिषणा तद्वशात् सत्त्वस्य स्फुरत्तात्मनः सूक्ष्मस्य आन्तरपरिस्पन्दस्य सिद्धिरभिव्यक्तिर्भवति । नाट्ये च सात्त्विकाभिनयसिद्धिर्बुद्धि कौशलादेव लभ्यते ।।१२।।

एवं स्फुरत्तात्मकसत्त्वासादनातेव अस्य योगिनः—

सिद्धः स्वतन्त्रभावः ।।१३।।

सिद्धः, संपन्नः, स्वतन्त्रभावः, सहजज्ञत्व-कर्तृत्वात्मकम् अशेषविश्ववशीकारि स्वातन्त्र्यम् । यदुक्तं श्रीश्रीनाथपादैः

`श्रयेत्स्वातन्त्र्यशक्तिं स्वां सा श्रीकाली परा कला ।`

इति । श्रीस्वच्छन्देऽपि

`सर्वतत्त्वानि भूतानि मन्त्रवर्णाश्च ये स्मृताः ।
नित्यं तस्य वशास्ते वै शिवभावनया सदा ।।`

इति ।।१३।।

एष स्वतन्त्रभावोऽस्य—

यथा तत्र तथान्यत्र ।।१४।।

यत्र देहे योगिनः स्वाभिव्यक्तिर्जाता तत्र यथा, तथा अन्यत्र सर्वत्र सदावहितस्य सा भवति । यथोक्तं श्रीस्वच्छन्दे

`स्वच्छन्दश्चैव स्वच्छन्दः स्वच्छन्दो विचरेत्सदा ।`

इति । श्रीस्पन्देऽपि

`लभते तत्प्रयत्नेन परीक्ष्यं तत्त्वमादरात् ।
यतः स्वतन्त्रता तस्य सर्वत्रेयमकृत्रिमा ।।`

इति ।।१४।।

न चैवमपि उदासीनेन अनेन भाव्यम् अपि तु—

बीजावधानम् ॥१५॥

कर्तव्यमिति शेषः बीजं विश्वकारणं स्फुरत्तात्मा परा शक्तिः । यदुक्तं श्रीमृत्युजिद्भट्टारके

`सा योनिः सर्वदेवानां शक्तीनां चाप्यनेकधा ।
अग्नीषोमात्मिका योनिस्ततः सर्वं प्रवर्तते ॥`

इत्यादि । तत्र परशक्त्यात्मनि बीजे, अवधानं भूयो भूयश्चित्तनिवेशनं कार्यम् ॥१५॥

एवं हि सति असौ योगी—

आसनस्थः सुखं ह्रदे निमज्जति ॥१६॥

आस्यते, नित्यमैकात्म्येन स्थीयते अस्मिन् इति आसनं, परं शाक्तं बलम्, यस्तत्र तिष्ठति, परिहृतपरापरध्यानधारणादिसर्वक्रियाप्रयासो नित्यमन्तर्मुखतया तदेव परामृशति यः, स सुखमनायासतया, ह्रदे, विश्वप्रवाहप्रसरहेतौ स्वच्छोच्छलत्तादियोगिनि परामृतसमुद्रे निमज्जति, देहादिसंकोचसंस्कारब्रोडनेन तन्मयीभवति । यदुक्तं श्रीमृत्युजिद्भट्टारके एव

`नोर्ध्वे ध्यानं प्रयुञ्जीत नाधस्तान्न च मध्यतः ।
नाग्रतः पृष्ठतः किञ्चिन्न पार्श्वे नोभयोरपि ॥
नान्तः शरीर संस्थं तु न बाह्ये भावयेत्क्वचित् ।
नाकाशे बन्धयेल्लक्ष्यं नाधो दृष्टिं निवेशयेत् ॥
न चक्षुर्मीलनं किञ्चिन्न किंचिद्दृष्टिबन्धनम् ।
अवलम्बं निरालम्बं सालम्बं नैव भावयेत् ॥
नेन्द्रियाणि न भूतानि शब्दस्पर्शरसादयः ।
एवं त्यक्त्वा समाधिस्थः केवलं तन्मयीभवेत् ॥

सावस्था परमा प्रोक्ता शिवस्य परमात्मनः ।
निराभासं पदं तत्तु तत्प्राप्य न विनिवर्तते ॥`

इति ॥१६॥

तदेवं नाडीसंहाराद्याणवोपायक्रमासादितमोहजयोन्मज्जच्छुद्धविद्यात्मक-शाक्तबलासादनप्रकर्षाद् आत्मीकृतपरामृतह्लदात्मकशाम्भवपदो योणी—

स्वमात्रानिर्माणमापादयति ॥१७॥

स्वस्य चैतन्यस्य संबन्धिनी मात्रा चिद्रसाश्यानतात्मा अंशः, तद्रूपं यथेष्टवेद्यवेदकावभासात्मकं निर्माणमापादयति, निर्मितत्वेन दर्शयति । यदुक्तं श्रीस्वच्छन्दे

`तदेव भवति स्थूलं स्थूलोपाधिवशात्प्रिये ।
स्थूलसूक्ष्मविभेदेन तदेकं संव्यवस्थितम् ॥`

इति । प्रत्यभिज्ञायामपि

`आत्मानमत एवायं ज्ञेयीकुर्यात्पृथक्स्थिति ।
ज्ञेयं न तु ....॥`

इति । आगमेऽपि

`जलं हिमं च यो वेद गुरुवक्त्रागमात्प्रिये ।
नास्त्येव तस्य कर्तव्यं तस्यापश्चिमजन्मता ॥`

इति अनेनैव आशयेन उक्तम् । एतदेव

`इति वा यस्य संवित्तिः क्रीडात्वेनाखिलं जगत् ।
स पश्यन्सततं युक्तो जीवन्मुक्तो न संशयः ॥`

इति अनेन स्पन्दे प्रतिपादितम् ॥१७॥

न चैवं स्वशक्तिनिर्मितभूत-भावशरीरवतोऽस्य जन्मादिबन्धः कश्चिदित्याह—

विद्याऽविनाशे जन्मविनाशः ॥१८॥

प्रोक्तायाः सहजविद्याया अविनाशे सततोन्मग्नतया स्फुरणे, जन्मनः अज्ञान-सहकारिकर्महेतुकस्य दुःखमयस्य देहेन्द्रियादिसमुदायस्य, नाशो विध्वंसः संपन्न एव । यदुक्तं श्री श्रीकण्ठ्याम्

`सप्रपंञ्चं परित्यज्य हेयोपादेयलक्षणम् ।
तृणादिकं तथा पर्णं पाषाणं सचराचरम् ॥
शिवाद्यवनिपर्यन्तं भावाभावोपबृंहितम् ।
सर्वं शिवमयं ध्यात्वा भूयो जन्म न प्राप्नुयात् ॥`

इति । श्रीस्वच्छन्दे

`स्वनिर्वाणं परं शुद्धं गुरुपारम्परागतम् ।
तद्विदित्वा विमुच्येत गत्वा भूयो न जायते ॥`

इति । श्रीमृत्युजित्यपि

`तत्त्वत्रयविनिर्मुक्तं शाश्वतं त्वचलं ध्रुवम् ।
दिव्येन योगमर्गेण दृष्ट्वा भूयो न जायते ॥`

इति ॥१८॥

यदा तु शुद्धविद्यास्वरूपम् अस्य निमज्जति तदा—

कवर्गादिषु माहेश्वर्याद्याः पशुमातरः ॥१९॥

अधिष्टात्र्यो भवन्ति इति शेषः ।

`या सा शक्तिर्जगद्धातुः कथिता समवायिनी ।
इच्छात्वं तस्य सा देवि सिसृक्षोः प्रतिपद्यते ।

सैकापि सत्यनेकत्वं यथा गच्छति तच्छृणु ॥
एवमेतदिति ज्ञेयं नान्यथेति सुनिश्चितम् ।
ज्ञापयन्ती जगत्यत्र ज्ञानशक्तिर्निगद्यते ॥
एवं भूतमिदं वस्तु भवत्विति यदा पुनः ।
जाता तदैव तत्तद्वत्कुर्वन्त्यत्र क्रियोच्यते ॥
एवं सैषा द्विरूपापि पुनर्भेदैरनन्तताम् ।
अर्थोपाधिवशात्प्राप्ता चिन्तामणिरिवेश्वरी ॥
तत्र तावत्समापन्नमातृ भावा विभिद्यते ।
द्विधा च नवधा चैव पञ्चाशद्वा च मालिनी ॥
बीजयोन्यात्मकाद्भेदाद्द्विधा बीजं स्वरा मताः ।
कादिभिश्च स्मृता योनिर्नवधा वर्गभेदतः ॥
बीजमत्र शिवः शक्तिर्योनिरित्यभिधीयते ।
वर्गाष्टकविभेदेन माहेश्वर्यादि चाष्टकम् ॥
प्रतिवर्णविभेदेन शतार्धकिरणोज्ज्वला ।
रुद्राणां वाचकत्वेन तत्संख्यानां निवेशिता ॥'

इति श्रीमालिनीविजयनिरूपितनीत्या पारमेश्वरी परावाक्प्रसरन्ती, इच्छा-ज्ञान-क्रियारूपतां श्रित्वा, बीजयोनि-वर्ग-वर्ग्यादिरूपा शिव-शक्ति-माहेश्वर्यादि-वाचक-आदि-क्षान्तरूपां मातृकात्मतां श्रित्वा, सर्वप्रमातृषु अविकल्पक-सविकल्पक-तत्तत्संवेदनदशासु, अन्तः परामर्शात्मना स्थूल-सूक्ष्मशब्दानुवेधं विदधाना, वर्ग-वर्ग्यादिदेवताधिष्ठानादिद्वारेण स्मय-हर्ष-भय-राग-द्वेषादिप्रपंचं प्रपञ्चयन्ती, असंकुचितस्वतन्त्रचिद्घनस्वस्वरूप-मावृण्वाना संकुचितपरतन्त्रदेहादिमयत्वमापादयति । तदुक्तं श्रीतिमिरोद्घाटेपि

'करन्ध्र चितिमध्यस्था ब्रह्मपाशावलम्बिकाः ।

पीठेश्वर्यो महाघोरा मोहयन्त्यो मुहुर्मुहुः ॥`

इति पूर्वमपि संवादितम् । `ज्ञानाधिष्ठानं मातृका` (१-४-) इति सामान्येन उक्तम्, इदं तु प्राप्ततत्त्वोऽपि प्रमाद्यन् माहेश्यादिभिः पशुजनाधिष्ठातृभूताभिरपि शब्दानुवेधद्वारेण मोह्यते इत्याशयेन इति विशेषः ॥१९॥

यत एवम्, अतः शुद्धविद्यास्वरूपमुक्तयुक्तिभिरासादितमपि यथा न नश्यति, तथा सर्वदशासु योगिना सावधानेन भवितव्यम् इत्याह—

त्रिषु चतुर्थं तैलवदासेच्यम् ॥२०॥

त्रिषु जागरादिषु पदेषु, चतुर्थं शुद्धविद्याप्रकाशरूपं तुर्यानन्दरसात्मकं धाम, तैलवदिति, यथा तैलं क्रमेण अधिकमधिकं प्रसरद् आश्रयं व्याप्नोति तथा आसेच्यम् । त्रिष्वपि पदेषु उन्मेषोपशान्त्यात्मकाद्यन्तकोट्योः परिस्फुरता तुर्यरसेन मध्यदशामपि अवष्टम्भयुक्तया व्याप्नुयात् येन तन्मयीभावमाप्नुयात् । `जाग्रत्स्वप्नसुषुप्तेषु तुर्याभोगसंभवः` (१-७) इत्यनेन उद्यम-शक्तिचक्रानुसंध्यवष्टम्भभाजः स्वरसप्रसरज्जागरादिपदेषु सत्तामात्रं तुर्यस्योक्तम् । `त्रितयभोक्ता वीरेशः` (१-११) इति शाम्भवोपायानुगुणहठपाकयुक्त्या जागरादिसंहारो दर्शितः । अनेन तु सूत्रेण आणवोचितावष्टम्भयुक्त्या दलकल्पं जागरादित्रयं तुर्यरसासिक्तं कार्यम् इत्युक्तम्, इति विशेषः ॥

अत्रोपायमाह—

मग्नः स्वचित्तेन प्रविशेत् ॥२१॥

`प्राणादिस्थूल भावं तु त्यक्त्वा सूक्ष्ममथान्तरम् ।
सूक्ष्मातीतं तु परमं स्पन्दनं लभ्यते यतः ॥`

इत्युपक्रम्य

` ............... प्रविशेत्तत्स्वचेतसा ॥`

इति श्रीमृत्युजिद्भट्टारक निरूपितनीत्या प्राणयाम-ध्यान-धारणादि-स्थूलोपायान् परित्यज्य, स्वचित्तेन, अविकल्पकरूपेण अन्तर्मुखान्तरविमर्श-चमत्कारात्मना संवेदनेन, प्रविशेत् समाविशेत्। कीदृक् सन् ? मग्नः शरीर-प्राणादिप्रमातृतां तत्रैव चिच्चमत्काररसे मज्जनेन प्रशमयन्। तदुक्तं श्रीस्वच्छन्दे

`व्यापारं मानसं त्यक्त्वा बोधरूपेण योजयेत् ।
तदा शिवत्वमभ्येति पशुर्मुक्तो भवार्णवात् ॥`

इति । श्रीविज्ञानभट्टारकेऽपि

`मानसं चेतना शक्तिरात्मा चेति चत्तुष्टयम् ।
यदा प्रिये परिक्षीणं तदा तद्भैरवं वपुः ॥`

इति । एतदेव ज्ञानगर्भे स्तोत्रे

`विहाय सकलाः क्रिया जननि मानसीः सर्वतो
विमुक्तकरणक्रियानुसृतिपारतन्त्र्योज्ज्वलम् ।
स्थितैस्त्वदनुभावतः सपदि वेद्यते सा परा
दशा नृभिरतन्द्रितासमसुखामृतस्यन्दिनी ॥`

इत्यनेन महागुरुभिर्निबद्धम् ॥२१॥

इत्थं च परमपदप्रविष्टस्य अस्य वस्तुस्वाभाव्यात् यदा पुनः प्रसरणं भवति तदा—

प्राणसमाचारे समदर्शनम् ॥२२॥

परस्फुरत्तात्मकशाक्तपरिमलसंस्कृतस्य प्राणस्य, सम्यक् इति विकसितसमग्रग्रन्थ्यात्मकान्तरावष्टम्भबलात्, आ ईषत् बहिर्मन्दमन्दं चारे प्रसरणे, समं चिदानन्दघनात्मतया एकरूपं, दर्शनं संवेदनम्, अर्थात् सर्वदशासु अस्य भवति इत्यर्थः । उक्तं च श्रीमदानन्दभैरवे

`उत्सृज्य लौकिकाचारमद्वैतं मुक्तिदं श्रयेत् ।
स समं सर्वदेवानां तथा वर्णाश्रमादिके ॥
द्रव्याणां समतादर्शी स मुक्तः सर्वबन्धनैः ।`

इति । अत एव श्रीप्रत्यभिज्ञायाम्

`बुद्धिप्राणप्रसरेऽपि बाह्यदेशाद्युपादानानाहित संकोचानां
विश्वात्मस्वरूपलाभ एव ॥`

इत्युक्तम् ॥२२॥

यदा तु अन्तर्मुखतुर्यविधानावष्टम्भप्रकर्षलभ्यं तुर्यातीतपदम् एवमयं न समाविशति, अपि तु पूर्वापरकोटिसंवेद्यतुर्यचमत्कारमात्रे एव संतुष्यन्नास्ते, तदा अस्य—

मध्येऽवरप्रसवः ॥२३॥

पूर्वापरकोट्योस्तुर्यरसमास्वादयतो, मध्ये मध्यदशायाम्, अवरः अश्रेष्ठः, प्रसवो व्युत्थानात्मा कुत्सितः सर्गो जायते । न तु `विद्यासंहारे तदुत्थस्वप्नदर्शनम्` (२-१०) इत्युक्तसूत्रार्थनीत्या सदा व्यामुह्यति इत्यर्थः । उक्तं च श्रीमालिनीविजये

`वासनामात्रलाभेऽपि योऽप्रमत्तो न जायते ।
तमनित्येषु भोगेषु योजयन्ति विनायकाः ॥
तस्मान्न तेषु संसक्तिं कुर्वीतोत्तमवाञ्छया ।`

इति प्रागपि संवादितम् ॥२३॥

एवमेव प्रसवेऽपि प्रवृत्ते यदि तुर्यरसावष्टम्भेन मध्यपदं सिञ्चति पुनरपि, तदा—

मात्रास्वप्रत्ययसंधाने नष्टस्य पुनरुत्थानम् ॥२४॥

मात्रासु पदार्थेषु स्वप्रत्ययसंधानम् ।

`चक्षुषा यच्च संधानं वाचा वा यश्च गोचरः ।
मनश्चिन्तयते यानि बुद्धिश्चैवाध्यवस्यति ॥
अहंकृतानि यान्येव यच्च वेद्यतया स्थितम् ।
यश्च नास्ति स तत्रैव त्वन्वेष्टव्यः प्रयत्नतः ॥`

इति श्रीस्वच्छन्दनिरूपितनीत्या `विश्वमिदम् अहम्` इति चिद्घनात्मरूपतां सर्वत्र अनुसंदधतः, पूर्वोक्तावरप्रसवात् नष्टस्य, अपहारिततुर्यैकघन-चमत्कारमयस्वभावस्य, पुनरुत्थानम् उन्मज्जनं तदैक्यसंपत्संपूर्णत्वं योगिनो भवति इत्यर्थः । तदुक्तं श्रीस्वच्छन्दे

`प्रसह्य चञ्चलीत्येव योगिनामपि यन्मनः ।`

इत्युपक्रम्य

`यस्य ज्ञेयमयो भावः स्थिरः पूर्णः समन्ततः ।
मनो न चलते तस्य सर्वावस्थागतस्य तु ॥
यत्र यत्र मनो याति ज्ञेयं तत्रैव चिन्तयेत् ।
चलित्वा यास्यते कुत्र सर्वं शिवमयं यतः ॥`

इति ।

`विषयेषु च सर्वेषु इन्द्रियार्थेषु च स्थितः ।
यत्र यत्र निरूप्येत नाशिवं विद्यते क्वचित् ॥`

इति च ॥२४॥

इत्थमासादितप्रकर्षो योगी—

शिवतुल्यो जायते ॥२५॥

तुर्यपरिशीलनप्रकर्षात् प्राप्ततुर्यातीतपदः परिपूर्णस्वच्छस्वच्छन्दचिदानन्दघनेन शिवेन भगवता तुल्यो, देहकलाया अविगलनात् तत्समो जायते । तद्विगलनेन साक्षाच्छिव एव असौ इत्यर्थः । तथा च श्रीकालिकाक्रमे

`तस्मान्नित्यमसंदिग्धं बुद्ध्वा योगं गुरोर्मुखात् ।
अविकल्पेन भावेनभावयेत्तन्मयत्वतः ॥
यावत्तत्समतां याति भगवान्भैरवोऽब्रवीत् ।`

इति ॥२५॥

एवमपि च `येनेदं तद्धि भोगतः` इत्याद्युक्तरीत्या उपनतभोगातिवाहनमात्रप्रयोजनात् देहस्थितिः अस्य न अतिक्रमणीया इत्याह—

शरीरवृत्तिर्व्रतम् ॥२६॥

प्रोक्तदृशा शिवतुल्यस्य योगिनः शिवाहंभावेन वर्तमानस्य, शरीरे वृत्तिर्वर्तनं यत्, तदेव व्रतम्, स्वस्वरूपविमर्शात्मकनित्योदितपरपूजातत्परस्य नियमेन अनुष्ठेयम् अस्य । तथा च श्रीस्वच्छन्दे

`सु प्रदीप्ते यथा वह्नौ शिखा दृश्येत चाम्बरे ।
देहप्राणस्थितोऽप्यात्मा तद्वल्लीयेत तत्पदे ॥`

इत्युक्त्या देहप्राणाद्यवस्थितस्यैव शिवसमाविष्टत्वमुक्तम् । न पुनस्तस्य देहस्थितिव्यतिरिक्तं व्रतमुपयुक्तम् । यदुक्तं श्रीत्रिकसारे

`देहोत्थिताभिर्मुद्राभिर्यः सदा मुद्रितो बुधः ।
स तु मुद्राधरः प्रोक्तः शेषा वै अस्थिधारकाः ॥`

इति । श्रीकुलपञ्चाशिकायामपि

`अव्यक्तलिङ्गिनं दृष्ट्वा संभाषन्ते मरीचयः ।
लिङ्गिनं नोपसर्पन्ति अतिगुप्ततरा यतः ॥`

इति ॥२६॥

एवं-विधस्य अस्य—

कथा जपः ॥२७॥

`अहमेव परो हंसः शिवः परमकारणम् ।`

इति-श्रीस्वच्छन्दनिरूपितनीत्या नित्यमेव पराहंभावनामयत्वात् ।

`तस्य देवातिदेवस्य परबोधस्वरूपिणः ।
विमर्शः परमा शक्तिः सर्वज्ञा ज्ञानशालिनी ॥`

इति-श्रीकालिकाक्रमनिरूपितनीत्या महामन्त्रात्मकाकृतकाहंविमर्शारूढस्य यद्यदालापादि तत्तदस्य स्वात्मदेवताविमर्शानवरतावर्तनात्मा जपो जायते । यदुक्तं श्रीविज्ञानभैरवे

`भूयो भूयः परे भावे भावना भाव्यते हि या ।
जपः सोऽत्र स्वयं नादो मन्त्रात्मा जप्य ईदृशः ॥

इति । तथा-

`सकारेण बहिर्याति हकारेण विशेत्पुनः ।
हंस-हंसेत्यमुं मन्त्रं जीवो जपति नित्यशः ॥
षट्शतानि दिवारात्रौ सहस्राण्येकविंशतिः ।
जपो देव्या विनिर्दिष्टः सुलभो दुर्लभो जडैः ॥`

इति ।।२७।।

इति ईदृग्जपव्रतवतोऽस्य चर्यामाह—

दानमात्मज्ञानम् ।।२८।।

प्रोक्तचैतन्यरूपस्य आत्मनो यत् ज्ञानं, साक्षात्कारः, तत् अस्य दानम्, दीयते परिपूर्णं स्वरूपम्, दीयते खण्ड्यते विश्वभेदः दायते शोध्यते मायास्वरूपम्, दीयते रक्ष्यते लब्धः शिवात्मा स्वभावश्च अनेन इति कृत्वा ।
अथ च दीयते इति दानम्; आत्मज्ञानमेव अनेन अन्तेवासिभ्यो दीयते ।
तदुक्तम्

`दर्शनात्स्पर्शनाद्वापि विततात्भवसागरात् ।
तारयिष्यन्ति योगीन्द्राः कुलाचारप्रतिष्ठिताः ।`

इति ।।२८।।

यथोक्तदृशा शीवतुल्यतया नित्यमेवं व्रत-जपचर्यानिष्ठत्वात् निजशाक्ति-चक्रारूढः स एव तत्त्व उपदेश्यानां प्रतिबोधक इत्याह—

योऽविपस्थो ज्ञाहेतुश्च ।।२९।।

अवीन् पशून् पाति इति अविपं `कवर्गादिषु माहेश्वर्याद्याः पशुमातरः` (३-१९) इत्यभिहितदृशा माहेश्वर्यादिशक्तिचक्रं, तत्र तिष्ठति विदितस्व-माहात्म्यत्वात् प्रभुत्वेन यः प्रतपति, स ज्ञाहेतुः; जानाति इति ज्ञा ज्ञान-शक्तिः; तस्या हेतुः, उपदेश्यान् ज्ञानशक्त्या प्रतिबोधयितुं क्षमः । अन्यस्तु शक्तिचक्रपरतन्त्रीकृतत्वात् स्वात्मनि अप्रभविष्णुः कथमन्यान् प्रबोधयेत् । यच्छब्दापेक्षया सूत्रेऽत्र तच्छब्देऽध्याहार्यः । च शब्दो ह्यर्थे ।

योऽयमविपस्थः स यस्मात् ज्ञानप्रबोधनहेतुस्तस्माद्युक्तमुक्तम् `दानमात्मज्ञानम्, (३-२८) इति ।

अन्ये तु `अक्षरसारूप्यात् प्रब्रूयात्` इति निरुक्तस्थित्या `यो` इति योगीन्द्रः, `वि` इति विज्ञानम्, `प` इति पदम्, `स्थ` इति पदस्थः इत्यस्य अन्त्यमक्षरम् । `ज्ञ` इति ज्ञाता, `हे` इति हेयः, `तु` इति तुच्छता, विसर्जनीयेन विसर्गशक्तिः, चकारेण अनुक्तसमुच्चयार्थेन कर्ता परामृश्यते इत्याश्रित्य, यो योगीन्द्रो विमर्शशक्त्या स्वरूपात्मविज्ञानपदस्थः, स ज्ञाता कर्ता च अवगन्तव्यः, तदा च अस्य हेयतां तुच्छतां निःसारतां, न तु उपादेयतामासादयति इति व्याचक्षते; एतच्च न नः प्रातिभाति, पदार्थसङ्गतेर्नातिचारुत्वात्; प्रतिसूत्रं च ईदृशव्याख्याक्रमस्य सहस्रशो दर्शयितुं शक्यत्वात् ॥२९॥

अस्य च—

स्वशक्तिप्रचयोऽस्य विश्वम् ॥३०॥

यतोऽयं शिवतुल्य उक्तस्ततो यथा—

`शक्तयोऽस्य जगत्कृत्स्नम् ....................।`

इत्याधाम्नायदृष्ट्या शिवस्य विश्वं स्वशक्तिमयं, तथा अस्यापि स्वस्याः संविदात्मनः शक्तेः, प्रचयः क्रियाशक्तिस्फुरणरूपो विकासो, विश्वम् ।

यदुक्तं श्रीमृत्युजिति

`यतो ज्ञानमयो देवो ज्ञानं च बहुधा स्थितम् ।
नियन्त्रितानां बद्धानां त्राणात्तन्नेत्रमुच्यते ॥`

कालिकाक्रमेऽपि

`तत्तद्रूपतया ज्ञानं बहिरन्तः प्रकाशते ।

ज्ञानादृते नार्थसत्ता ज्ञानरूपं ततो जगत् ॥
न हि ज्ञानादृते भावाः केनचिद्विषयीकृताः ।
ज्ञानं तदात्मतां यातमेतस्मादवसीयते ॥
अस्तिनास्तिविभागेन निषेधविधियोगतः ।
ज्ञानात्मता ज्ञेयनिष्ठा भावानां भावनाबलात् ॥
युगपद्वेदनाज्ज्ञानज्ञेययोरेकरूपता ।`

इति ॥३०॥

न केवलं सृष्टिदशायां निजशक्तिविकासोऽस्य विश्वं, यत् तत्पृष्ठपातिनौ—

स्थितिलयौ ॥३१॥

`स्वशक्तिप्र चयः` इत्यनुवर्तते। क्रियाशक्त्याभासितस्य वि श्वस्य तत्तत्प्रमात्रपेक्षं कंचित्कालं बहिर्मुखत्वावभासनरूपा या स्थितिः, चिन्मयप्रमातृविश्रान्त्यात्मा च यो लयः, तावेतौ एतस्य स्वशक्तिप्रचय एव, तत्तद्वेद्यं हि आभासमानं विलीयमानं च निजसंविच्छक्त्यात्मकमेव, अन्यथा अस्य संवेदनानुपपत्तेः । अत एव श्रीकालिकाक्रमे

`अस्तिनास्तिविभागेन .......................।`

इत्यादि स्थितिलयपरत्वेनोक्तम् । तथा

`सर्वं शुद्धं निरालम्बं ज्ञानं स्वप्रत्ययात्मकम् ।
यः पश्यति स मुक्तात्मा जीवन्नेव न संशयः ॥`

इति ॥३१॥

नन्वेवं सृष्टिस्थितिलयावस्थासु अन्योन्यभेदावभासमयीषु अस्य स्वरूपान्यथात्वमायातम् । इत्याशङ्काशान्त्यर्थमाह—

तत्प्रवृत्तावप्यनिरासः संवेत्तृभावात् ॥३२॥

तेषां सृष्ट्यादीनां प्रवृत्तावपि उन्मज्जनेऽपि, नास्य योगिनः संवेत्तृभावात् तुर्यचमत्कारात्मकविमर्शमयात् उपलब्धृत्वात्, निरासश्च्लनम्, तन्निरासे कस्यचिदप्यप्रकाशनात् । यदुक्तं तत्तैव

`नाशे ऽविद्याप्रपञ्चस्य स्वभावो न विनश्यति ।
उत्पत्तिध्वंसविरहात्तस्मान्नाशो न वास्तवः ।
यतोऽविद्या समुत्पत्तिध्वंसाभ्यामुपचर्यते ।
यत्स्वभावेन नष्टं न तन्नष्टं कथमुच्यते ॥`

इति । एतदेव स्पन्दे

`अवस्था युगलं चात्र कार्यकर्तृत्वशब्दितम् ।
कार्यता क्षयिणी तत्र कर्तृत्वं पुनरक्षयम् ॥`

यथा ।

`कार्योन्मुखः प्रयत्नो यः केवलं सोऽत्र लुप्यते ।
तस्मिँल्लुप्ते विलुप्तोऽस्मीत्यबुधः प्रतिपद्यते ॥

न तु योऽन्तर्मुखो भावः सर्वज्ञत्वगुणास्पदम् ।
तस्य लोपः कदाचित्स्यादन्यस्यानुपलम्भनात् ॥`

इत्यनेनोक्तम् ॥३२॥

अस्य योगिनः—

सुखदुःखयोर्बहिर्मननम् ॥३३॥

वेद्यास्पर्शज्ञातयोः सुखदुःखयोर्बहिरिव नीलादिवत् इदन्ताभासतया मननं संवेदनं, न तु लौकिकवत् अहन्तास्पर्शनेन, अस्य हि `स्वशक्तिप्र चयोऽस्य विश्वम्` (३-३०) इत्युक्तसूत्रार्थनीत्या सर्वम् अहन्ताच्छादितत्वेन स्फुरति, न तु नियतं सुखदुःखाधेव इत्येवंपरमेतत् । योगी हि प्रशान्तपुर्यष्टकप्रमातृभावः कथं सुखदुःखाभ्यां स्पृश्यते । तथा च श्रीप्रत्यभिज्ञासूत्रविमर्शिन्याम् ।

`ग्राहकभूमिकोत्तीर्णानां वास्तवप्रमातृदशाप्रपन्नानां तत्तत्स्वहेतूपस्थापितसुखदुःखसाक्षात्कारेऽपि न तेषां सुखदुःखादि, नोत्पद्यत एव वा सुखादि हेतुवैकल्यात्, सहजानन्दाविर्भावस्तु तदा स्यात् ॥`

इत्युक्तम् । अत एव

`न दुःखं न सुखं यत्र न ग्राह्यं ग्राहको न च ।
न चास्ति मूढभावोऽपि तदस्ति परमार्थतः ॥`

इति स्पन्दे निरूपितम् ॥३३॥

यतश्च उत्तीर्णपुर्यष्टकप्रमातृभावस्य योगिनो नान्तःसुखदुःखसंस्पर्शः, अत एवासौ—

तद्विमुक्तस्तु केवली ॥३४॥

ताभ्यां सुखदुःखाभ्यां विशेषेण मुक्तः संस्कारमात्रेणापि अन्तर् असंस्पृष्टः, केवली, केवलं चिन्मात्रप्रमातृतारूपं यस्य । तदुक्तं श्रीकालिकाक्रमे

`सुखदुःखादिविज्ञानविकल्पानल्पकल्पितम् ।
भित्त्वा द्वैतमहामोहं योगी योगफलं लभेत् ॥`

इति । तु-शब्दो वक्ष्यमाणापेक्षया विशेषद्योतकः, एवमुत्तरसूत्रगतोऽपि एतत्सूत्रापेक्षया ॥३४॥

यदाह—

मोहप्रतिसंहतस्तु कर्मात्मा ॥३५॥

मोहेन अज्ञानेन, प्रतिसंहतः तदेकघनः, तत एव सुखदुःखाश्रयो यः, स पुनः कर्मात्मा नित्यं शुभाशुभकलङ्कितः । तदुक्तं तत्रैव

`यदविद्यावृततया विकल्पविधियोगतः ।
शिवादीन्नैव झटिति समुद्भावयतेऽखिलान् ॥
ततः शुभाशुभा भावा लक्ष्यन्ते तद्वशत्वतः ।
अशुभेभ्यश्च भावेभ्यः परं दुःखं प्रजायते ॥`

इति ॥३५॥

एवमीदृशस्यापि कर्मात्मनो यदा अनर्गलमाहेशशक्तिपात-वशोन्मिषितसहजस्वातन्त्र्ययोगो भवति, तदा अस्य—

भेदतिरस्कारे सर्गान्तरकर्मत्वम् ॥३६॥

शरीरप्राणाद्यहन्ताभिमानात्मनः सकलप्रलयाकालादिप्रमात्रुचितस्य भेदस्य, तिरस्कारे स्थितस्यापि चिद्घनस्वभावोन्मज्जनाद् अपहस्तने सति, क्रमेण मन्त्र-मन्त्रेश्वर-मन्त्रमहेश्वरात्मकस्वमाहात्म्यावाप्तौ, सर्गान्तरकर्मत्वं यथाभिलषितनिर्मेयनिर्मातृत्वं भवति । तथा च श्रीस्वच्छन्दे

`त्रिगुणेन तु जप्तेन स्वच्छन्दसदृशो भवेत् ।`

इति स्वच्छन्दसादृश्येन भेदतिरस्कारमस्य उक्त्वा

`ब्रह्मविष्णिवन्द्रदेवानां सिद्धदैत्योरगेशिनाम् ॥
भयदाता च हर्ता च शापानुग्रहकृद्भवेत् ।
दर्पं हरति कालस्य पातयेद्भूधरानपि ॥`

इत्युक्तम् ॥३६॥

न च एतदस्य असंभाव्यम्, यतः—

करणशक्ति स्वतोऽनुभवात् ।।३७।।

स्वतः स्वस्मादेवानुभवात् संकल्पस्वप्नादौ, करणशक्तिः तत्तदसाधारणार्थ-निर्मातृत्वम् आत्मनः सिद्धमेव । अनेनैव आशयेन श्रीप्रत्यभिज्ञायाम्

`अत एव यथाभीष्ट समुल्ले खावभासनात् ।
ज्ञानक्रिये स्फुटे एव सिद्धेसर्वस्य जीवतः ।।`

इत्युक्तम् । तथासंभवात् यदि चैतत् गाढाभिनिवेशेन विमृशति, सदा सर्वसाधारणा अभीष्टार्थनिर्मातृतापि भवति । तदुक्तं तत्त्वगर्भे

`यदा तु तेऽपि सुव्यक्तस्वसामर्थ्यगुणोज्ज्वलाः ।
भवेद्दृढतरादूरदारिता दार्ढ्यदीनता ।
तदा च तेषां संकल्पः कल्पपादपतां व्रजेत् ।।`

इति ।।३७।।

यतश्च करणशक्तिशब्दोक्त्या तुर्यत्मा स्वातन्त्र्यशक्तिरेव बोधरूपस्य प्रमातुः सारम्, अतो मायाशक्त्यपहस्तिततत्स्वरूपोत्तेजनाय—

त्रिपदाद्यनुप्राणनम् ।।३८।।

त्रयाणां भावौन्मुख्यतदभिष्वङ्गतदन्तर्मुखीभावनामयानां सृष्टिस्थितिलय-शब्दोक्तानां पदानामवस्थानां, यद् आदि प्रधानं त्रिचमत्कृतित्वेन आनन्दघनं तुर्याख्यं पदं मायाशक्त्याच्छादितमपि तत्तद्विषयोपभोगाद्यवसरेषु विद्युद्वदाभासमानं, तेन तत्तदवसरेषु क्षणमात्रोदितेनापि, अनुप्राणनम् अन्तर्मुखतद्विमर्शावस्थितितारतम्येन अनुगततया प्राणनम्, आत्मनस्तेनैव

जीवितेनापि चीवितस्य उत्तेजनं कुर्यात् । तदुक्तं श्री विज्ञानभैरवे

`अन्तः स्वानुभवानन्दा विकल्पोन्मुक्तगोचरा ।
यावस्था भरिताकारा भैरवी भैरवात्मनः ॥
तद्वपुस्तत्त्वतो ज्ञेयं विमलं विश्वपूरणम् ।`

इत्याद्युपक्रम्य

`शक्ति संगमसंक्षुब्धशक्त्यावेशावसानिकम् ।
यत्सुखं ब्रह्मतत्त्वस्य तत्सुखं स्वाक्यमुच्यते ॥
लेहनामन्थनाकोटैः स्त्रीसुखस्य भरात्स्मृतेः ।
शक्त्यभावेऽपि देवेशि भवेदानन्दसंप्लवः ॥
आनन्दे महति प्राप्ते दृष्टे वा बान्धवे चिरात् ।
आनन्दमुद्गतं ध्यात्वा तन्मयस्तल्लयीभवेत् ॥
जग्धिपानकृतोल्लासरसानन्दविजृम्भणात् ।
भावयेद्भरितावस्थां महानन्दस्ततो भवेत् ॥
गीतादिविषयास्वादासमसौख्यैकतात्मनः ।
योगिनस्तन्मयत्वेन मनोरूढेस्तदात्मता ॥`

इत्यादिना उपायप्रदर्शनेन प्रपञ्चितम् । एतच्च

`अतिक्रुद्धः प्रहृष्टो वा किं करोमीति वा मृशन् ।
धावन्वा यत्पदं गच्छेत्तत्र स्पंदः प्रतिष्ठितः ॥`-२२(कारिका)

इतयादिना

` ..................... प्रबुद्धःस्यादनावृतः ॥`

इत्यन्तेन प्रदर्शितम् । एतत् स्पन्दनिर्णये निराकांक्षं मयैव निर्णीतम् । `त्रिषु चतुर्थम् ......` (३-२०) इति सूत्रेण जागरादौ तुर्यानुप्राणनमुक्तम् । अनेन सर्वदशागतादिमध्यान्तेषु सृष्टिस्थितिसंहारनिरूपितया भङ्ग्या निरूपितेषु इति विशेषः ॥३८॥

एतच्च त्रिपदाद्यनुप्राणनमन्तर्मुखत्वावष्टम्भत्वदशायामेवासाद्य न संतुष्येत, अपि तु—

चित्तस्थितिवच्छरीरकरणबाह्येषु ॥३९॥

`त्रिंदाद्यनुप्राणनम्` इत्येव । यथा अन्तर्मुखरूपायां चित्तस्थितौ तुर्येणानुप्राणनं कुर्यात्, तथा शरीरकरणबाह्याभासात्मिकायां बहिर्मुखतायामपि अन्तरविमर्शावष्टम्भबलात् क्रमात्क्रमं तारतम्यभाजा तेन अनुप्राणनं कुर्यात् । यदुक्तं श्रीविज्ञानभैरवे

`सर्वं जगत्स्वदेहं वा स्वानन्दभरितं स्मरेत् ।
युगपत्स्वामृतेनैव परानन्दमयो भवेत् ॥`

इति । एवं हि आनन्दात्मा स्वातन्त्र्यशक्तिः सर्वदशासु स्फुटीभूता सती यथेष्टनिर्माणकारिणी भवति ॥३९॥

यदा तु अयमेव आन्तरीं तुर्यदशाम् आत्मत्वेन न विमृशति, तदा देहादिप्रमातृताभावाद् अपूर्णमन्यतात्मकाणवमलरूपात्—

अभिलाषाद्बहिर्गतिः संवाह्यस्य ॥४०॥

शक्तिचक्राधिष्ठितैः कञ्चुकान्तःकरणबहिष्करणतन्मात्रभूतैः सह, संवाह्यते योनेर्योन्यन्तरं नीयते इति संवाह्यः, कर्मात्मरूपः पशुः तस्य

` ...................अभिलाषो मलोऽत्र तु ।`

इति श्रीस्वच्छन्दोक्तनीत्या अपूर्णमन्यतात्मकाविद्याख्याणवमलरूपाद् अभिलाषाद्धेतोर्बहिर्गतिः, विषयोन्मुखत्वमेव भवति, न तु अन्तर्मुखरूपावहितत्वं जातुचित् । यदुक्तं कालिकाक्रमे

`यदविद्यावृततया विकल्पविधियोगतः ।
शिवादीन्नैव झटिति समुद्भावयतेखिलान् ॥
ततः शुभाशुभा भावा लक्ष्यन्ते तद्वशत्वतः ।
अशुभेभ्यश्च भावेभ्यः परं दुःखं प्रजायते ॥
अतथ्यां कल्पनां कृत्वा पच्यन्ते नरकादिषु ।
स्वोत्थैर्दोषैश्च दह्यन्ते वेणवो वह्निना यथा ॥
मायामयैः सदा भावैरविद्यां परिभुञ्जते ।
मायामयीं तनुं यान्ति ते जनाः क्लेशभाजनम् ॥`

इति ॥४०॥

यदा तु पारमेशशक्तिपातवशोन्मिषितं स्व स्वभावमेव विमृशति, तदा अभिलाषाभावाद् न अस्य बहिर्गतिः, अपि तु आत्मारामतैव नित्यमित्याह—

तदारूढप्रमितेस्तत्क्षयाज्जीवसंक्षयः ॥४१॥

तदिति पूर्वनिर्दिष्टसंवेत्रात्मनि पुर्यपदे, आरूढा तद्विमर्शनपरा प्रमितिः संवित् यस्य योगिनस्तस्य । तदिति अभिलाषक्षयात्, जीवस्य संवाह्यात्मनः पुर्यष्टकप्रमातृभावस्य, क्षयः प्रशमः; चित्प्रमातृतयैव स्फुरति इत्यर्थः । यदुक्तं तत्रैव

`यथा स्वप्नानुभूार्थान्प्रबुद्धो नैव पश्यति ।
तथा भावनया योगी संसारं नैव पश्यति ॥`

इति । तथा

`निरस्य सदसद्वृत्तीः संश्रित्य पदमान्तरम् ।
विहाय कल्पनाजालमद्वैतेन परापरम् ॥

य: स्वात्मनिरतो नित्यं कालग्रासैकतत्पर: ।
कैवल्यपदभाग्योगी स निर्वाणपदं लभेत् ॥`

इति । कैवल्यपदभागिति इन्द्रियतन्मात्राभिरसंवाह्य: ॥४१॥

नत्वेवं जीवसंक्षये सति अस्य देहपात: प्राप्त:, न च असौ सुप्रबुद्धस्यापि देहिन: सद्य एव दृश्यते, तत्कथमयं तदारूढप्रमिति:? इत्याशङ्क्याह—

भूतकञ्चुकी तदा विमुक्तो भूय: पतिसम: पर: ॥४२॥

तदेति अभिलाषक्षयात्, जीवसंक्षये पुर्यष्टकप्रमातृताभिमानविगलने सति, अयं भूतकञ्चुकी, शरीरारम्भीणि भूतानि कञ्चुकमिव व्यतिरिक्तं प्रावरणमिव, न तु अहन्तापदस्पर्शीनि यस्य, तथाभूत: सन् विमुक्तो निर्वाणभाक्, यतो भूयो बाहुल्येन पतिसम: चिद्घनपारमेश्वरस्वरूपाविष्ट:, तत एव पर: पूर्ण, `शरीरवृत्तिर्व्रतम्` (३-२६) इत्युक्तसूत्रार्थनीत्या दलकल्पे देहादौ स्थितोऽपि, न तत्प्रमातृतासंस्कारेणापि स्पृष्ट: । तदुक्तं श्रीकुलरत्नमालायां

`यदागुरुवर: सम्यक् कथयेत्तन्न संशय: ।
मुक्तस्तेनैव कालेन यन्त्रस्तिष्ठति केवलम् ॥
किं पुनश्चैकतानस्तु परे ब्रह्मणि य: सुधी: ।
क्षणमात्रस्थितो योगी स मुक्तो मोचयेत्प्रजा: ॥`

इति । श्रीमृत्युजित्यपि

`निमेषोन्मेषमात्रं तु तत्त्वं यद्युपलभ्यते ।
तदैव किल मुक्तोऽसौ न पुनर्जन्म चाप्नुयात् ॥`

इति । कुलसारेऽपि

`अहो तत्त्वस्य माहात्म्यं ज्ञातमात्रस्य सुन्दरि ।
श्रोत्रान्तरं तु संप्राप्ते तत्क्षणादेव मुच्यते ॥`

इति ।।४२।।

ननु भूतकञ्चुकित्वमपि अस्य कस्मात् तदैव न निवर्तते ।
इत्याह—

नैसर्गिकः प्राणसंबन्धः ।।४३।।

निसर्गात् स्वातन्त्र्यात्मनः स्वभावात् आयातो नैसर्गिकः, प्राणसंबन्धः, संवित् किल भगवती विश्ववैचित्र्यम् अवबिभासयिषुः संकोचावभासपूर्वकं संकुचदशेषविश्वस्फुरत्तात्मकप्राणनारूपग्राहकभूमिकां श्रित्वा ग्राह्यरूपजगदाभासात्मना स्फुरतीति नैसर्गिकः, स्वातन्त्र्यात् प्रथममुद्भासितोऽस्याः प्राणसंबन्धः । तथा च श्रीवाजसनेयायाम्

`या सा शक्तिः परा सूक्ष्मा व्यापिनी निर्मला शिवा ।
शक्तिचक्रस्य जननी परानन्दामृतात्मिका ।।
महाघोरेश्वरी चण्डा सृष्टिसंहारकारिका ।
त्रिवहं त्रिविधं त्रिस्थं बलात्कालं प्रकर्षति ।।`

इति संविद एव भगवत्याः प्राणक्रमेण नाडित्रयवाहिसोमसूर्यवह्न्यात्मावस्थितातीतानागतवर्तमानरूपबाह्यकालोल्लसनविलापनकारित्वमुक्तम् ।
तदुक्तं स्वच्छन्देऽपि

`प्राणः प्राणमयः प्राणो विसर्गापूरणं प्रति ।
नित्यमापूरयत्येष प्राणिनामुरसि स्थितः ।।`

इति । प्राणस्य

`हकारस्तु स्मृतः प्राणः स्वप्रवृत्तो हलाकृतिः ।`

इतियुक्तनीत्या श्रीस्वच्छन्दभट्टारकरूपप्राणमयत्वात् विसर्गापूरतया सृष्टिसंहारकारित्वमभिहितम् इति युक्तमुक्तम् `नैसर्गिकः प्राणसंबन्धः`

इति । अत एव श्रीभट्टकल्लटेन प्राणाख्यनिमित्तदार्ढ्यम्
`प्राक् संवित् प्राणे परिणता ।`
इति तत्त्वार्थचिन्तामणावुक्तम् ।।४३।।

अतश्च स्थितेऽपि नैसर्गिके प्राणसंबन्धे यस्तदारूढ आन्तरीं कला विमृशन्नास्ते स लोकोत्तर एव इत्याह—

नासिकान्तर्मध्यसंयमात् किमत्र सव्यापसव्यसौषुम्नेषु ।।४४।।

सर्वनाडीचक्रप्रधानरूपेषु सव्यापसव्यसौषुम्नेषु दक्षिणवाममध्यनाडीपदेषु, या नासिका, नसते कौटिल्येन वहति इति कृत्वा, कुटिलवाहिनी प्राणशक्तिः, तस्याः अन्तरिति आन्तरी संवित्, तस्या अपि मध्यं सर्वान्तरतमतया प्रधानम् ।

`तस्य देवातिदेवस्य परबोधस्वरूपिणः ।
विमर्शः परमा शक्तिः सर्वज्ञा ज्ञानशालिनी ।।`

इति श्रीकालिक्रमोक्तनीत्या यत् विमर्शमयं रूपं तत्संयमात् अन्तर्निभालन-प्रकर्षात्, किमत्र उच्यते, अयं हि सर्वदशासु देदीप्यमानो निर्व्युत्थानः परः समाधिः । तदुक्तं श्रीविज्ञानभैरवे

`ग्राह्यग्राहकसंवित्तिः सामान्या सर्वदेहिनाम् ।
योगिनां नु विशेषोऽयं संबन्धे सावधानता ।।`

इति ।।४४।।

एवमीदृशस्य योगफलं दर्शयन् प्रकरणमुपसंहरति-

भूयः स्यात्प्रतिमीलनम् ।।४५।।

चैतन्यात्मनः स्वरूपात् उदितस्य अस्य विश्वस्य भूयः पुनः, विगलितभेद-संस्कारात्मना बाहुल्येन च प्रतिमीलनम्, चैतनयाभिमुख्येन निमीलनं, पुनरपि चैतन्यात्मस्वस्वरूपोन्मीलनरूपं परयोगाभिनिविष्टस्य योगिनो भवति । तदुक्तं श्रीस्वच्छन्दे

`उन्मनापरतो देवि तत्रात्मानं नियोजयेत् ।
तस्मिन्युक्तस्ततो ह्यात्मा तन्मयश्च प्रजायते ॥`

इति । तथा च

`उद्बोधितो यथा वह्निर्निर्मलोऽतीव भास्वरः ।
न भूयः प्रविशेत्काष्ठे तथात्माध्वन उद्धृतः ॥
मलकर्मकलाद्यैस्तु निर्मलो विगतक्लमः ।
तत्रस्थोऽपि न बध्येत यतोऽतीव सुनिर्मलः ॥`

इति । भूयः स्यादित्यभिदधतोऽयमाशयः, यत् शिवत्वमस्य योगिनो न अपूर्वम्, अपि तु स्वभाव एव, केवलं मायाशक्त्युत्थापितस्वविकल्प-दौरात्म्यात् भासमानमपि तत् नायं प्रत्यवम्रष्टुं क्षमः, इत्यस्य उक्तोपायप्र-दर्शनक्रमेण तदेव अभिव्यज्यते इति शिवम् ॥४५॥

इति शिवसूत्रविवृत्तौ

आणवोपायप्रकाशनं

तृतीय उन्मेषः ॥३॥

`सेयमागमसंवादस्पन्दसंगतिसुन्दरा ।
वृत्तिः शैवरहस्यार्थे शिवसूत्रेषु दर्शिता ॥१॥
शिवरहस्यनिदर्शनसंस्रवन्-

नवनवामृतसाररसोल्बणाम् ।
सुकृतिनो रसयन्तु भवच्छिदे
स्फुटमिमां शिवसूत्रविमर्शिनीम् ।।२।।
इयमरोचकिनां रुचिवर्धिनी
परिणतिं तनुते परमां मतेः ।
रसनमात्रत एव सुधौघवत्
मृतिजराजननादिभयापहृत् ।।३।।
देहप्राणसुखादिभिः परिमिताहन्तास्पदैः संवृत-
श्चैतन्यं चिनुते निजं न सुमहन्महेश्वरं स्वं जनः ।
मध्ये बोधसुधाब्धि विश्वमभितस्तत्फेनपिण्डोपमं
यः पश्येदुपदेशतस्तु कथितः साक्षात्स एकः शिवः ।।४।।
तरत तरसा संसाराब्धिं विधत्त परे पदे
पदमविचलं नित्यालोकप्रमोदसुनिर्भरे ।
विमृशत शिवप्रोक्तं सूत्रं रहस्यसमुज्ज्वलं
प्रसभविलसत्सद्युक्त्यान्तः समुत्प्लवदायि तत् ।।५।।

इति श्रीमान्महामाहेश्वराचार्यवर्याभिनवगुप्तपादपाद्मोपजीविश्रीक्षेमराज-विरचितायां शिवसूत्रविमार्शिन्यामाणवोपायप्रकाशनं नाम तृतीय उन्मेषः ।।३।।

समाप्ता चेयं शिवसूत्रविमर्शिनी ।।
कृतिः श्रीक्षेमराजस्य क्षेमायास्तु विमर्शिनाम् ।
शिवस्वात्मैक्यबोधार्था शिवसूत्रविमर्शिनी ।।
।। ॐ ।।

Contents

deep sleep: in the state of deep sleep, 40; in the waking state, 40; state within a dream, 40
degraded individual consciousness, 215
deha: *kañcukatād*, 234; *pramātṛi*, 241–42
depression, 156
desire, 23, 47–49, 60, 65–67, 79, 97, 143, 176, 218, 225–28
Devanāgarī, 104
devatas, 76
devatā, 78
dhāraṇā, 16, 40, 107–8, 141, 145–46, 148–49, 169
dhyāna, 6, 16, 141, 145–46, 148–49, 169
difference, 13, 35, 43, 50, 91, 101, 123, 127, 139, 144, 151, 165, 172, 181, 184–85, 202, 223, 225, 237–28
differentiated: knowledge, 18, 22, 25–26, 131, 151, 179; nature, 19
dikcarī, 27, 199
disciples, 4, 9–10, 14, 23, 27, 34, 60, 86–87, 92–94, 103, 111, 194, 197, 199
discipline, 81
divine aspects, 12
doer, 25, 200, 207
drama, 156, 158–63
dreaming: state of deep sleep, 40; waking state, 39
dreamless, 39, 53, 62, 120, 138, 153, 157–58, 173, 180, 186, 204, 223
dream state within a dream, 40
dṛiśyaṁ śarīram, 49
dualism, 116
duḥkha, 131, 208

eating, 192, 222
eclipse, 191
ecstasy, 148, 180, 182–83, 220
ecstasy of consciousness (*citta camatkāra*), 183
ego, 20, 27, 49, 129, 131–32, 138, 158, 175, 183, 188, 209, 214, 226, 228, 231, 241
eightfold subtle body, 209
ekāgratā, 105
elementary, 141–42, 144–45, 164, 173, 212, 234
elements, 23–24, 33–34, 53–54, 63, 95, 105–8, 110, 115, 132–35, 137–39, 141–44, 170, 174, 190, 209, 212, 231, 234
elevate, 10, 199
embodiment, 22–23, 59, 89, 95–96, 105, 127, 169, 201, 208, 212
emotions, 34, 173
energies (*śakticakra*), 42, 65, 198
energy of absolute independence (*svātantrya śakti*), 225, 234; action, 68–69, 95, 99–102, 106–7, 111, 113, 176, 203; bliss, 95, 100–101, 106–7, 111; consciousness, 68, 94–95, 100–102, 106–7, 111; illusion (*māyā śakti*), 133; knowledge, 69, 95, 100–101, 106–7, 111, 135, 176, 199; will, 47, 59–60, 63–64, 66, 68–69, 95, 97, 100–101, 106–7, 111, 176
enjoyer, 47, 193
enjoying, 42, 47, 52, 54, 58, 191
enjoyment, 25, 28, 47, 84, 122, 132, 156, 220
enjoys, 42, 58, 101, 181, 186, 220–21
enlightenment, 92, 133–34
enslaved, 183
entangled, 129, 131–32, 135, 138, 145
entangles, 113, 179
entangling, 54
essence, 69, 80, 108–9, 115, 123, 162, 179, 219, 241
ether, 27, 89, 106, 115, 132, 143, 170
eunuch, 99–100, 102
evil, 75
existence and nonexistence, 205
expansion, 73, 75, 102, 121, 133–34, 153–54, 160, 201, 203–4, 206, 208
experiencer, 42–43, 64, 114, 214–15, 242

experiencing, 43, 57–58, 83, 109, 138, 146–47, 150, 171, 214, 229
external perception, 106
extroverted, 68, 105, 221, 224

f-a-t-h-e-r, 28
faint impressions *saṁskārāḥ,* 149
faith, 81, 194
fallen, 103, 175
father, 28, 120, 178
fear, 106, 135, 179, 210, 216, 223, 241
feeling of incompletion, 26, 226
flash of lightning, 220–221
freedom, 19–21, 23, 150, 166, 171
fullness, 9, 12–13, 45, 74, 92, 108, 117, 136, 147, 189, 195, 197

gandha, 106, 132, 138, 170, 175, 226
gandha (smell), 24
gap, 121, 204, 215, 226
garbhe, 87
garland of letters, 176–78
Garuḍa, 215
ghoratarī, 193
ghorā, 193
gocarī, 27, 199
goddess, 47, 81–82, 233–35, 239
God consciousness: held by the trick of awareness, 221–23; in *samādhi,* 119, 186; subjective, 57, 75–77; supreme state of, 9, 16–17, 115, 135, 183–84, 233, 242
Gorakhanātha, 103
grace of his master, 6, 94, 111, 172, 220
grammar, 46, 129
grammarian, 99, 107–8, 112
guṇas, 132
guru, 92
gururupāyaḥ, 92

haṁsa, 196
haṭhapākayuktyā, 181
haviḥ, 114
hell, 37, 64, 227
hero, 36, 42–43, 111, 158, 161–63, 197
heroic yogī, 33–34, 36–37, 41–43, 181
heroine, 111
hṛidaye, 52

I-consciousness, 73, 86, 127, 192, 195–96, 208–10, 226, 231–32
I-ness, 53, 114, 183, 209
icchā: *śakti,* 63–64, 84, 95, 101, 106–7, 176; *śakttirūmā kumāri,* 46
idam, 50, 108
iḍā, piṅgalā, and *suṣumnā nāḍi,* 236
imaginary independence, 165
imitation, 109, 162
impressions of pleasures and pain, 26
impurities, 19, 22–24, 70, 227, 235, 240
independent supreme God consciousness., 13–16, 17
Indra, 215
indriya: *śaktis,* 42; *vṛittis,* 42
inference, 56
inferior, 3–4, 6, 73, 84–85, 104–5, 110–11, 130, 140–41, 188–90, 192–93
inherent difference (*vibhāgam*), 161
initiate, 122
initiation, 54, 60
intellect, 5, 14–15, 24, 27, 129, 131–32, 135, 138, 158, 162, 167–68, 175, 188, 209, 226, 228
intellectual: acts, 131; organs, 129, 131–32; state, 24
introverted successive unbroken consciousness, 221
iśvara, 108
iṣana, 101

jaḍa (insentient), 12
jagrat, 3, 181, 209
jala (water), 24
japaḥ, 195
jīva, 19, 104, 228, 232
jīvanmukta, 55, 172
joyful, 44, 156
joyous, 47, 82, 117, 160, 178, 208

The Author
Swami Lakshmanjoo

Swami Lakshmanjoo was born in Srinagar, Kashmir on May 9, 1907. He was the last and the greatest of the saints and masters of the tradition of Kashmir Shaivism. Having a deep understanding of the philosophy and practices of Kashmir Shaivism, he was like a splendid and rare jewel. Beginning from childhood he spent his whole life studying and practicing the teachings of this unique sacred tradition. Because of his intellectual power and strength of awareness, he realized both spiritually and intellectually the reality of its thought.

Being born with a photographic memory learning was always easy. In addition to complete knowledge of Kashmir Shavisim he had a vast knowledge of the traditional religious and philosophical texts of India. When translating or teaching he would freely draw on other texts to clarify, expand and substantiate his teaching. He could recall an entire text by simply remembering the first few words of the verse.

In time his reputation as a learned philospher and spiritual adept spread. Spiritual leaders and scholars journeyed from all over the world to receive his blessing and to ask him questions about various aspects of Kashmir Shaiva philosophy. He gained renown as a devotee of Lord Shiva and as a master of the nondual tradition of Kashmir Shaivism.

Throughout his life Swami Lakshmanjoo taught his disciples and devotees the ways of devotion and awareness. He shunned fame and recognition and did not seek his own glory. He knew Kashmir Shaivism was a most precious jewel and that by God's grace, those who desired to learn would be attracted to its teachings. His earnest wish was that Kashmir Shaivism be preserved and made available to all who desired to know it.

On September 27, 1991 Swami Lakshmanjoo attained the great liberation and left his physical body.

Lakshmanjoo ACADEMY

The teachings of Swami Lakshmanjoo are a response to the urgent need of our time: the transformation of consciousness and the evolution of a more enlightened humanity.

The Universal Shaiva Fellowship and its educational branch, The Lakshmanjoo Academy, a fully accredited non-profit organization, was established under Swamij's direct inspiration, for the purpose of realizing Swamiji's vision of making Kashmir Shaivism available to the whole world. It was Swamiji's wish that his teachings be made available without the restriction of caste, creed or color. The Universal Shaiva Fellowship and the Lakshmanjoo Academy have preserved Swamiji's original teachings and are progressively making these teachings available in book, audio and video formats.

This knowledge is extremely valuable and uplifting for all of humankind. It offers humanity a clear and certain vision in a time of uncertainty. It shows us the way home and gives us the means for its attainment.

For information on Kashmir Shaivism or to support the work of The Universal Shaiva Fellowship and the Lakshmanjoo Academy and its profound consciousness work,

visit the Lakshmanjoo Academy website or

email us at info@LakshmanjooAcademy.org.

www.LakshmanjooAcademy.org

Instructions to download audio files

1. Open this link to download the free audio . . .
https://www.universalshaivafellowship.org/ShivaSutras

It will **direct** you to "**Shiva Sutras - Audio**" in our shopping cart.

2. Select "**Add to basket** " which will send you to the next page.

3. Copy "**Shiva**" into the "**Add Gift Certificate or Coupon"** box

4. Click "**Checkout**" and fill in your details to process the free downloads.

If you have any difficulties please contact us at:
www.LakshmanjooAcademy.org/contact

Made in United States
North Haven, CT
10 June 2024

53449915R00211